ROCKET RACCOON
A CHASING TALE

WRITER
SKOTTIE YOUNG

ARTISTS
SKOTTIE YOUNG (#1-5)
& JAKE PARKER (#5-6)

COLOR ARTIST
JEAN-FRANÇOIS BEAULIEU

LETTERER: **JEFF ECKLEBERRY**
COVER ART: **SKOTTIE YOUNG**
ASSISTANT EDITORS: **DEVIN LEWIS**
EDITOR: **SANA AMANAT**
SENIOR EDITOR: **NICK LOWE**
SPECIAL THANKS TO STEPHEN WACKER

COLLECTION EDITOR: **JENNIFER GRÜNWALD** • ASSISTANT EDITOR: **SARAH BRUNSTAD**
ASSOCIATE MANAGING EDITOR: **ALEX STARBUCK** • EDITOR, SPECIAL PROJECTS: **MARK D. BEAZLEY**
SENIOR EDITOR, SPECIAL PROJECTS: **JEFF YOUNGQUIST** • SVP PRINT, SALES & MARKETING: **DAVID GABRIEL**
BOOK DESIGN: **JEFF POWELL**

EDITOR IN CHIEF: **AXEL ALONSO** • CHIEF CREATIVE OFFICER: **JOE QUESADA**
PUBLISHER: **DAN BUCKLEY** • EXECUTIVE PRODUCER: **ALAN FINE**

ROCKET RACCOON VOL. 1: A CHASING TALE. Contains material originally published in magazine form as ROCKET RACCOON #1-6. First printing 2015. ISBN# 978-0-7851-9045-5. Published by MARVEL WORLDWIDE, INC., a subsidiary of MARVEL ENTERTAINMENT, LLC. OFFICE OF PUBLICATION: 135 West 50th Street, New York, NY 10020. Copyright © 2015 MARVEL No similarity between any of the names, characters, persons, and/or institutions in this magazine with those of any living or dead person or institution is intended, and any such similarity which may exist is purely coincidental. **Printed in the U.S.A.** ALAN FINE, President, Marvel Entertainment; DAN BUCKLEY, President, TV, Publishing and Brand Management; JOE QUESADA, Chief Creative Officer; TOM BREVOORT, SVP of Publishing; DAVID BOGART, SVP of Operations & Procurement, Publishing; C.B. CEBULSKI, VP of International Development & Brand Management; DAVID GABRIEL, SVP Print, Sales & Marketing; JIM O'KEEFE, VP of Operations & Logistics; DAN CARR, Executive Director of Publishing Technology; SUSAN CRESPI, Editorial Operations Manager; ALEX MORALES, Publishing Operations Manager; STAN LEE, Chairman Emeritus. For information regarding advertising in Marvel Comics or on Marvel.com, please contact Jonathan Rheingold, VP of Custom Solutions & Ad Sales, at jrheingold@marvel.com. For Marvel subscription inquiries, please call 800-217-9158. **Manufactured between 8/21/2015 and 9/28/2015 by R.R. DONNELLEY, INC., SALEM, VA, USA.**

10 9 8 7 6 5 4 3 2 1

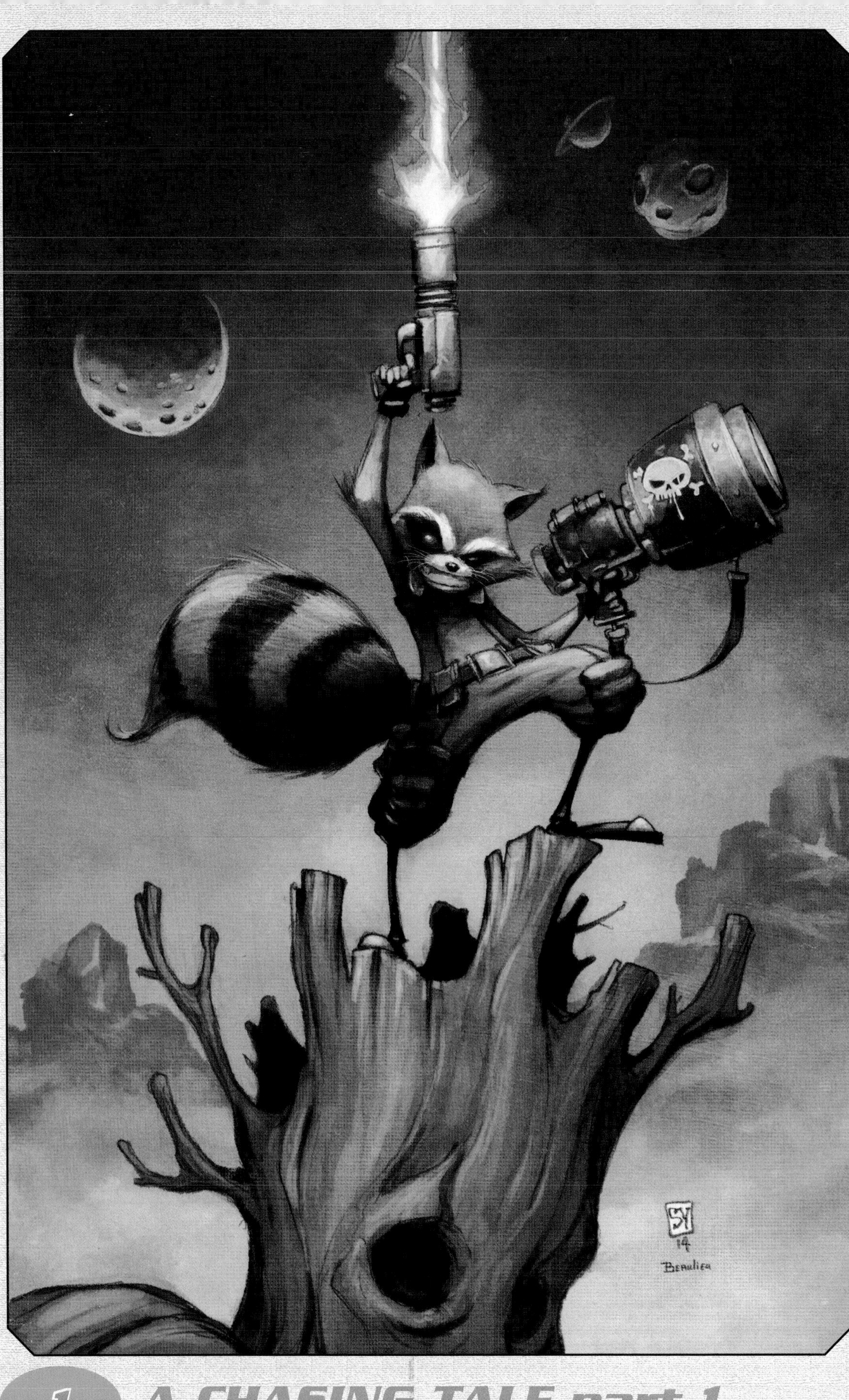
SY
'14
Beaulieu

1 A CHASING TALE part 1

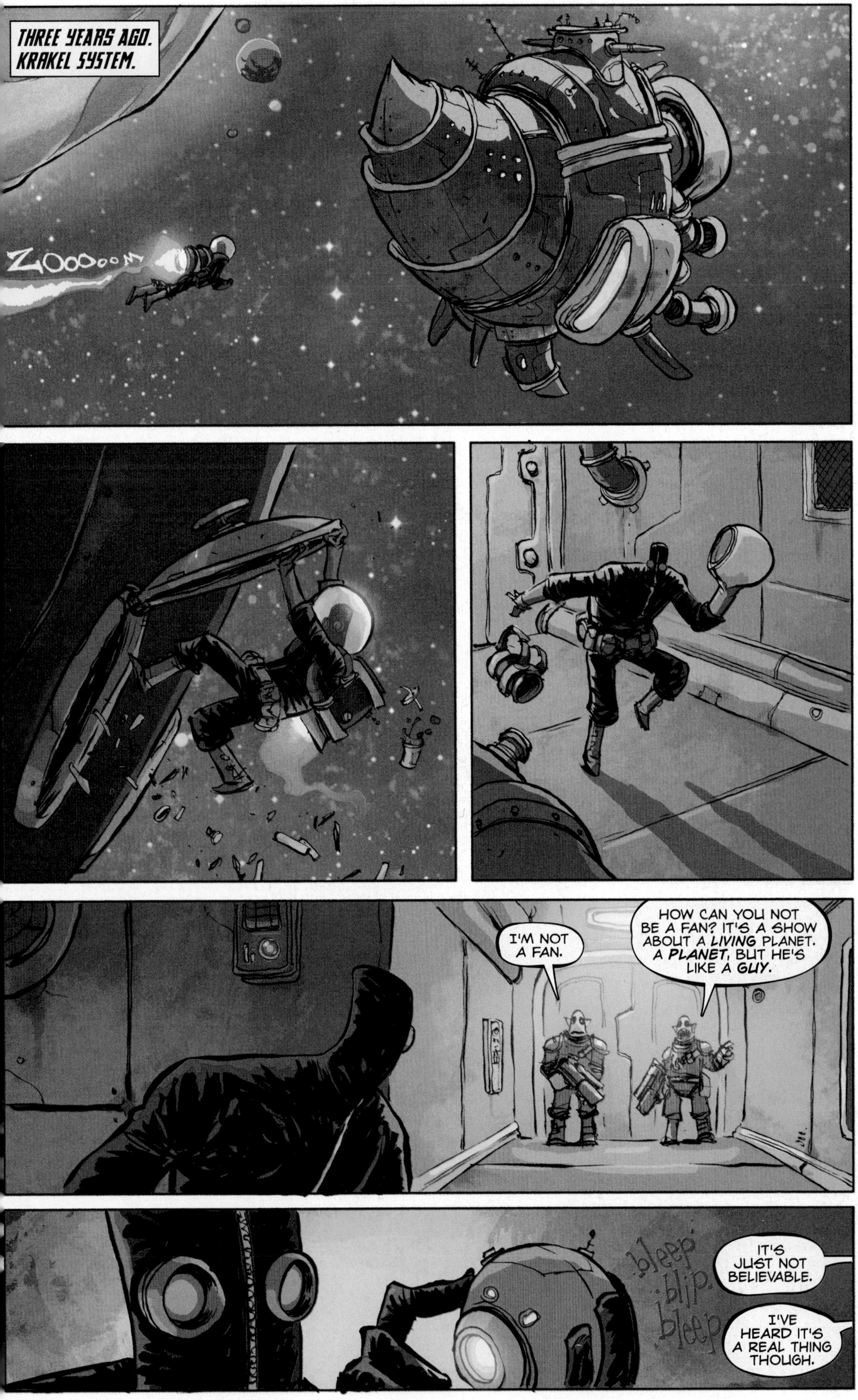
THREE YEARS AGO. KRAKEL SYSTEM.
ZOOOoom
I'M NOT A FAN.
HOW CAN YOU NOT BE A FAN? IT'S A SHOW ABOUT A LIVING PLANET. A PLANET, BUT HE'S LIKE A GUY.
bleep blip bleep
IT'S JUST NOT BELIEVABLE.
I'VE HEARD IT'S A REAL THING THOUGH.

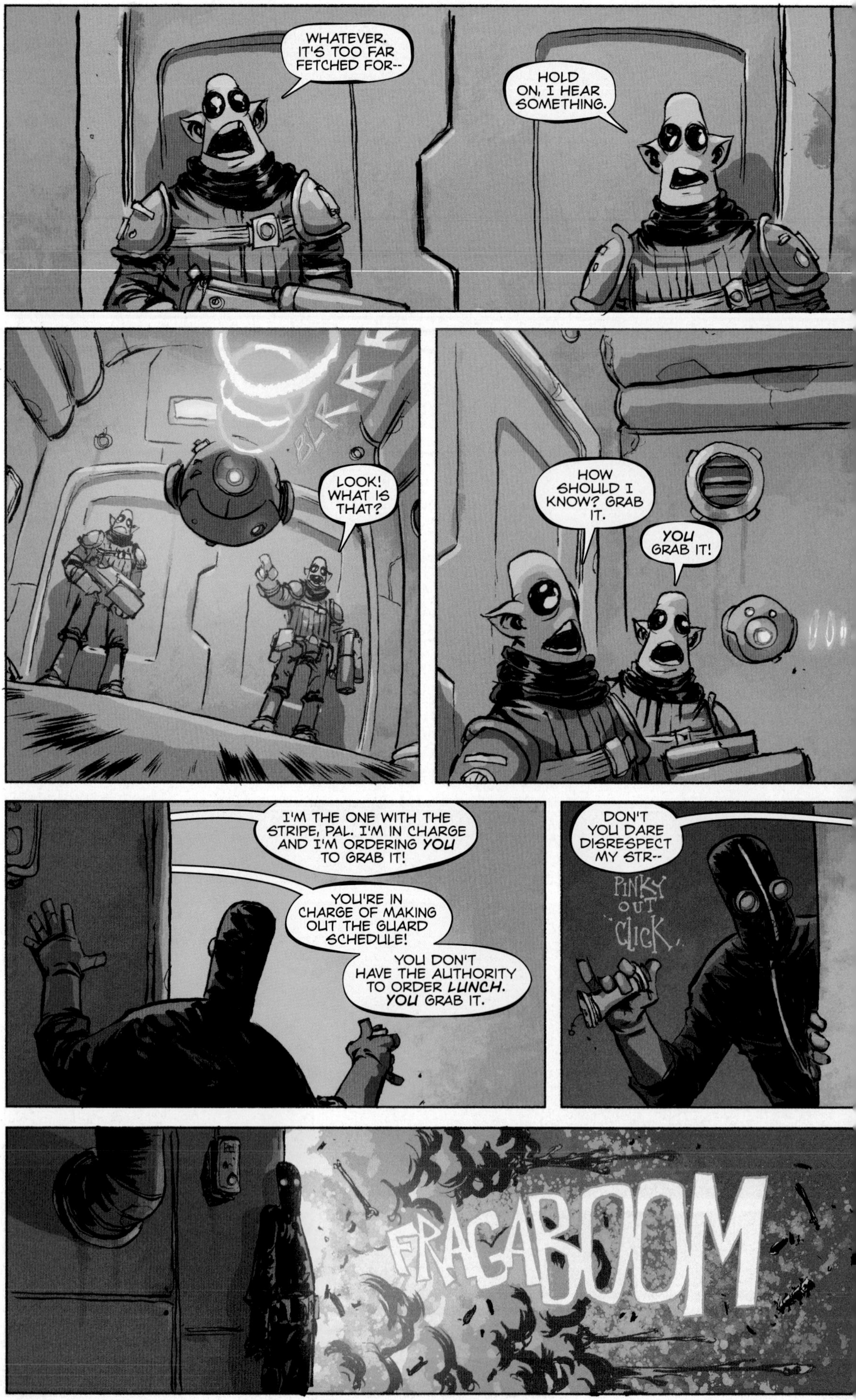
WHATEVER. IT'S TOO FAR FETCHED FOR--
HOLD ON, I HEAR SOMETHING.
BLRRR
LOOK! WHAT IS THAT?
HOW SHOULD I KNOW? GRAB IT.
YOU GRAB IT!
I'M THE ONE WITH THE STRIPE, PAL. I'M IN CHARGE AND I'M ORDERING YOU TO GRAB IT!
YOU'RE IN CHARGE OF MAKING OUT THE GUARD SCHEDULE!
YOU DON'T HAVE THE AUTHORITY TO ORDER LUNCH. YOU GRAB IT.
DON'T YOU DARE DISRESPECT MY STR--
PINKY OUT CLICK
FRAGABOOM

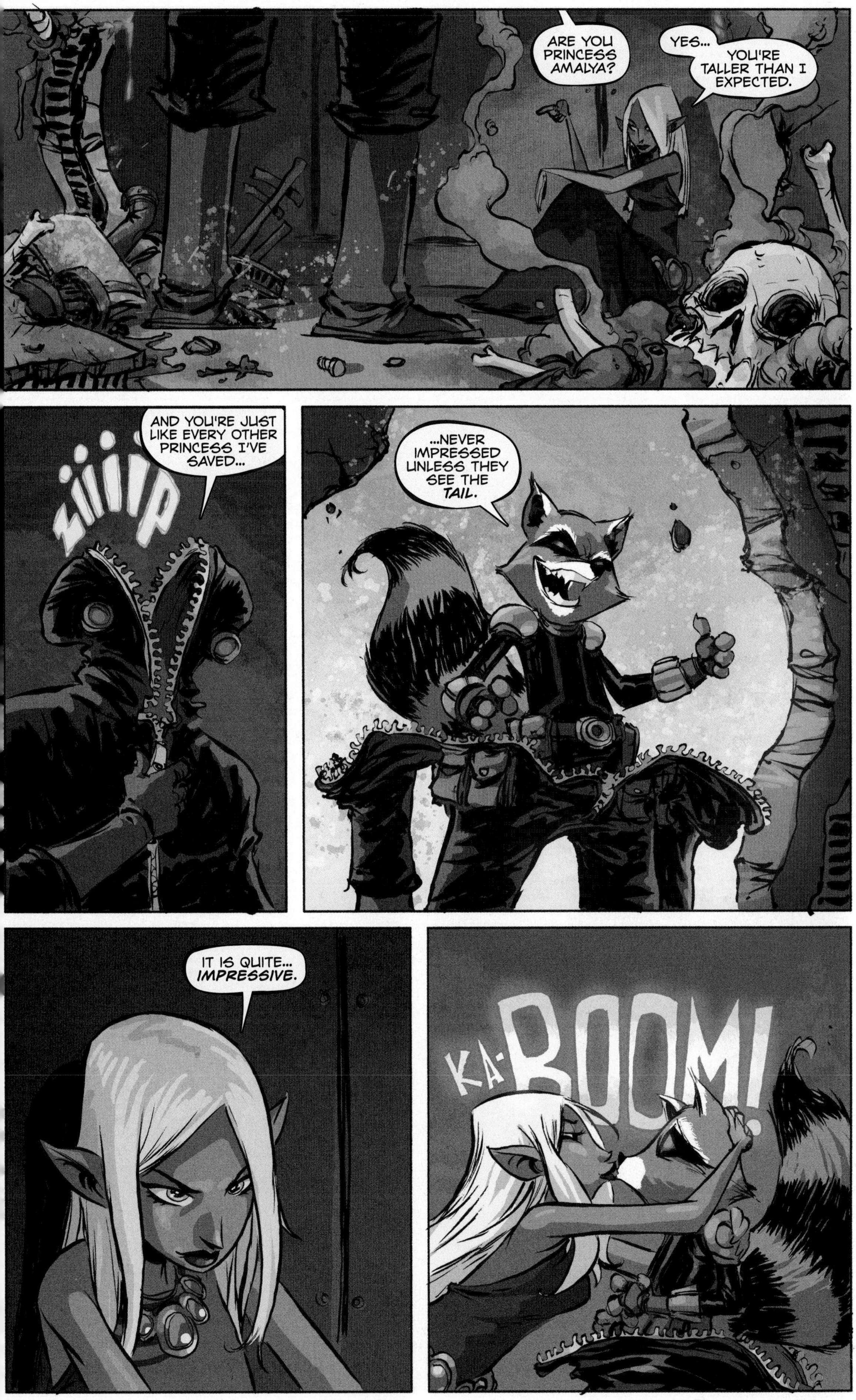
ARE YOU PRINCESS AMALYA?
YES... YOU'RE TALLER THAN I EXPECTED.
ZIIIIP
AND YOU'RE JUST LIKE EVERY OTHER PRINCESS I'VE SAVED...
...NEVER IMPRESSED UNLESS THEY SEE THE TAIL.
IT IS QUITE... IMPRESSIVE.
KA-BOOM!

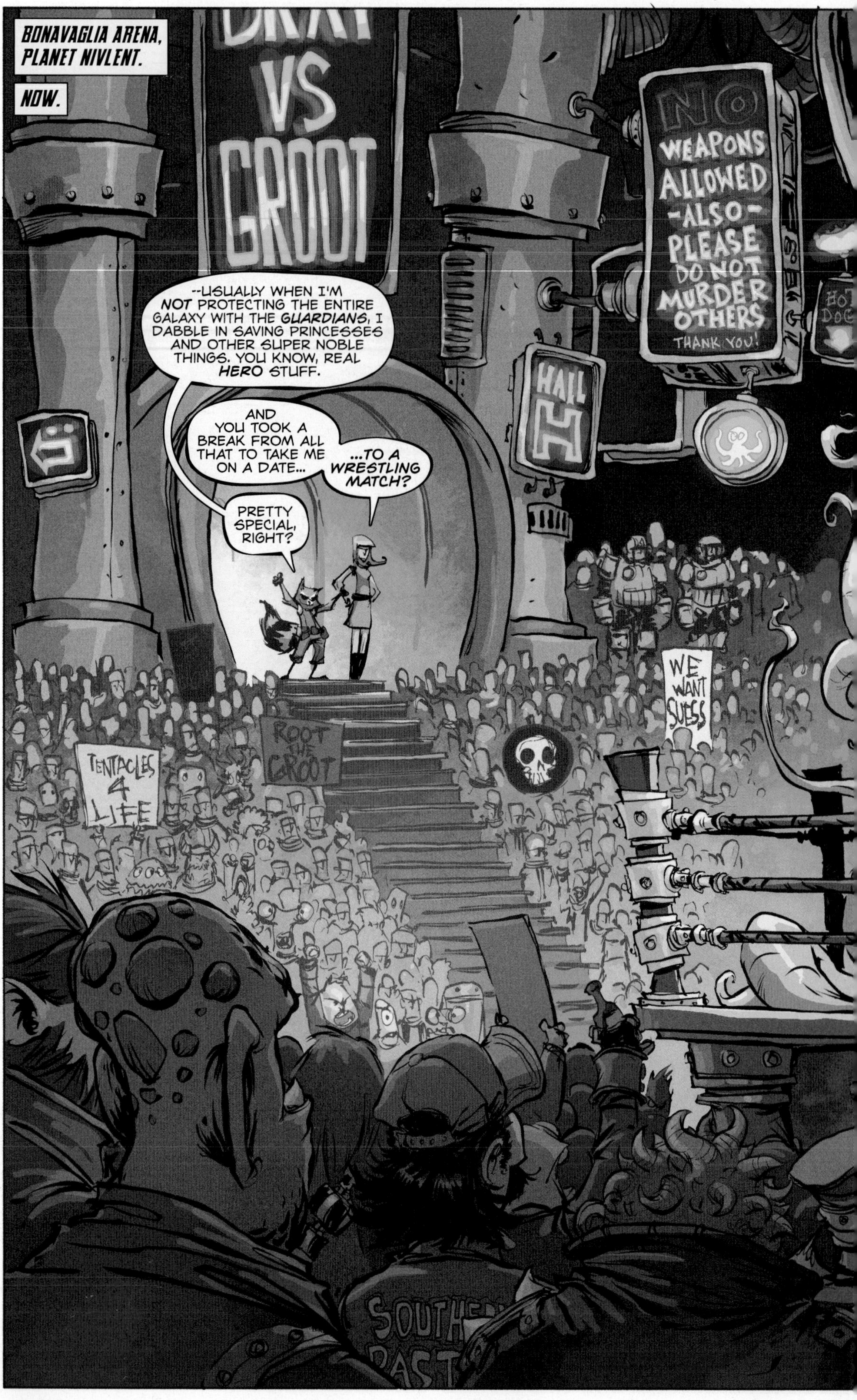
BONAVAGLIA ARENA, PLANET NIVLENT.
NOW.
VS GROOT
NO WEAPONS ALLOWED -ALSO- PLEASE DO NOT MURDER OTHERS THANK YOU!
HALL H
--USUALLY WHEN I'M NOT PROTECTING THE ENTIRE GALAXY WITH THE GUARDIANS, I DABBLE IN SAVING PRINCESSES AND OTHER SUPER NOBLE THINGS. YOU KNOW, REAL HERO STUFF.
AND YOU TOOK A BREAK FROM ALL THAT TO TAKE ME ON A DATE...
...TO A WRESTLING MATCH?
PRETTY SPECIAL, RIGHT?
WE WANT SUESS
ROOT THE GROOT
TENTACLES 4 LIFE

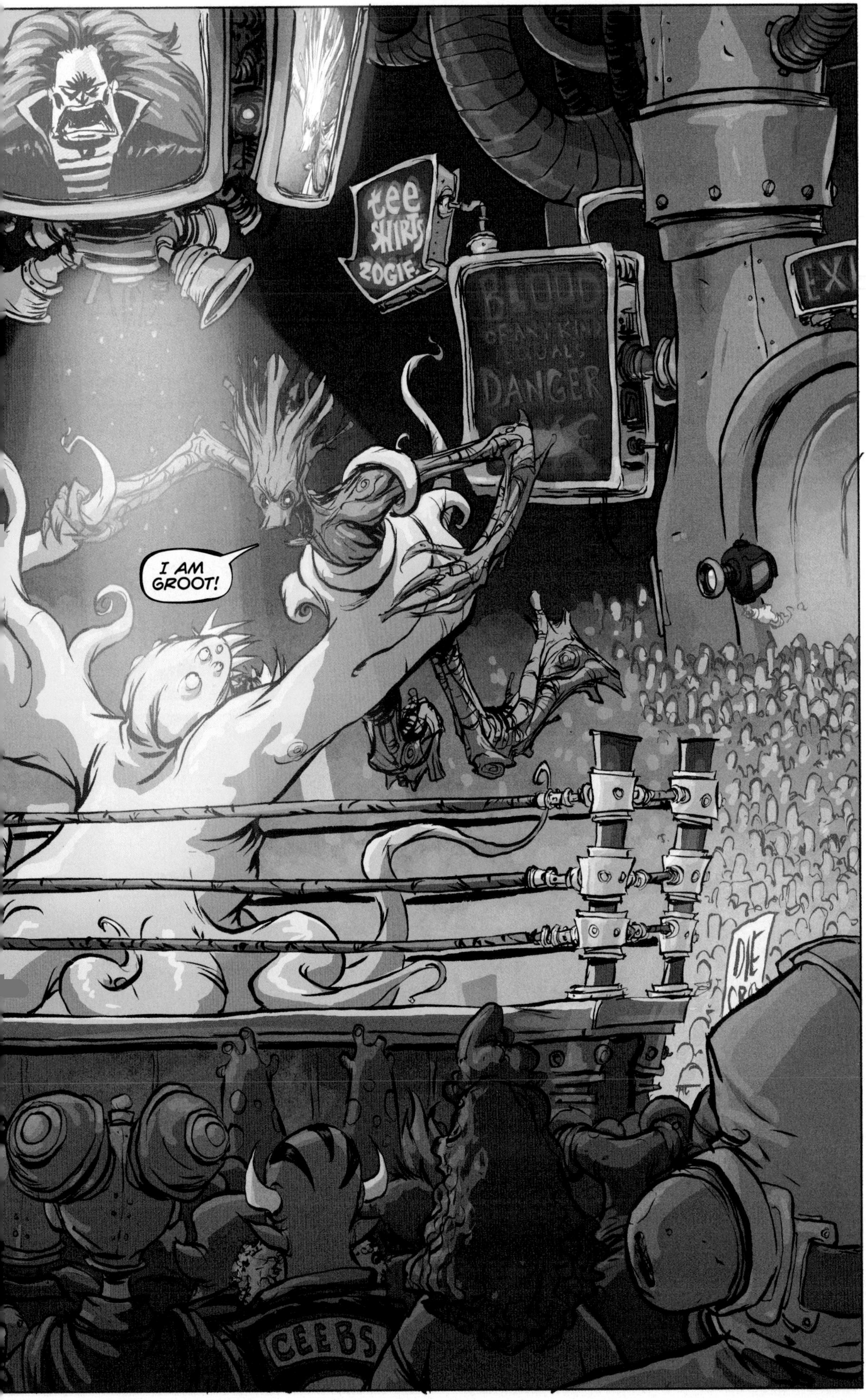
tee SHIRTS ZOGIE!
BLOOD
DANGER
I AM GROOT!
CEEBS

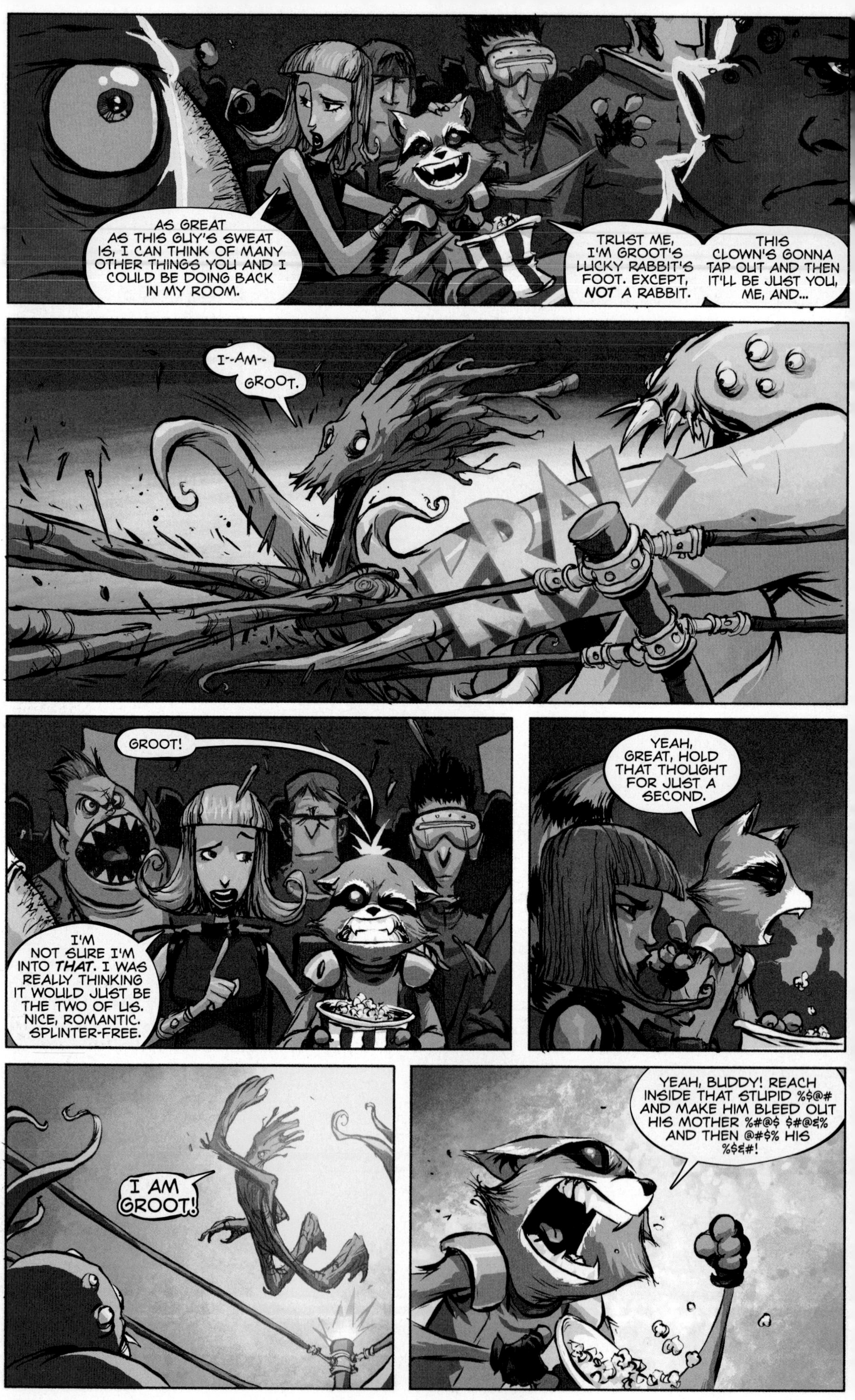
AS GREAT AS THIS GUY'S SWEAT IS, I CAN THINK OF MANY OTHER THINGS YOU AND I COULD BE DOING BACK IN MY ROOM.
TRUST ME, I'M GROOT'S LUCKY RABBIT'S FOOT. EXCEPT, *NOT* A RABBIT.
THIS CLOWN'S GONNA TAP OUT AND THEN IT'LL BE JUST YOU, ME, AND...
I--AM-- GROOT.
GROOT!
I'M NOT SURE I'M INTO *THAT*. I WAS REALLY THINKING IT WOULD JUST BE THE TWO OF US. NICE, ROMANTIC. SPLINTER-FREE.
YEAH, GREAT, HOLD THAT THOUGHT FOR JUST A SECOND.
I AM GROOT!
YEAH, BUDDY! REACH INSIDE THAT STUPID %$@# AND MAKE HIM BLEED OUT HIS MOTHER %#@$ $#@£% AND THEN @#$% HIS %$£#!

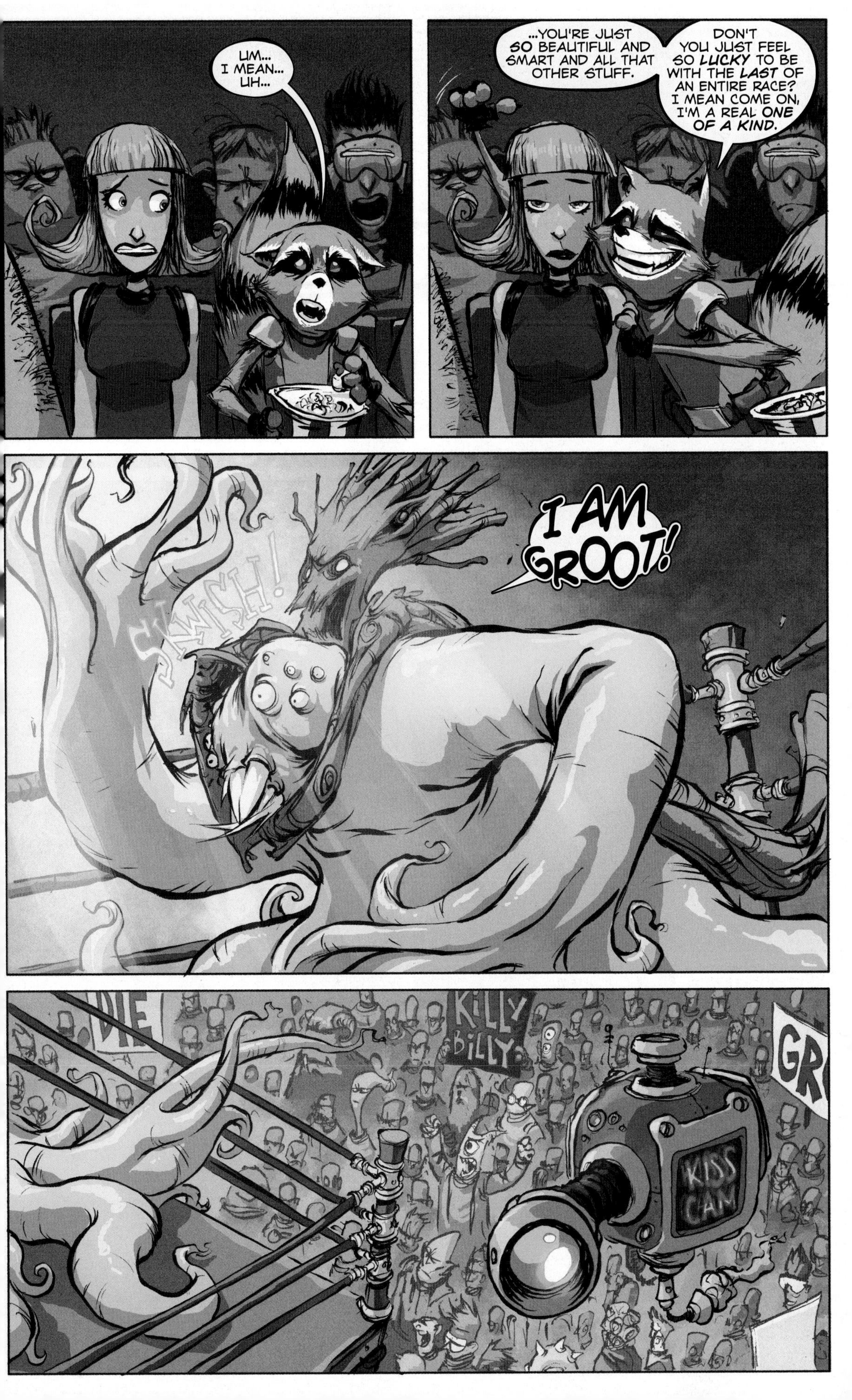
UM... I MEAN... UH...
...YOU'RE JUST SO BEAUTIFUL AND SMART AND ALL THAT OTHER STUFF.
DON'T YOU JUST FEEL SO LUCKY TO BE WITH THE LAST OF AN ENTIRE RACE? I MEAN COME ON, I'M A REAL ONE OF A KIND.
SWISH!
I AM GROOT!
DIE
KILLY BILLY
GR
KISS CAM

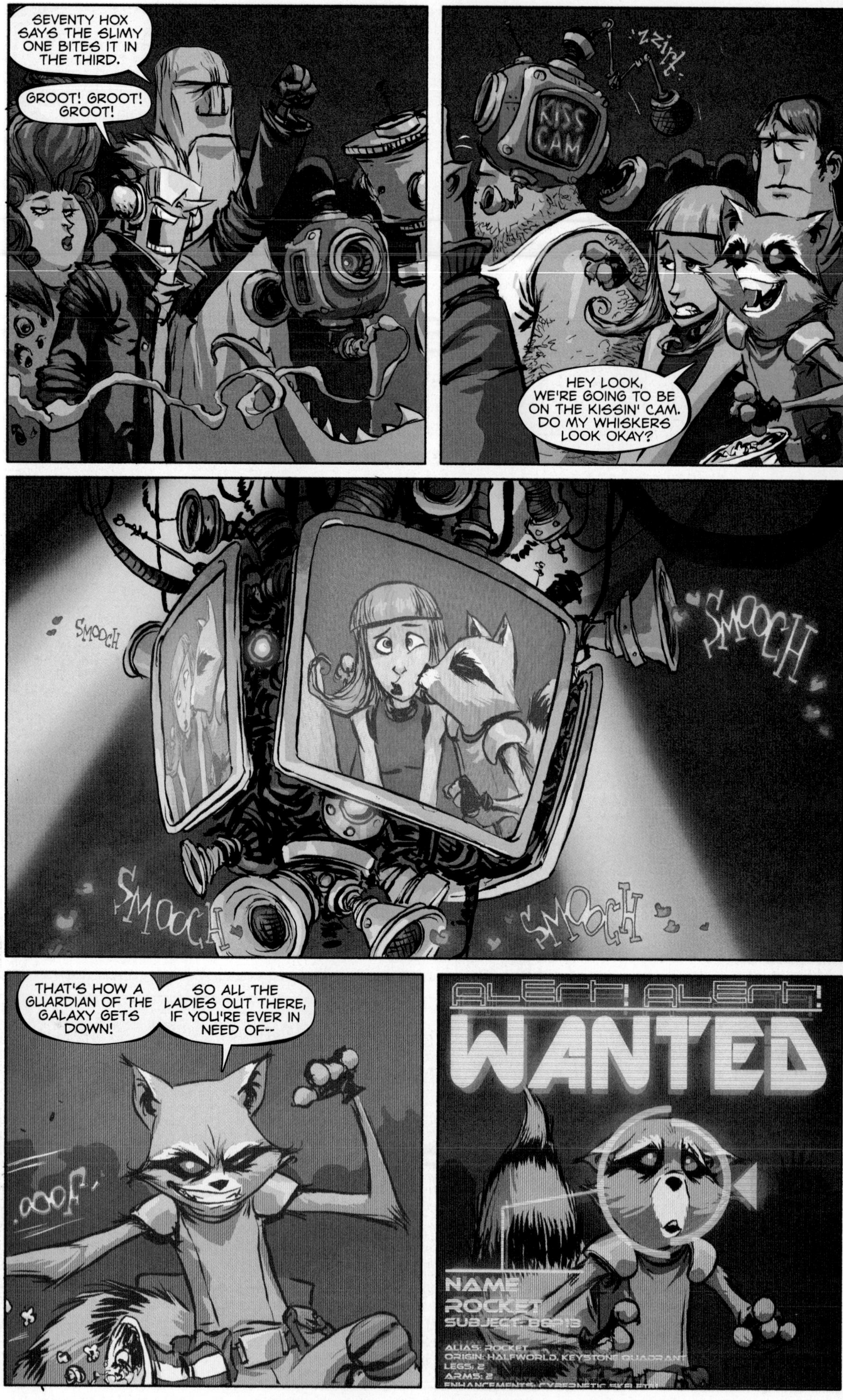
SEVENTY HOX SAYS THE SLIMY ONE BITES IT IN THE THIRD.
GROOT! GROOT! GROOT!
'ZZirt
KISS CAM
HEY LOOK, WE'RE GOING TO BE ON THE KISSIN' CAM. DO MY WHISKERS LOOK OKAY?
SMOOCH
SMOOCH
SMOOCH
SMOOCH
THAT'S HOW A GUARDIAN OF THE GALAXY GETS DOWN!
SO ALL THE LADIES OUT THERE, IF YOU'RE EVER IN NEED OF--
.OOOF!
ALERT! ALERT!
WANTED
NAME
ROCKET
ALIAS: ROCKET
ORIGIN: HALFWORLD, KEYSTONE QUADRANT
LEGS: 2
ARMS: 2

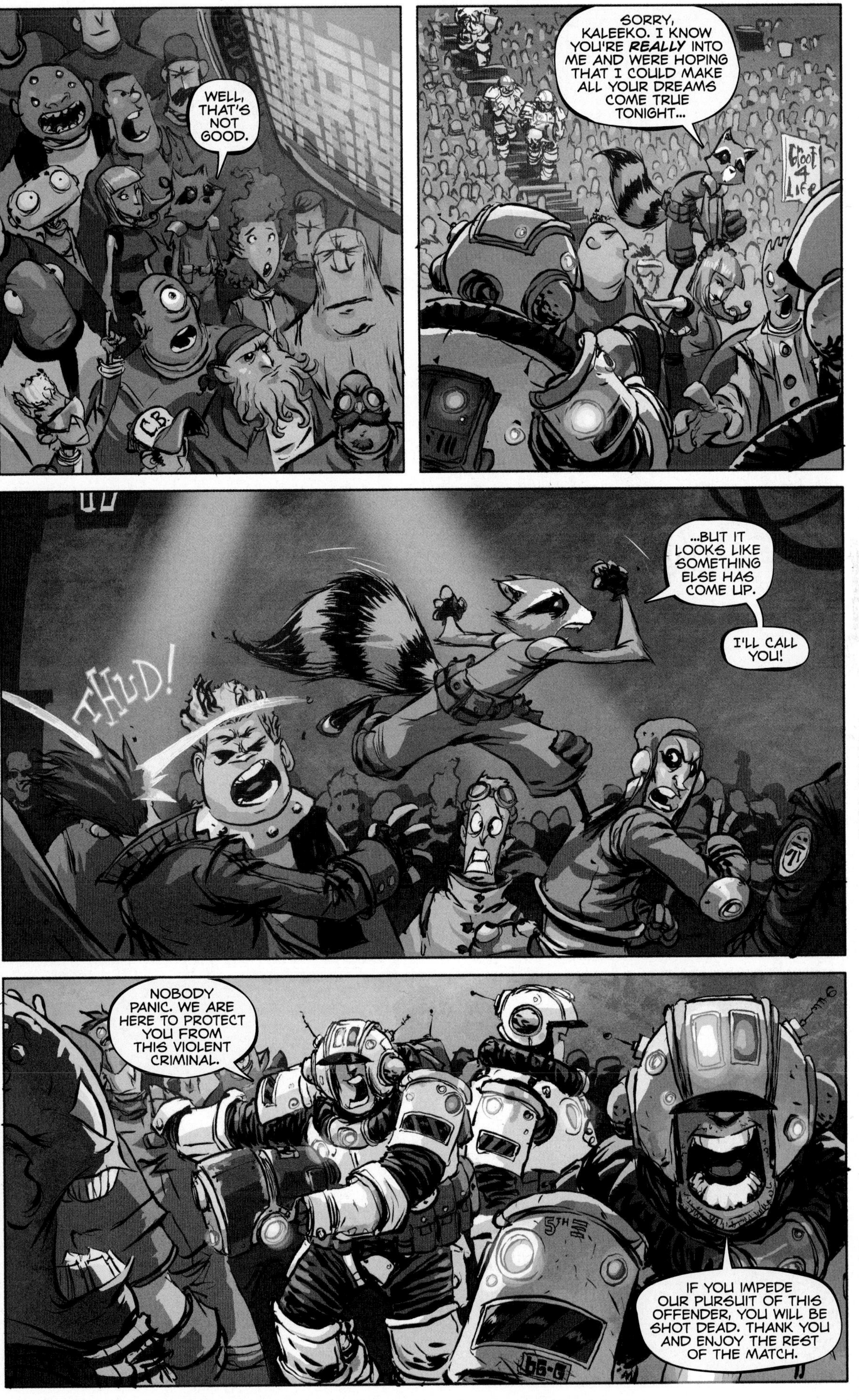
WELL, THAT'S NOT GOOD.
SORRY, KALEEKO. I KNOW YOU'RE *REALLY* INTO ME AND WERE HOPING THAT I COULD MAKE ALL YOUR DREAMS COME TRUE TONIGHT...
Groot 4 Life
...BUT IT LOOKS LIKE SOMETHING ELSE HAS COME UP.
I'LL CALL YOU!
THUD!
NOBODY PANIC. WE ARE HERE TO PROTECT YOU FROM THIS VIOLENT CRIMINAL.
IF YOU IMPEDE OUR PURSUIT OF THIS OFFENDER, YOU WILL BE SHOT DEAD. THANK YOU AND ENJOY THE REST OF THE MATCH.

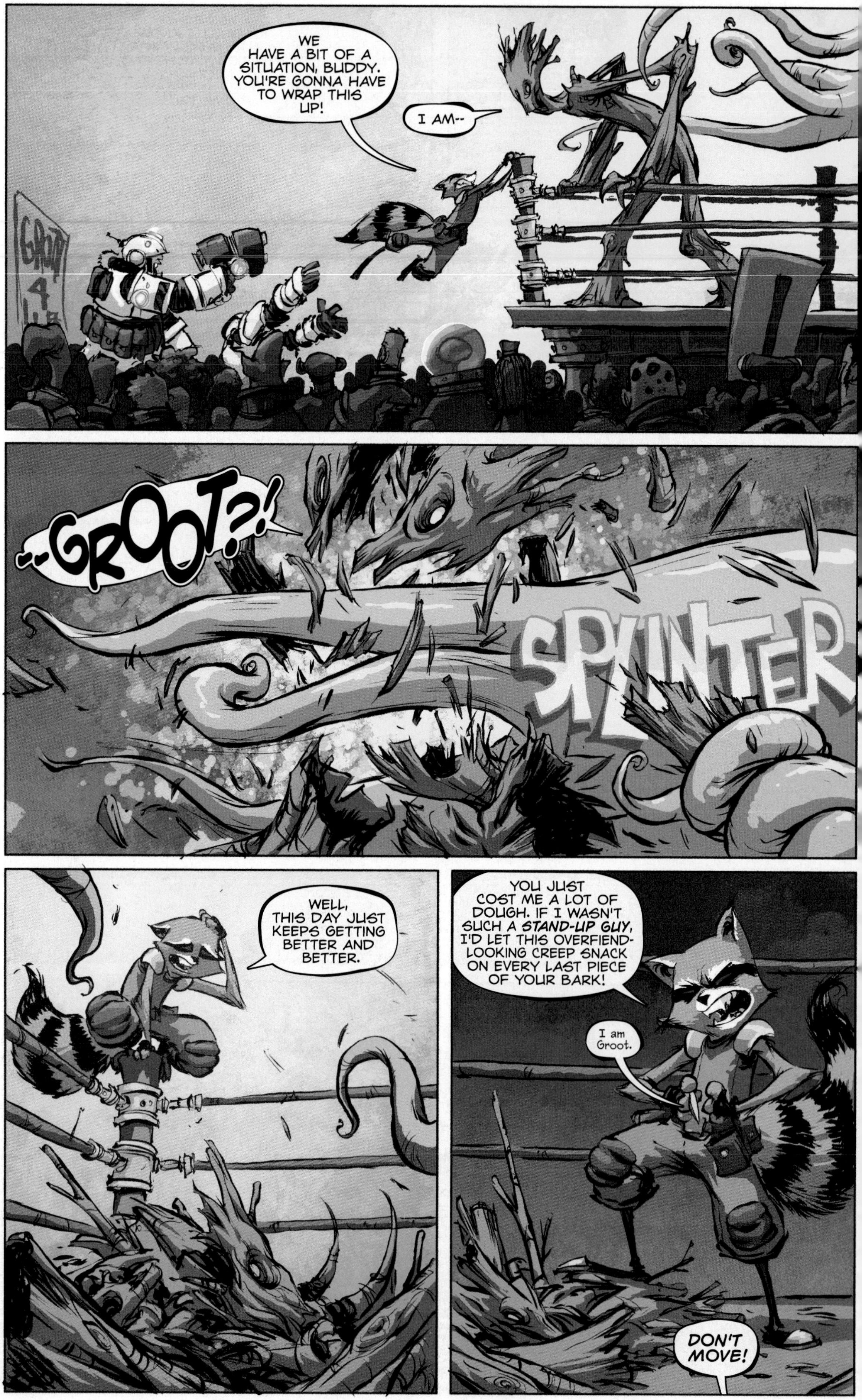
WE HAVE A BIT OF A SITUATION, BUDDY. YOU'RE GONNA HAVE TO WRAP THIS UP!
I AM--
--GROOT?!
SPLINTER
WELL, THIS DAY JUST KEEPS GETTING BETTER AND BETTER.
YOU JUST COST ME A LOT OF DOUGH. IF I WASN'T SUCH A *STAND-UP GUY*, I'D LET THIS OVERFIEND-LOOKING CREEP SNACK ON EVERY LAST PIECE OF YOUR BARK!
I am Groot.
DON'T MOVE!

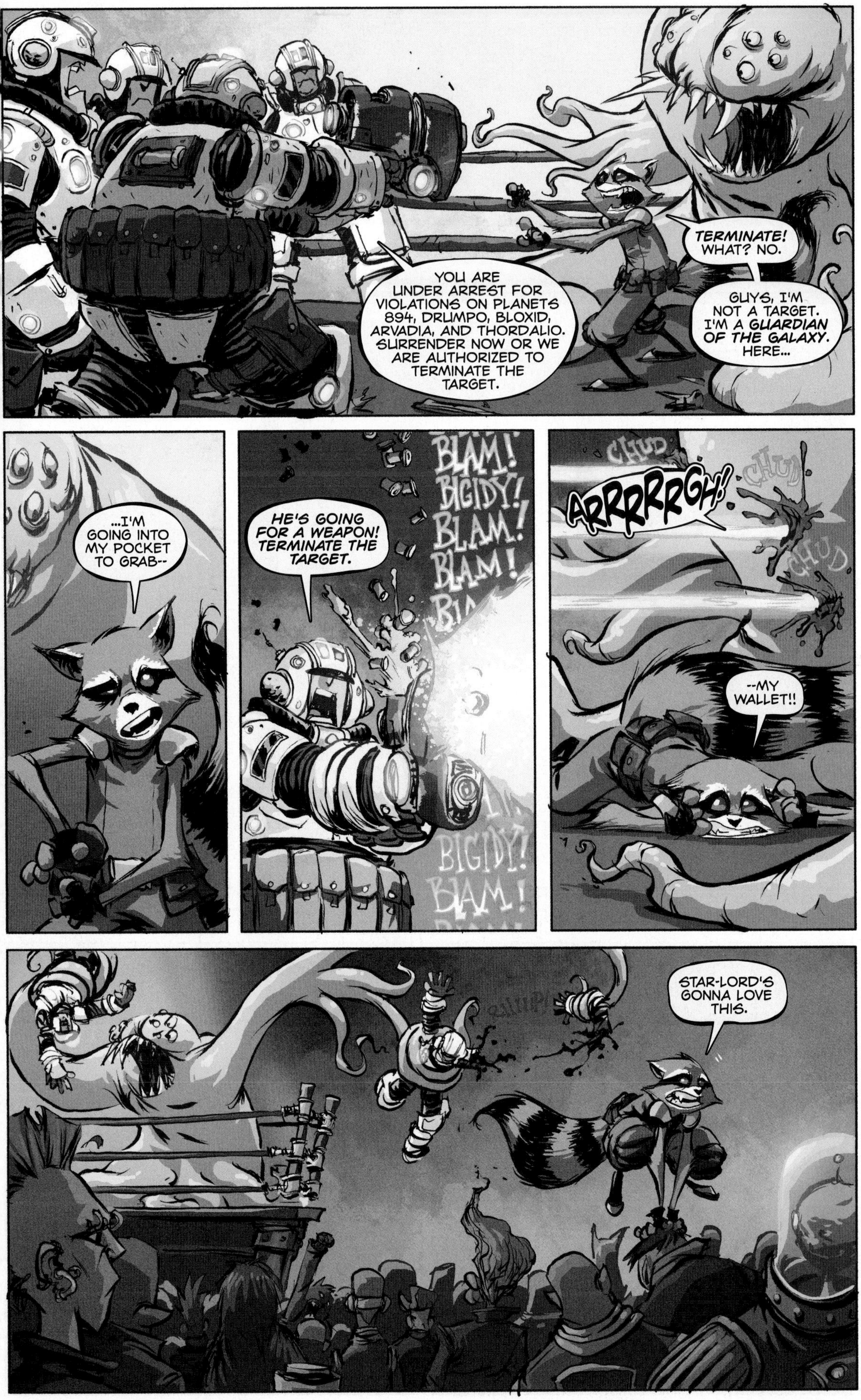
YOU ARE UNDER ARREST FOR VIOLATIONS ON PLANETS 894, DRUMPO, BLOXID, ARVADIA, AND THORDALIO. SURRENDER NOW OR WE ARE AUTHORIZED TO TERMINATE THE TARGET.
TERMINATE! WHAT? NO.
GUYS, I'M NOT A TARGET. I'M A GUARDIAN OF THE GALAXY. HERE...
...I'M GOING INTO MY POCKET TO GRAB--
BLAM! BIGIDY! BLAM! BLAM!
HE'S GOING FOR A WEAPON! TERMINATE THE TARGET.
BIGIDY! BLAM!
CHUD
ARRRRRGH!
CHUD
CHUD
--MY WALLET!!
STAR-LORD'S GONNA LOVE THIS.

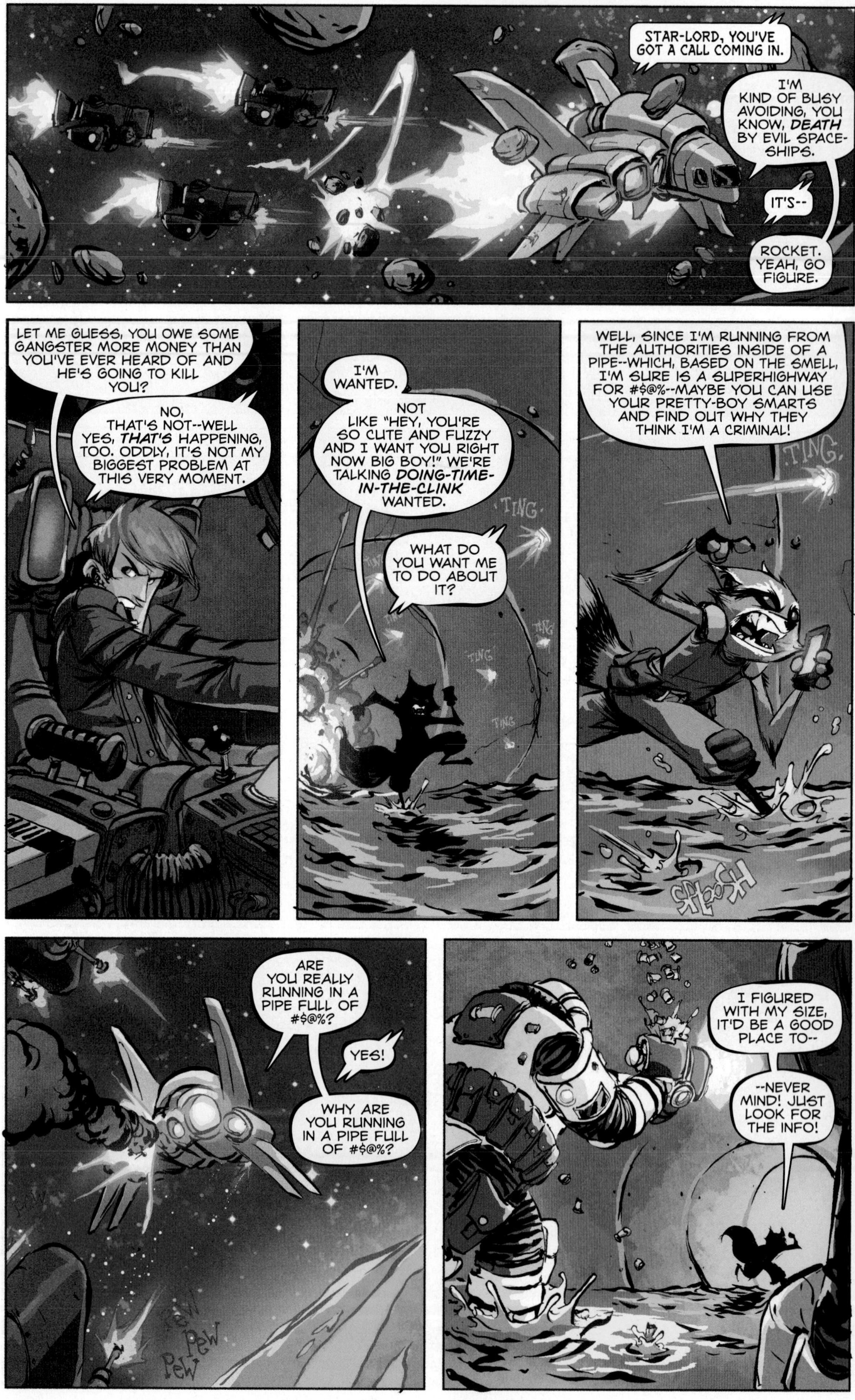

STAR-LORD, YOU'VE GOT A CALL COMING IN.
I'M KIND OF BUSY AVOIDING, YOU KNOW, *DEATH* BY EVIL SPACE-SHIPS.
IT'S--
ROCKET. YEAH, GO FIGURE.
LET ME GUESS, YOU OWE SOME GANGSTER MORE MONEY THAN YOU'VE EVER HEARD OF AND HE'S GOING TO KILL YOU?
NO, THAT'S NOT--WELL YES, *THAT'S* HAPPENING, TOO. ODDLY, IT'S NOT MY BIGGEST PROBLEM AT THIS VERY MOMENT.
I'M WANTED.
NOT LIKE "HEY, YOU'RE SO CUTE AND FUZZY AND I WANT YOU RIGHT NOW BIG BOY!" WE'RE TALKING *DOING-TIME-IN-THE-CLINK* WANTED.
TING
WHAT DO YOU WANT ME TO DO ABOUT IT?
TING
TING
TING
WELL, SINCE I'M RUNNING FROM THE AUTHORITIES INSIDE OF A PIPE--WHICH, BASED ON THE SMELL, I'M SURE IS A SUPERHIGHWAY FOR #$@%--MAYBE YOU CAN USE YOUR PRETTY-BOY SMARTS AND FIND OUT WHY THEY THINK I'M A CRIMINAL!
TING
ARE YOU REALLY RUNNING IN A PIPE FULL OF #$@%?
YES!
WHY ARE YOU RUNNING IN A PIPE FULL OF #$@%?
PEW
PEW
PEW
I FIGURED WITH MY SIZE, IT'D BE A GOOD PLACE TO--
--NEVER MIND! JUST LOOK FOR THE INFO!

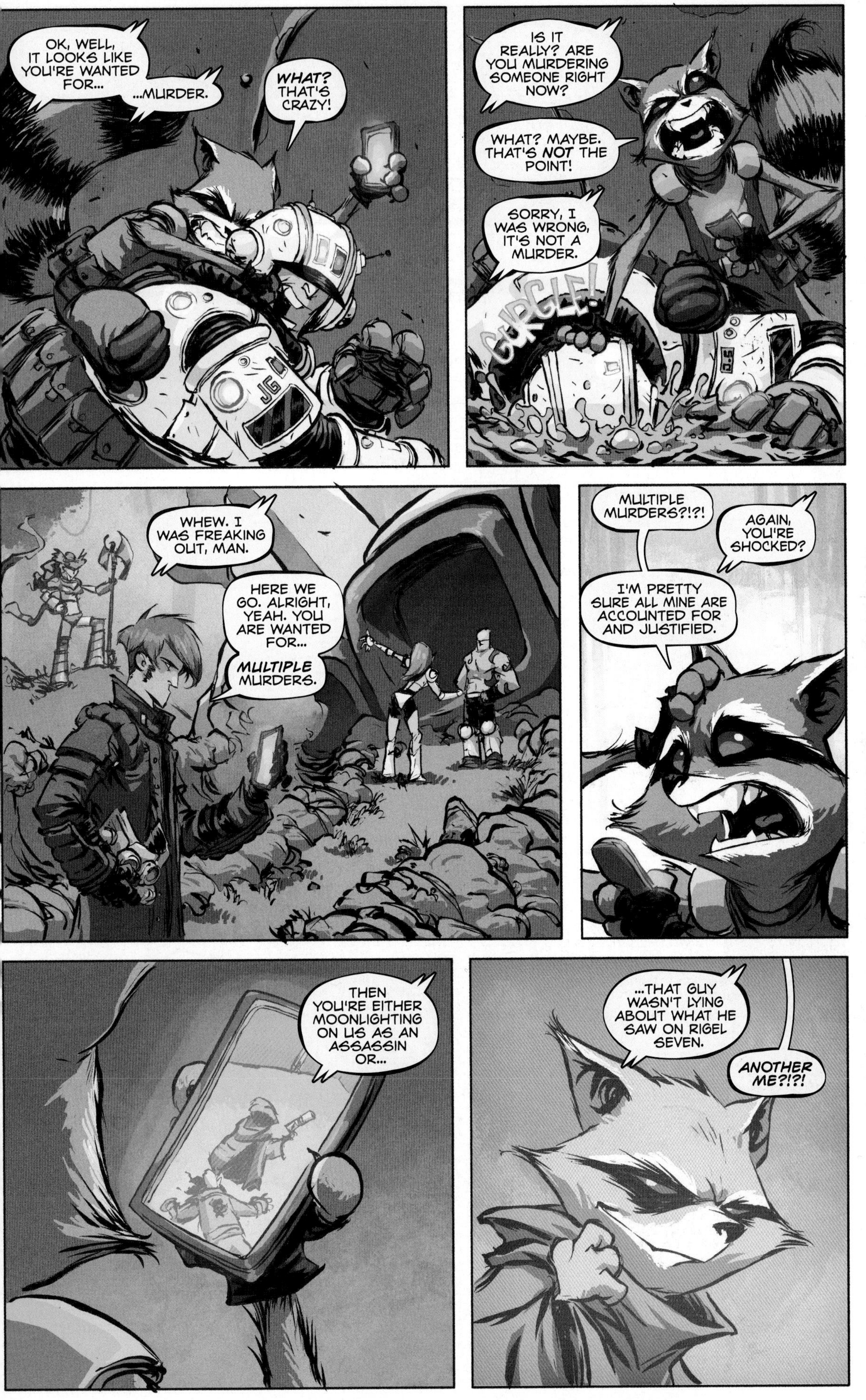
OK, WELL, IT LOOKS LIKE YOU'RE WANTED FOR...
...MURDER.
WHAT? THAT'S CRAZY!
IS IT REALLY? ARE YOU MURDERING SOMEONE RIGHT NOW?
WHAT? MAYBE. THAT'S NOT THE POINT!
SORRY, I WAS WRONG, IT'S NOT A MURDER.
GURGLE!
WHEW. I WAS FREAKING OUT, MAN.
HERE WE GO. ALRIGHT, YEAH. YOU ARE WANTED FOR...
MULTIPLE MURDERS.
MULTIPLE MURDERS?!?!
AGAIN, YOU'RE SHOCKED?
I'M PRETTY SURE ALL MINE ARE ACCOUNTED FOR AND JUSTIFIED.
THEN YOU'RE EITHER MOONLIGHTING ON US AS AN ASSASSIN OR...
...THAT GUY WASN'T LYING ABOUT WHAT HE SAW ON RIGEL SEVEN.
ANOTHER ME?!?!

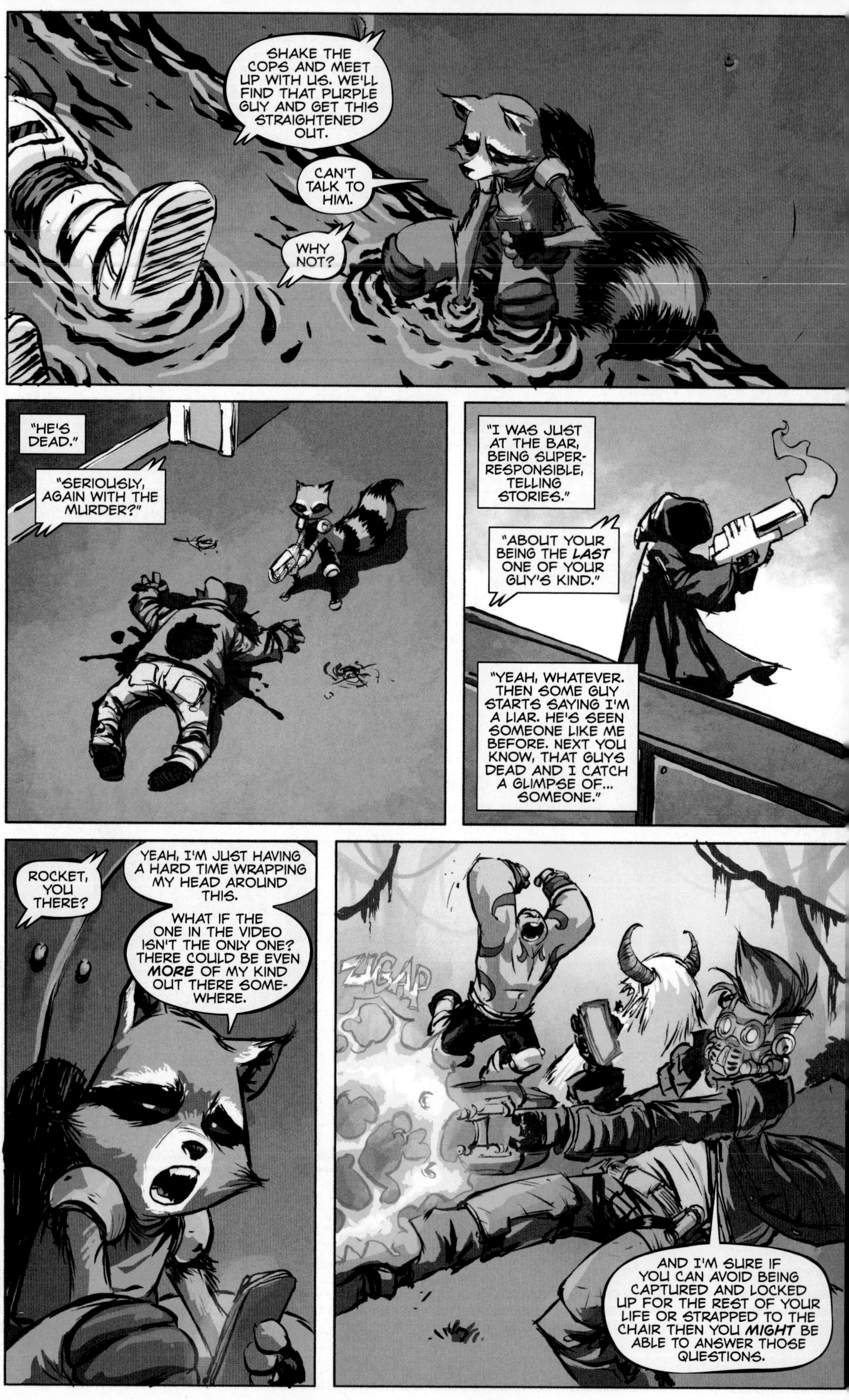
SHAKE THE COPS AND MEET UP WITH US. WE'LL FIND THAT PURPLE GUY AND GET THIS STRAIGHTENED OUT.
CAN'T TALK TO HIM.
WHY NOT?
"HE'S DEAD."
"SERIOUSLY, AGAIN WITH THE MURDER?"
"I WAS JUST AT THE BAR, BEING SUPER-RESPONSIBLE, TELLING STORIES."
"ABOUT YOUR BEING THE LAST ONE OF YOUR GUY'S KIND."
"YEAH, WHATEVER. THEN SOME GUY STARTS SAYING I'M A LIAR. HE'S SEEN SOMEONE LIKE ME BEFORE. NEXT YOU KNOW, THAT GUYS DEAD AND I CATCH A GLIMPSE OF... SOMEONE."
ROCKET, YOU THERE?
YEAH, I'M JUST HAVING A HARD TIME WRAPPING MY HEAD AROUND THIS.
WHAT IF THE ONE IN THE VIDEO ISN'T THE ONLY ONE? THERE COULD BE EVEN MORE OF MY KIND OUT THERE SOME-WHERE.
ZIGAP
AND I'M SURE IF YOU CAN AVOID BEING CAPTURED AND LOCKED UP FOR THE REST OF YOUR LIFE OR STRAPPED TO THE CHAIR THEN YOU MIGHT BE ABLE TO ANSWER THOSE QUESTIONS.

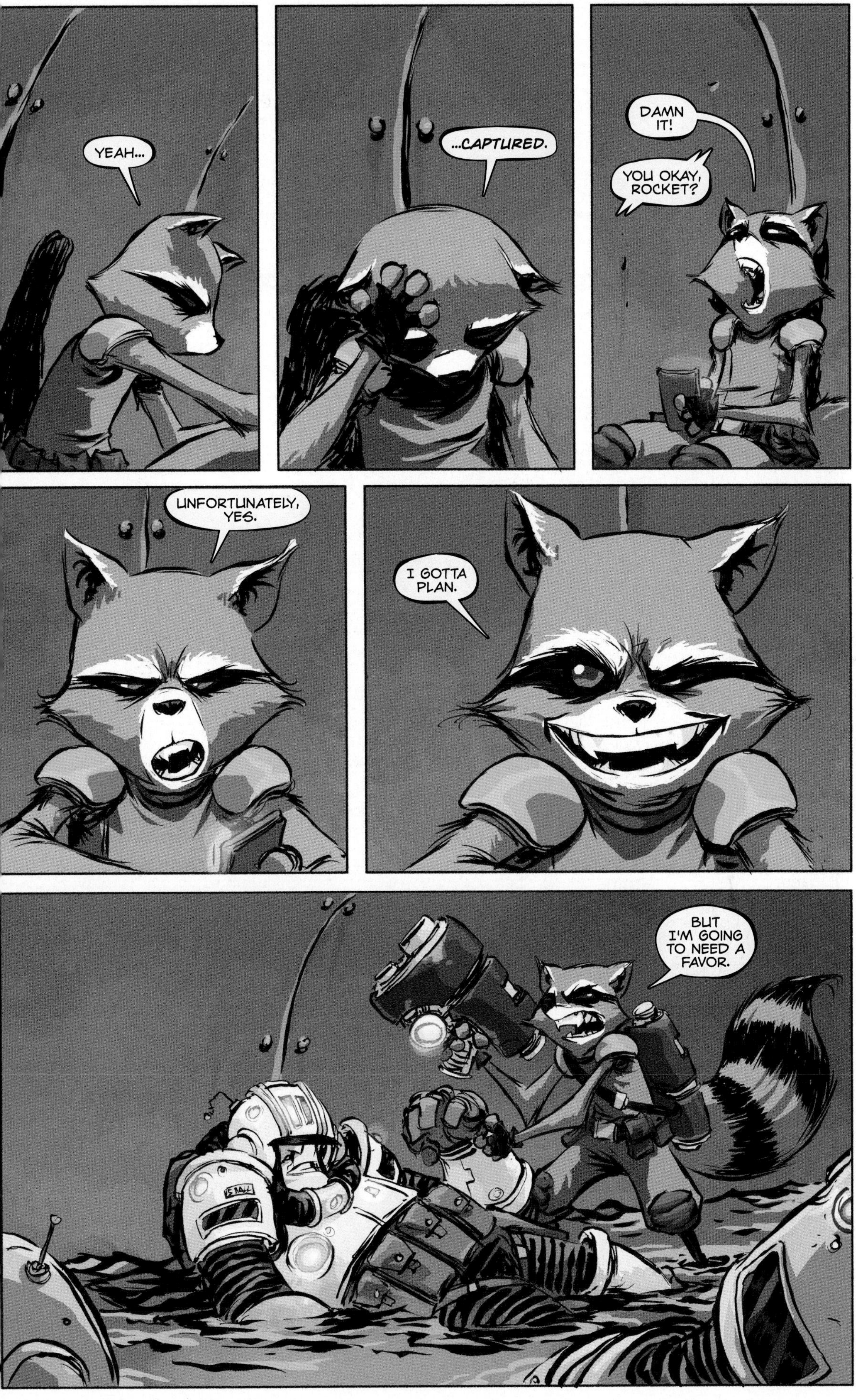
YEAH...
...CAPTURED.
DAMN IT!
YOU OKAY, ROCKET?
UNFORTUNATELY, YES.
I GOTTA PLAN.
BUT I'M GOING TO NEED A FAVOR.

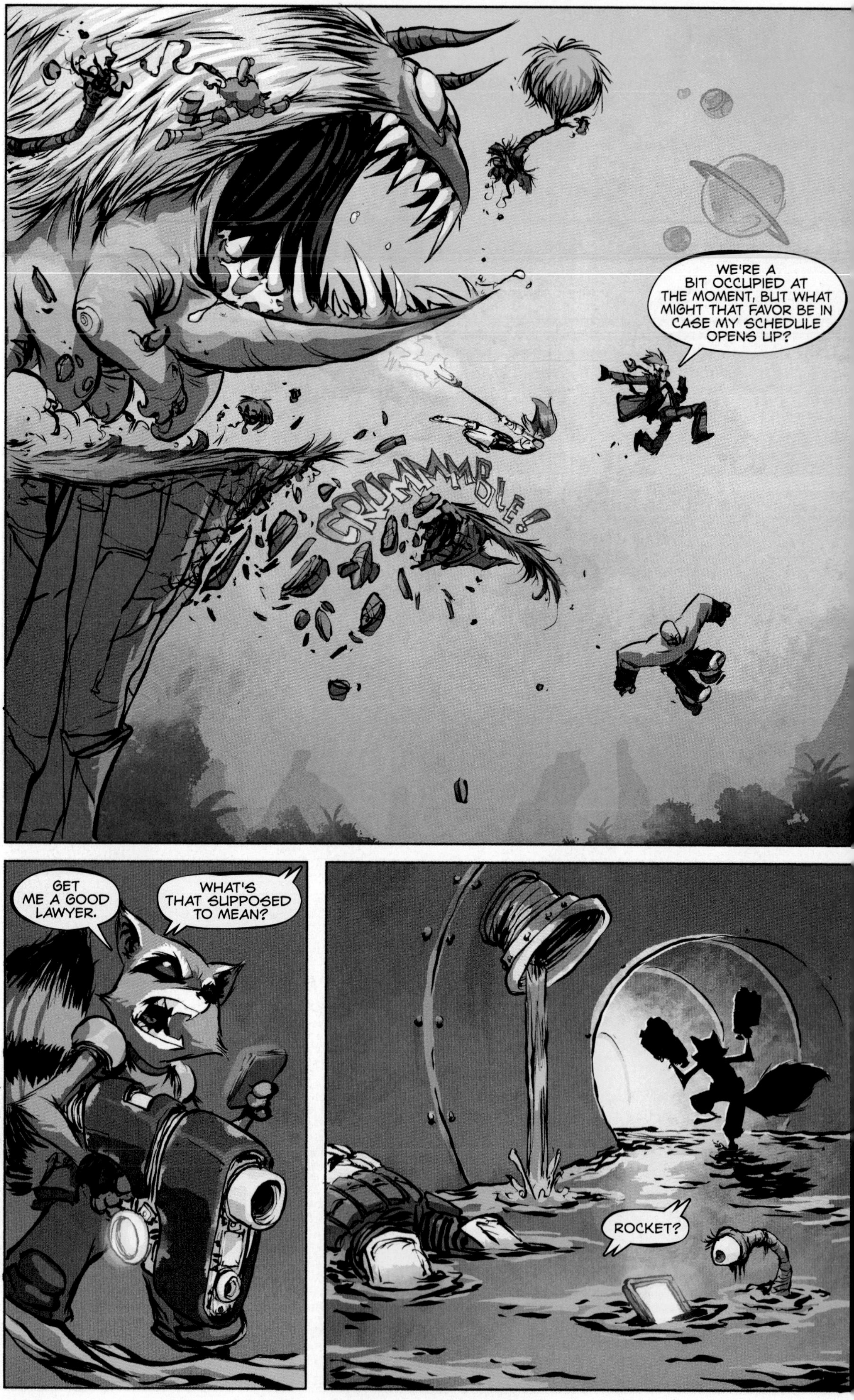
WE'RE A BIT OCCUPIED AT THE MOMENT, BUT WHAT MIGHT THAT FAVOR BE IN CASE MY SCHEDULE OPENS UP?
CRUMMMMBLE!
GET ME A GOOD LAWYER.
WHAT'S THAT SUPPOSED TO MEAN?
ROCKET?

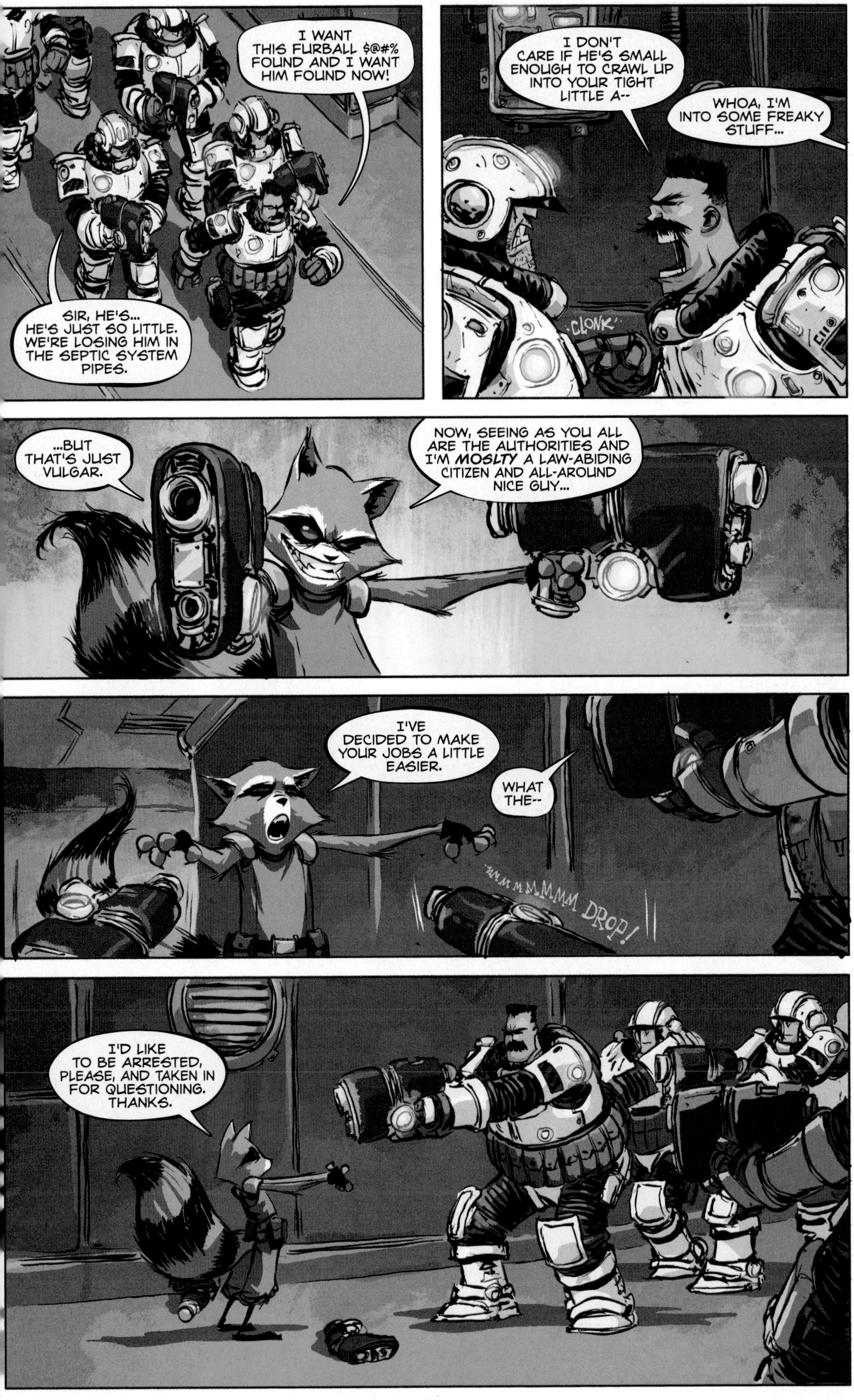
I WANT THIS FURBALL $@#% FOUND AND I WANT HIM FOUND NOW!
SIR, HE'S... HE'S JUST SO LITTLE. WE'RE LOSING HIM IN THE SEPTIC SYSTEM PIPES.
I DON'T CARE IF HE'S SMALL ENOUGH TO CRAWL UP INTO YOUR TIGHT LITTLE A--
WHOA, I'M INTO SOME FREAKY STUFF...
CLONK
...BUT THAT'S JUST VULGAR.
NOW, SEEING AS YOU ALL ARE THE AUTHORITIES AND I'M *MOSLTY* A LAW-ABIDING CITIZEN AND ALL-AROUND NICE GUY...
I'VE DECIDED TO MAKE YOUR JOBS A LITTLE EASIER.
WHAT THE--
DROP!
I'D LIKE TO BE ARRESTED, PLEASE, AND TAKEN IN FOR QUESTIONING. THANKS.

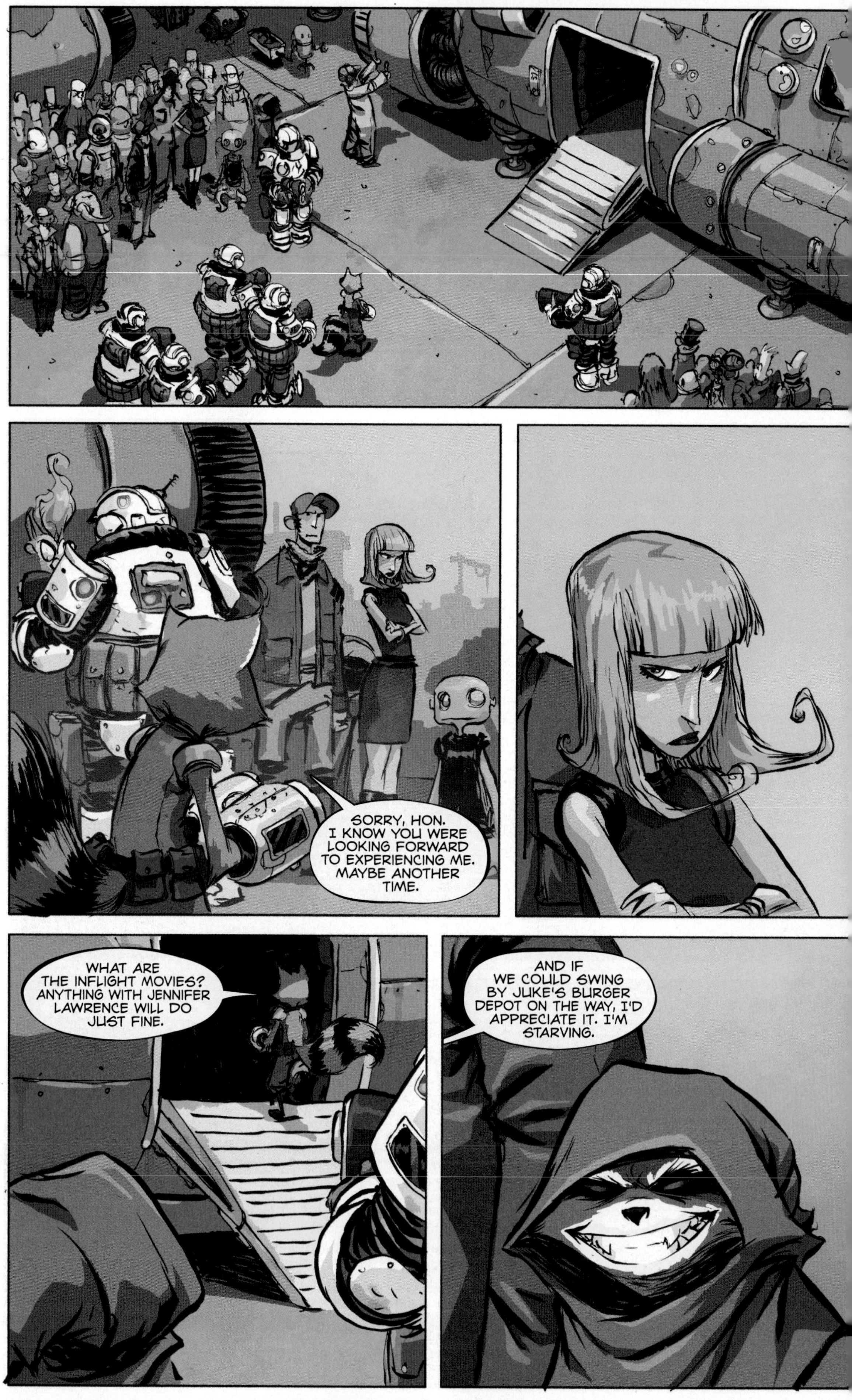
SORRY, HON. I KNOW YOU WERE LOOKING FORWARD TO EXPERIENCING ME. MAYBE ANOTHER TIME.
WHAT ARE THE INFLIGHT MOVIES? ANYTHING WITH JENNIFER LAWRENCE WILL DO JUST FINE.
AND IF WE COULD SWING BY JUKE'S BURGER DEPOT ON THE WAY, I'D APPRECIATE IT. I'M STARVING.

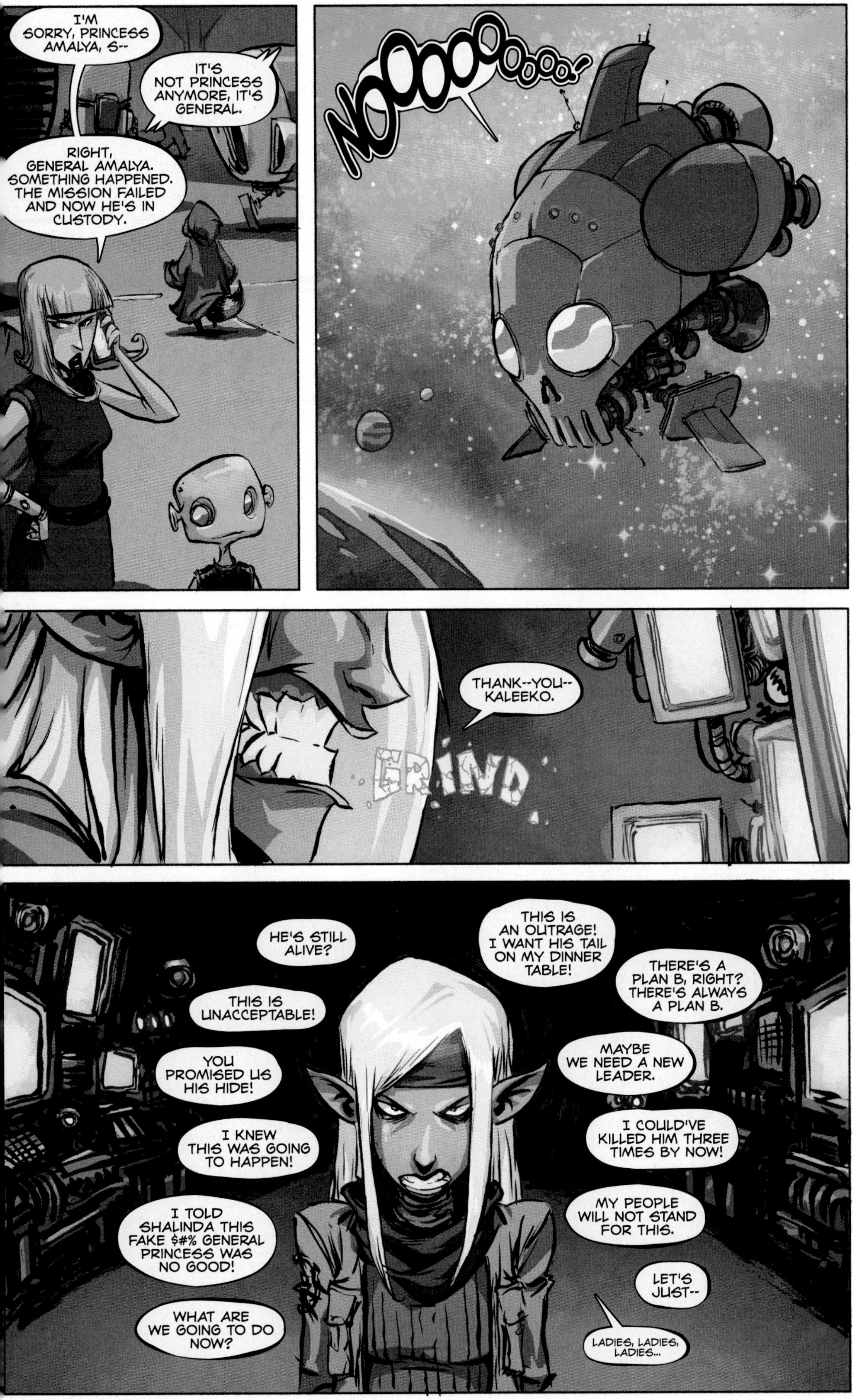
I'M SORRY, PRINCESS AMALYA, S--
IT'S NOT PRINCESS ANYMORE, IT'S GENERAL.
RIGHT, GENERAL AMALYA. SOMETHING HAPPENED. THE MISSION FAILED AND NOW HE'S IN CUSTODY.
NOOOOOOooo!
THANK--YOU--KALEEKO.
GRIND
HE'S STILL ALIVE?
THIS IS AN OUTRAGE! I WANT HIS TAIL ON MY DINNER TABLE!
THERE'S A PLAN B, RIGHT? THERE'S ALWAYS A PLAN B.
THIS IS UNACCEPTABLE!
YOU PROMISED US HIS HIDE!
MAYBE WE NEED A NEW LEADER.
I KNEW THIS WAS GOING TO HAPPEN!
I COULD'VE KILLED HIM THREE TIMES BY NOW!
I TOLD SHALINDA THIS FAKE $#% GENERAL PRINCESS WAS NO GOOD!
MY PEOPLE WILL NOT STAND FOR THIS.
LET'S JUST--
WHAT ARE WE GOING TO DO NOW?
LADIES, LADIES, LADIES...

LADIES!!!

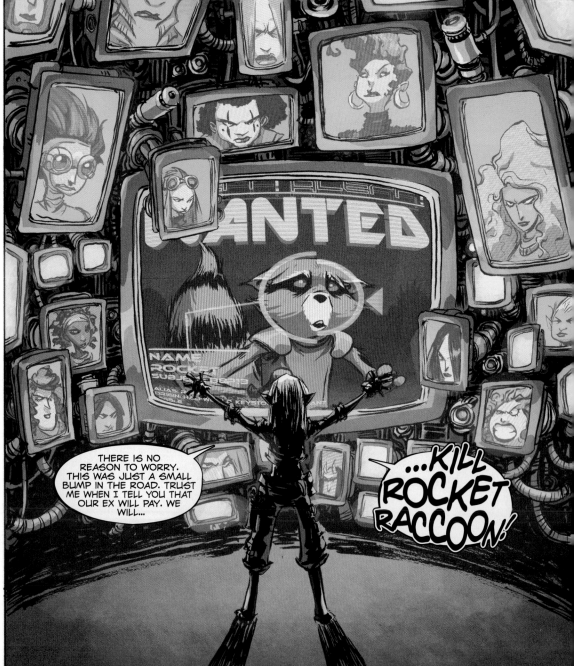

WANTED

NAME
ROCKET

THERE IS NO REASON TO WORRY. THIS WAS JUST A SMALL BUMP IN THE ROAD. TRUST ME WHEN I TELL YOU THAT OUR EX WILL PAY. WE WILL...

...KILL ROCKET RACCOON!

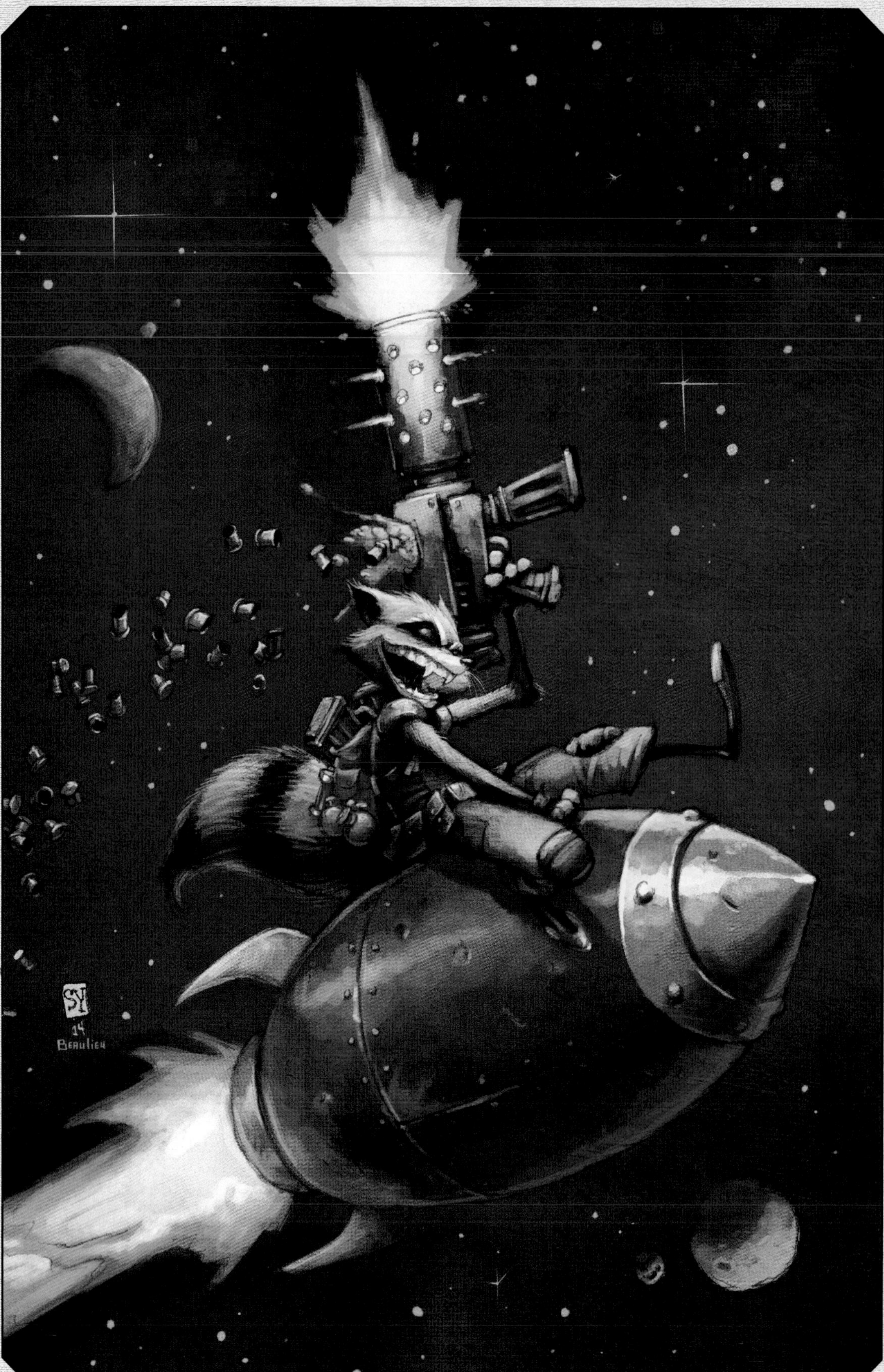
14
Beaulieu

2 A CHASING TALE part 2

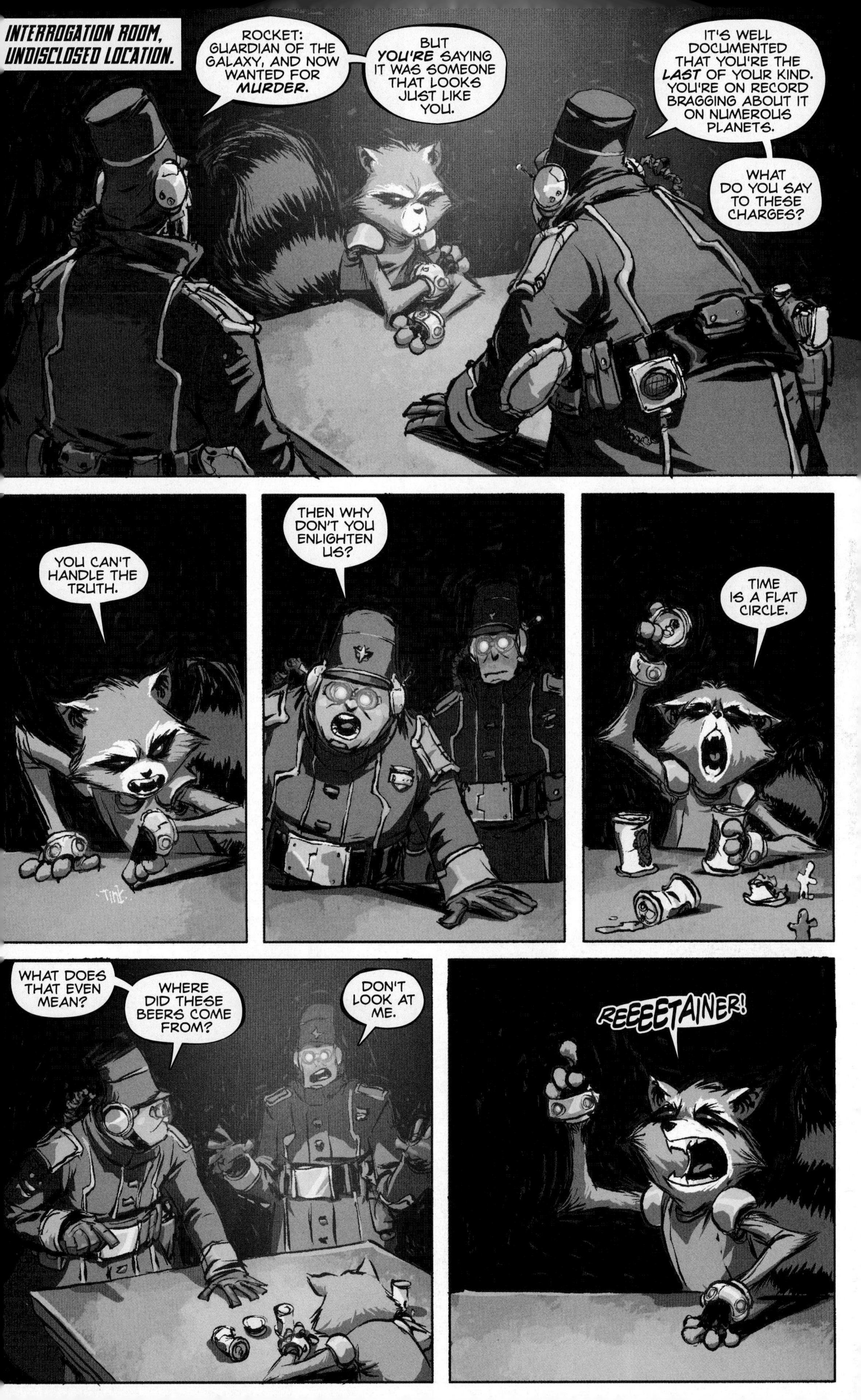
INTERROGATION ROOM, UNDISCLOSED LOCATION.
ROCKET: GUARDIAN OF THE GALAXY, AND NOW WANTED FOR MURDER.
BUT YOU'RE SAYING IT WAS SOMEONE THAT LOOKS JUST LIKE YOU.
IT'S WELL DOCUMENTED THAT YOU'RE THE LAST OF YOUR KIND. YOU'RE ON RECORD BRAGGING ABOUT IT ON NUMEROUS PLANETS.
WHAT DO YOU SAY TO THESE CHARGES?
YOU CAN'T HANDLE THE TRUTH.
TINK
THEN WHY DON'T YOU ENLIGHTEN US?
TIME IS A FLAT CIRCLE.
WHAT DOES THAT EVEN MEAN?
WHERE DID THESE BEERS COME FROM?
DON'T LOOK AT ME.
REEEEETAINER!

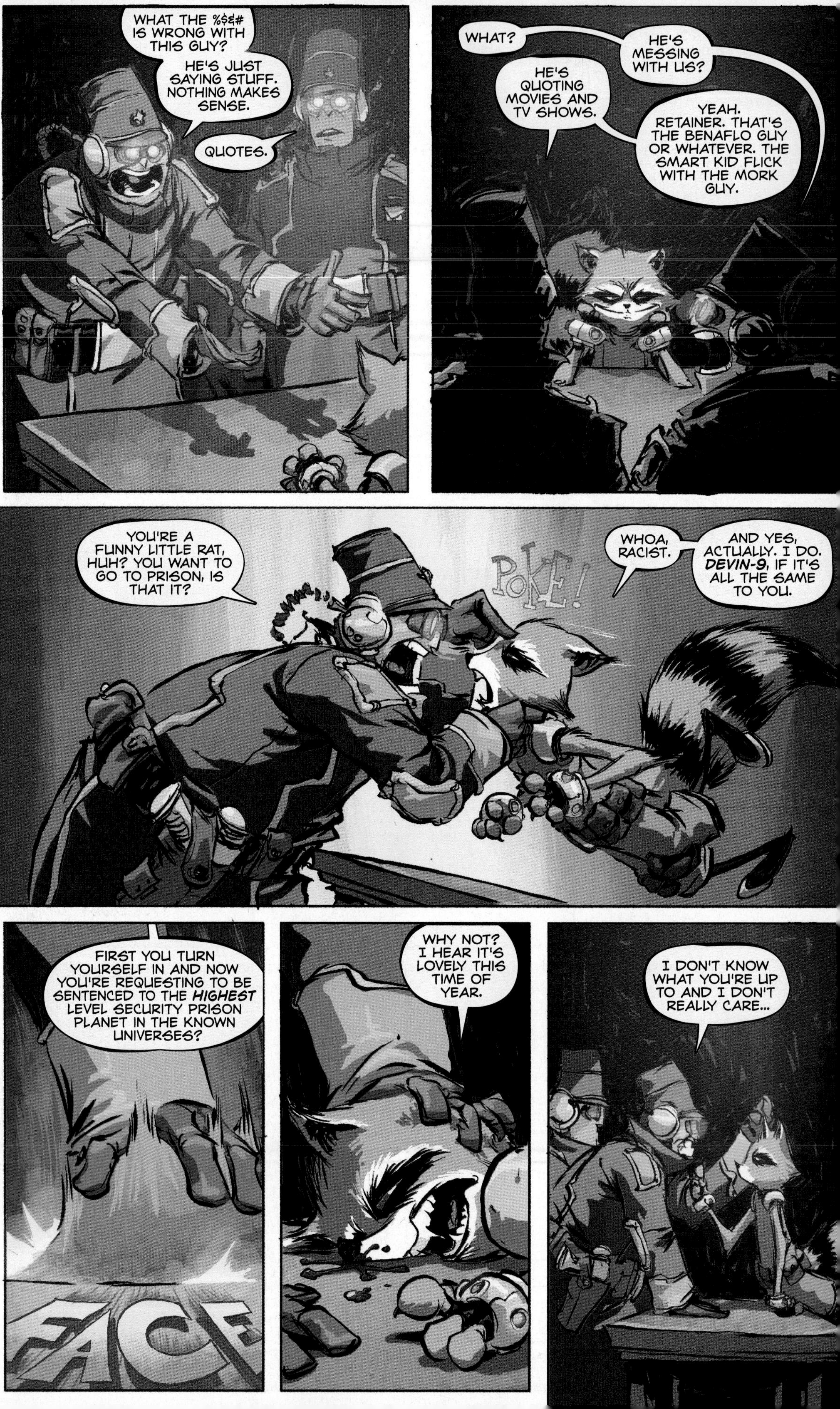
WHAT THE %$&# IS WRONG WITH THIS GUY?
HE'S JUST SAYING STUFF. NOTHING MAKES SENSE.
QUOTES.
WHAT?
HE'S QUOTING MOVIES AND TV SHOWS.
HE'S MESSING WITH US?
YEAH. RETAINER. THAT'S THE BENAFLO GUY OR WHATEVER. THE SMART KID FLICK WITH THE MORK GUY.
YOU'RE A FUNNY LITTLE RAT, HUH? YOU WANT TO GO TO PRISON, IS THAT IT?
POKE!
WHOA, RACIST.
AND YES, ACTUALLY. I DO. DEVIN-9, IF IT'S ALL THE SAME TO YOU.
FIRST YOU TURN YOURSELF IN AND NOW YOU'RE REQUESTING TO BE SENTENCED TO THE HIGHEST LEVEL SECURITY PRISON PLANET IN THE KNOWN UNIVERSES?
FACE
WHY NOT? I HEAR IT'S LOVELY THIS TIME OF YEAR.
I DON'T KNOW WHAT YOU'RE UP TO AND I DON'T REALLY CARE...

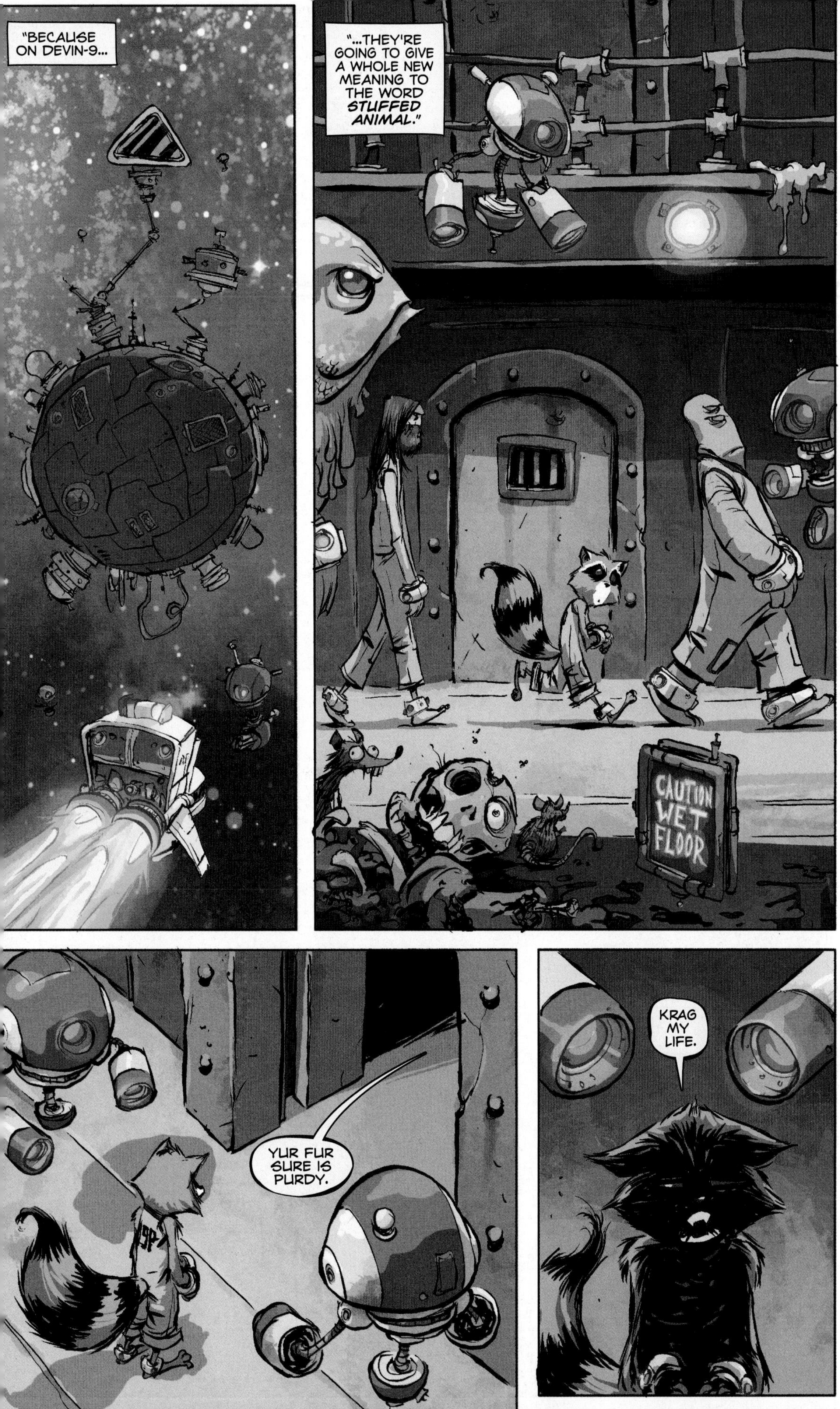
"BECAUSE ON DEVIN-9...
"...THEY'RE GOING TO GIVE A WHOLE NEW MEANING TO THE WORD STUFFED ANIMAL."
CAUTION WET FLOOR
YUR FUR SURE IS PURDY.
KRAG MY LIFE.

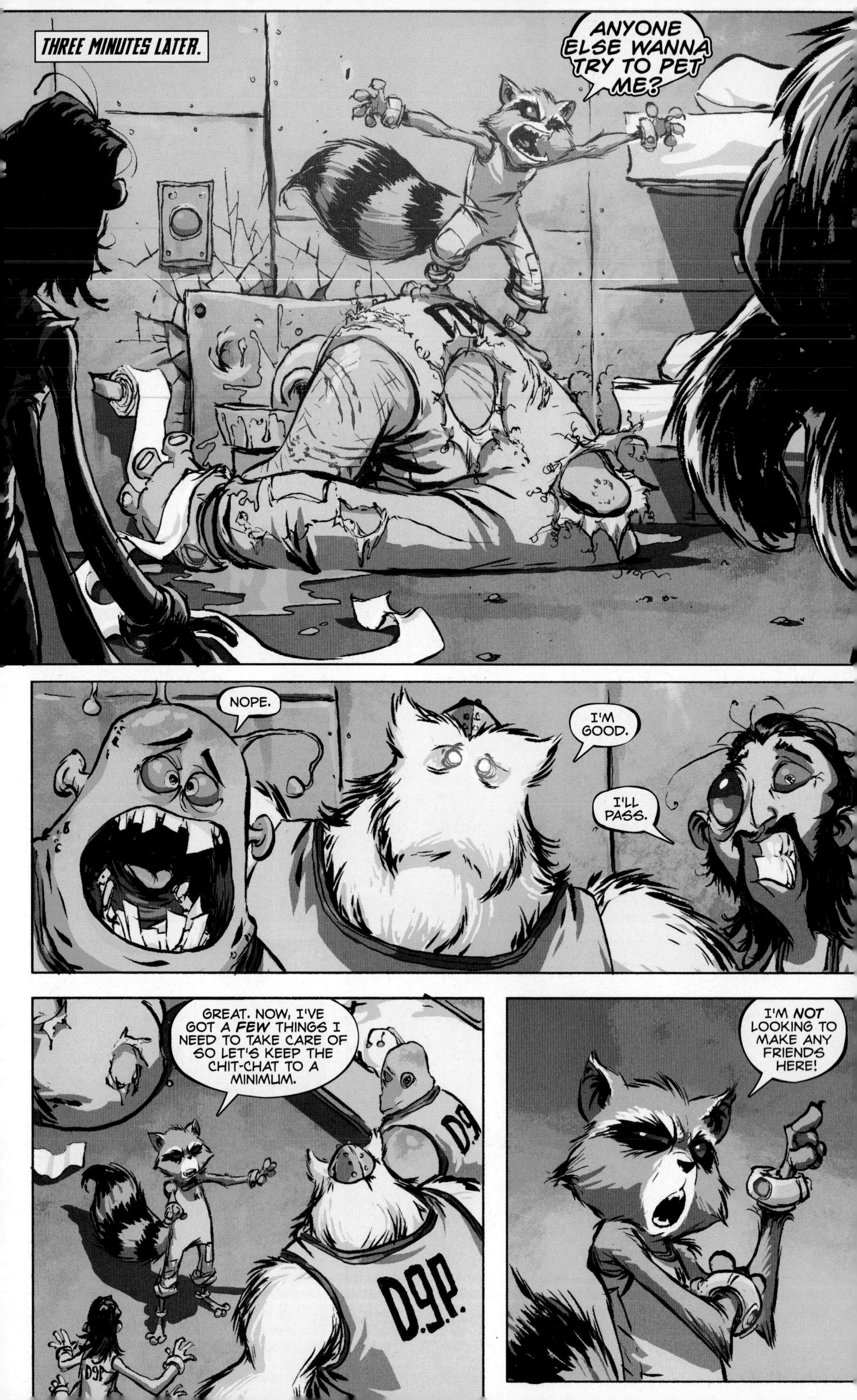
THREE MINUTES LATER.
ANYONE ELSE WANNA TRY TO PET ME?
NOPE.
I'M GOOD.
I'LL PASS.
GREAT. NOW, I'VE GOT A *FEW* THINGS I NEED TO TAKE CARE OF SO LET'S KEEP THE CHIT-CHAT TO A MINIMUM.
I'M *NOT* LOOKING TO MAKE ANY FRIENDS HERE!

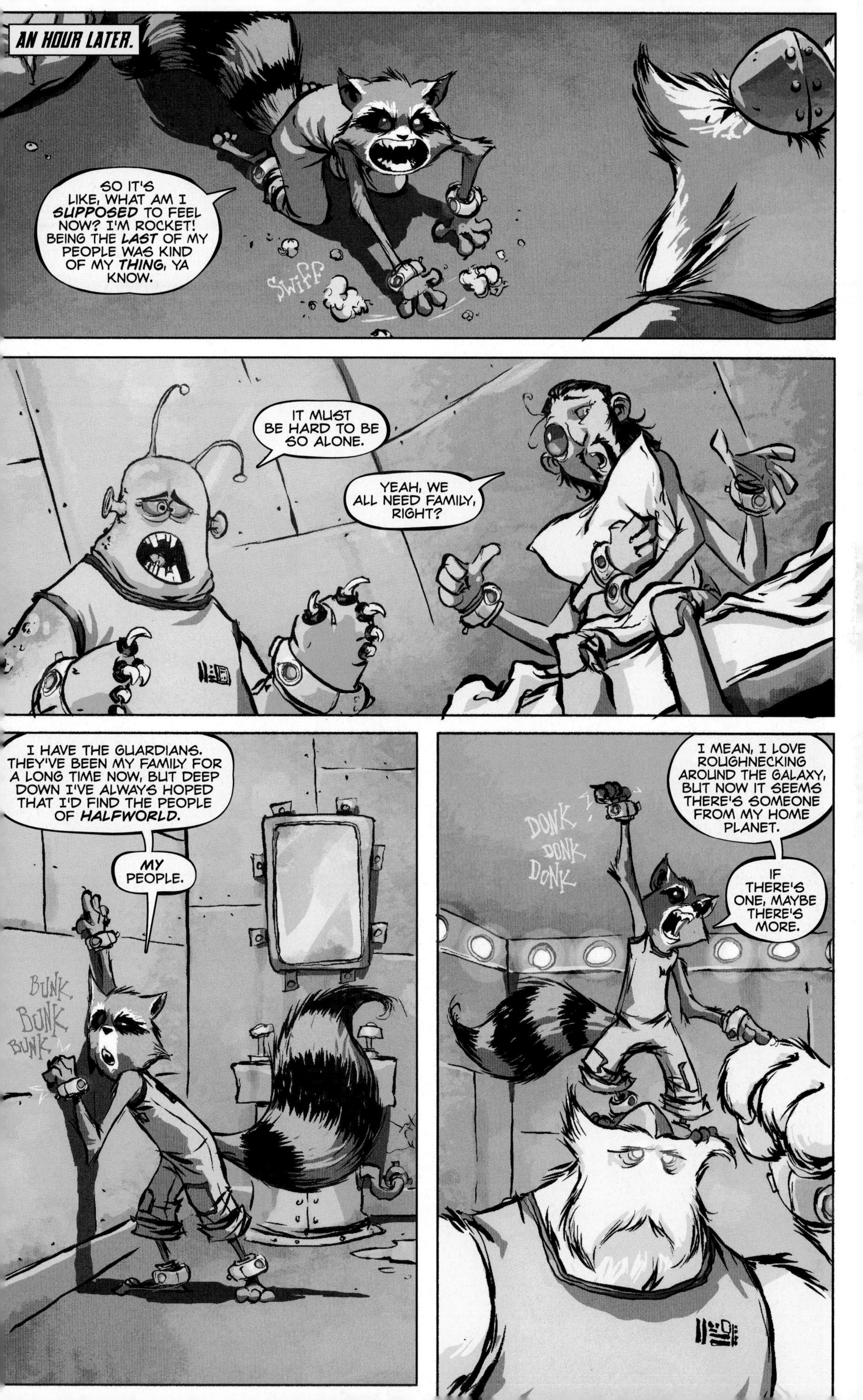
AN HOUR LATER.
SO IT'S LIKE, WHAT AM I SUPPOSED TO FEEL NOW? I'M ROCKET! BEING THE LAST OF MY PEOPLE WAS KIND OF MY THING, YA KNOW.
SWIFF
IT MUST BE HARD TO BE SO ALONE.
YEAH, WE ALL NEED FAMILY, RIGHT?
I HAVE THE GUARDIANS. THEY'VE BEEN MY FAMILY FOR A LONG TIME NOW, BUT DEEP DOWN I'VE ALWAYS HOPED THAT I'D FIND THE PEOPLE OF HALFWORLD.
MY PEOPLE.
BUNK BUNK BUNK
I MEAN, I LOVE ROUGHNECKING AROUND THE GALAXY, BUT NOW IT SEEMS THERE'S SOMEONE FROM MY HOME PLANET.
IF THERE'S ONE, MAYBE THERE'S MORE.
DONK DONK DONK

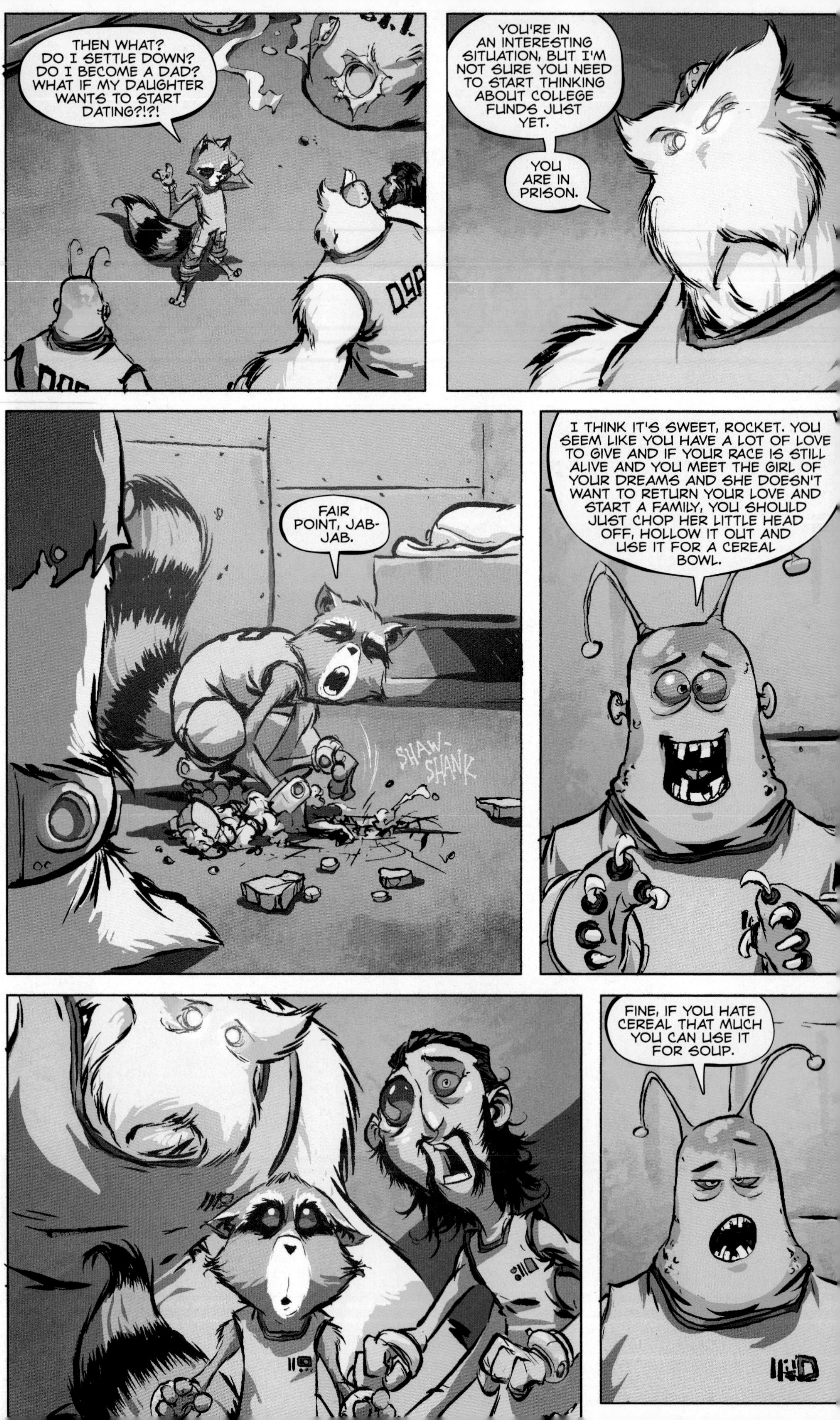

THEN WHAT? DO I SETTLE DOWN? DO I BECOME A DAD? WHAT IF MY DAUGHTER WANTS TO START DATING?!?!
YOU'RE IN AN INTERESTING SITUATION, BUT I'M NOT SURE YOU NEED TO START THINKING ABOUT COLLEGE FUNDS JUST YET.
YOU ARE IN PRISON.
FAIR POINT, JAB-JAB.
SHAW-SHANK
I THINK IT'S SWEET, ROCKET. YOU SEEM LIKE YOU HAVE A LOT OF LOVE TO GIVE AND IF YOUR RACE IS STILL ALIVE AND YOU MEET THE GIRL OF YOUR DREAMS AND SHE DOESN'T WANT TO RETURN YOUR LOVE AND START A FAMILY, YOU SHOULD JUST CHOP HER LITTLE HEAD OFF, HOLLOW IT OUT AND USE IT FOR A CEREAL BOWL.
FINE, IF YOU HATE CEREAL THAT MUCH YOU CAN USE IT FOR SOUP.

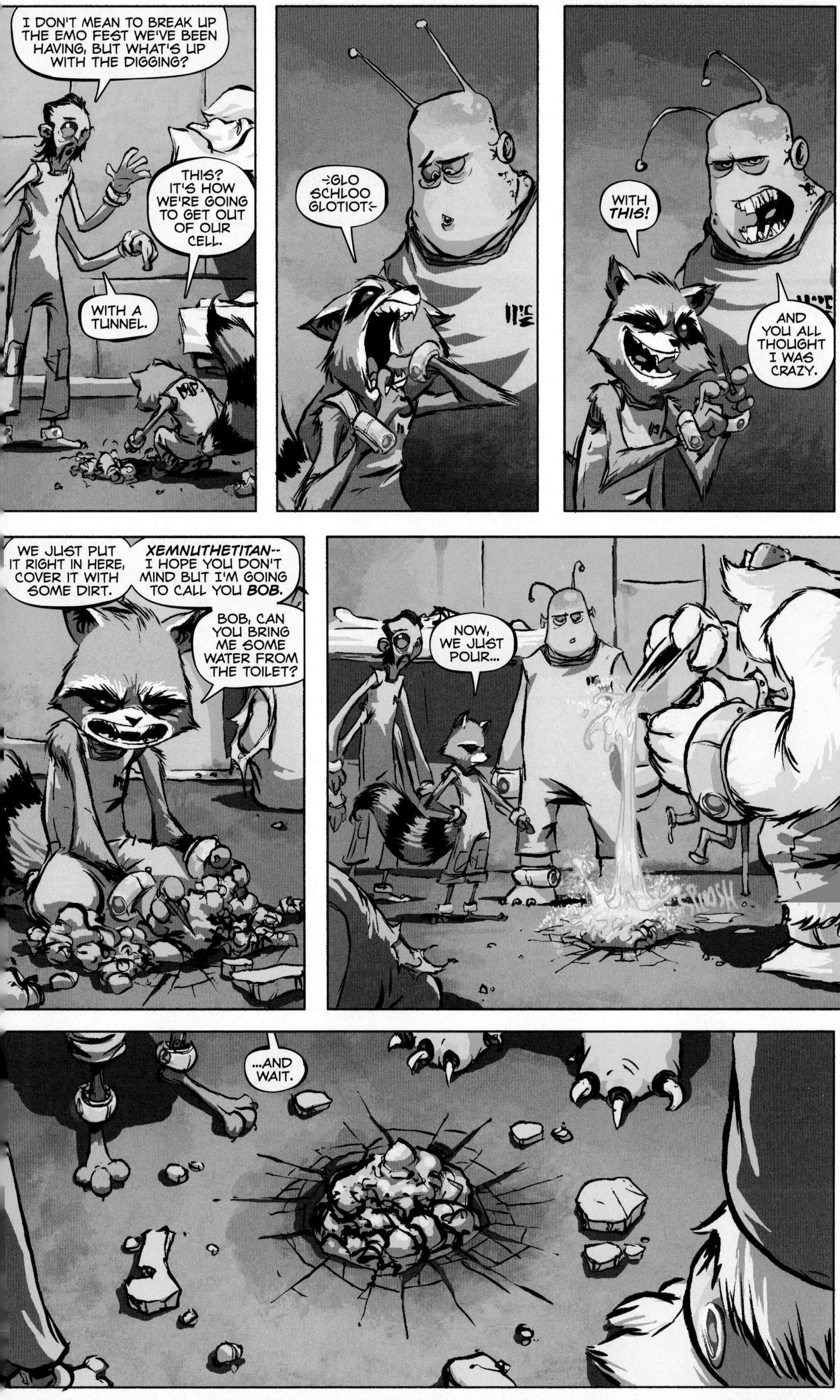

I DON'T MEAN TO BREAK UP THE EMO FEST WE'VE BEEN HAVING, BUT WHAT'S UP WITH THE DIGGING?
THIS? IT'S HOW WE'RE GOING TO GET OUT OF OUR CELL.
WITH A TUNNEL.
GLO SCHLOO GLOTIOT
WITH THIS!
AND YOU ALL THOUGHT I WAS CRAZY.
WE JUST PUT IT RIGHT IN HERE, COVER IT WITH SOME DIRT.
XEMNUTHETITAN-- I HOPE YOU DON'T MIND BUT I'M GOING TO CALL YOU BOB.
BOB, CAN YOU BRING ME SOME WATER FROM THE TOILET?
NOW, WE JUST POUR...
SPLOOSH
...AND WAIT.

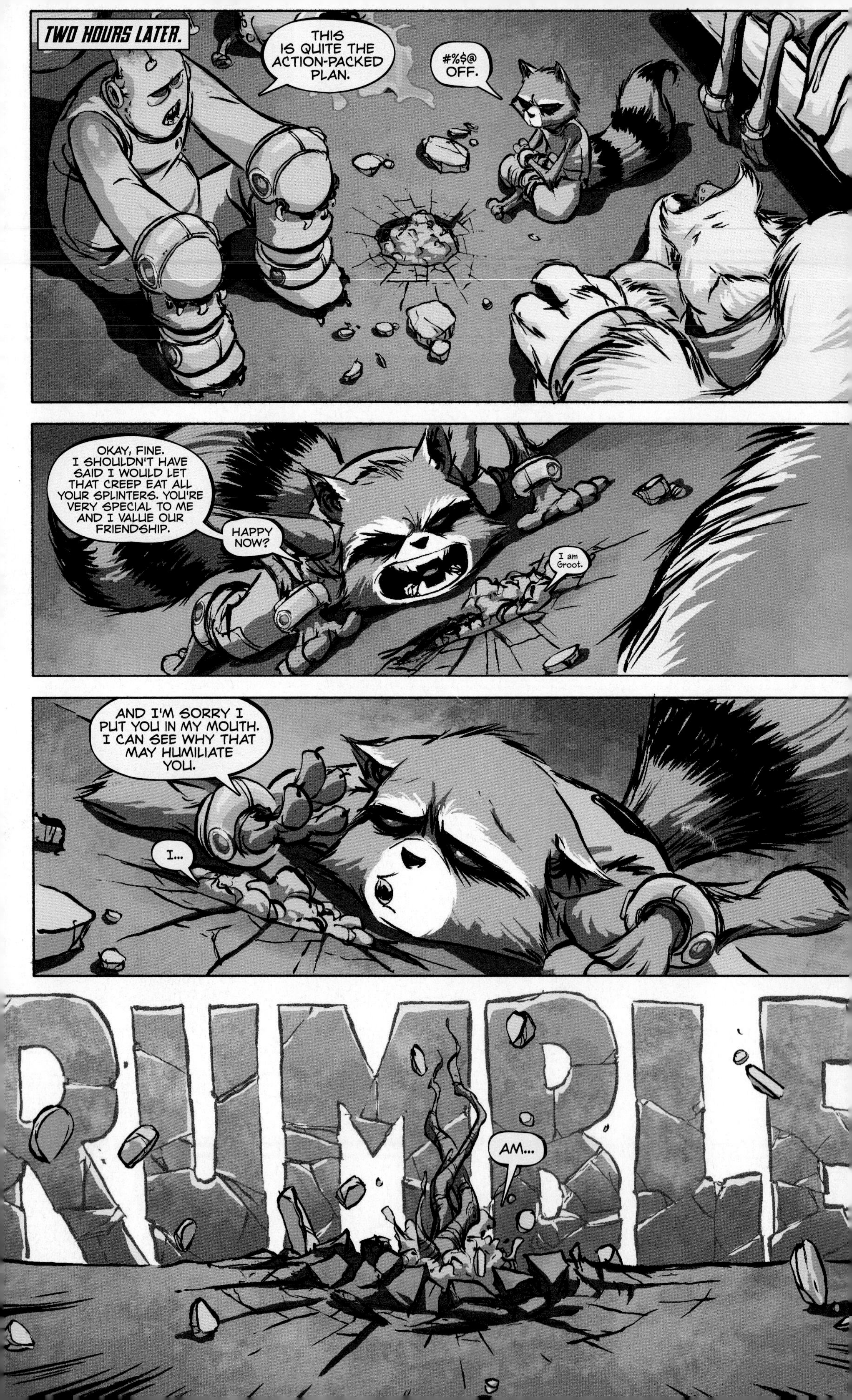
TWO HOURS LATER.
THIS IS QUITE THE ACTION-PACKED PLAN.
#%$@ OFF.
OKAY, FINE. I SHOULDN'T HAVE SAID I WOULD LET THAT CREEP EAT ALL YOUR SPLINTERS. YOU'RE VERY SPECIAL TO ME AND I VALUE OUR FRIENDSHIP.
HAPPY NOW?
I am Groot.
AND I'M SORRY I PUT YOU IN MY MOUTH. I CAN SEE WHY THAT MAY HUMILIATE YOU.
I...
RUMBLE
AM...

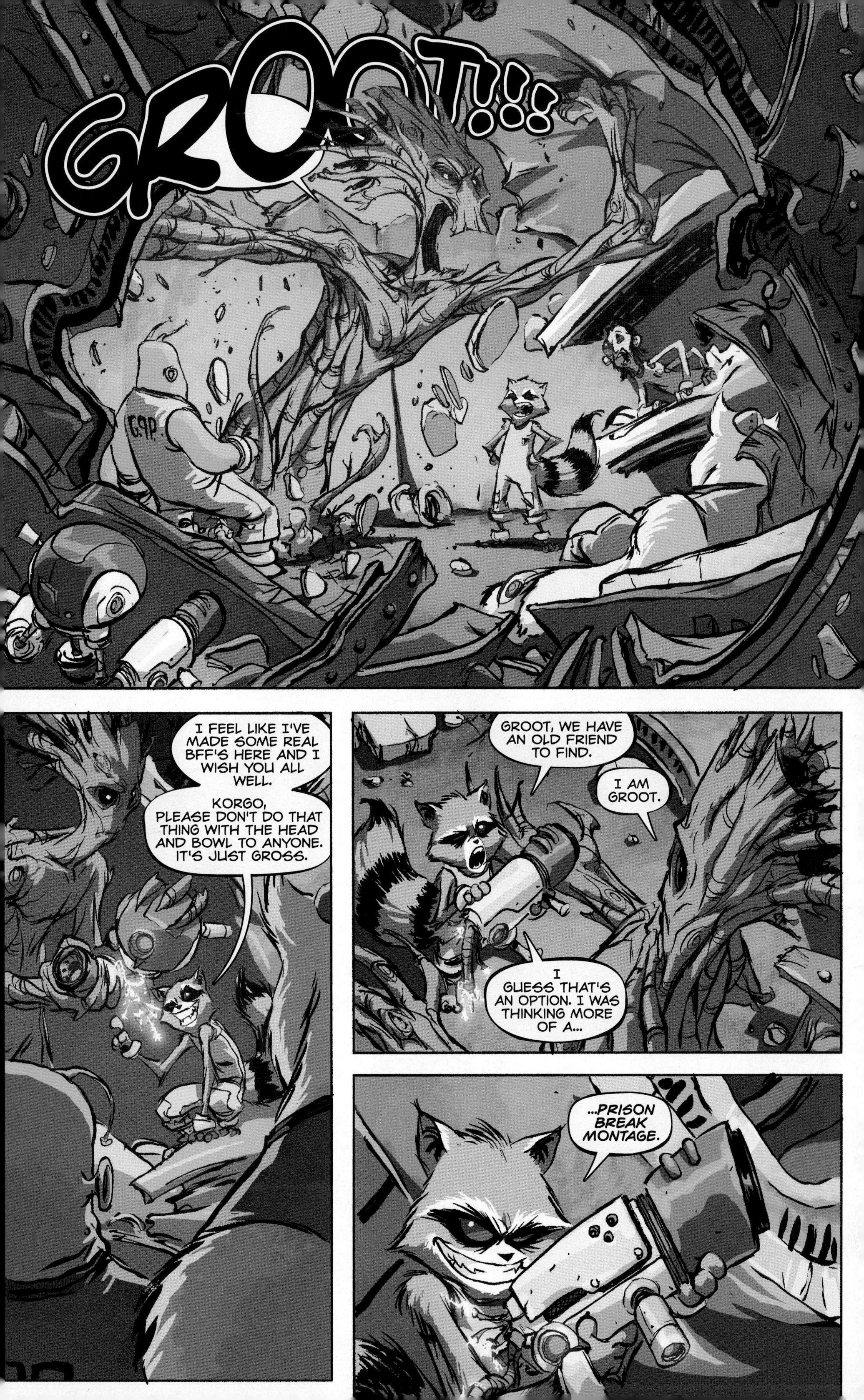

GROOT!!!
I FEEL LIKE I'VE MADE SOME REAL BFF'S HERE AND I WISH YOU ALL WELL.
KORGO, PLEASE DON'T DO THAT THING WITH THE HEAD AND BOWL TO ANYONE. IT'S JUST GROSS.
GROOT, WE HAVE AN OLD FRIEND TO FIND.
I AM GROOT.
I GUESS THAT'S AN OPTION. I WAS THINKING MORE OF A...
...PRISON BREAK MONTAGE.

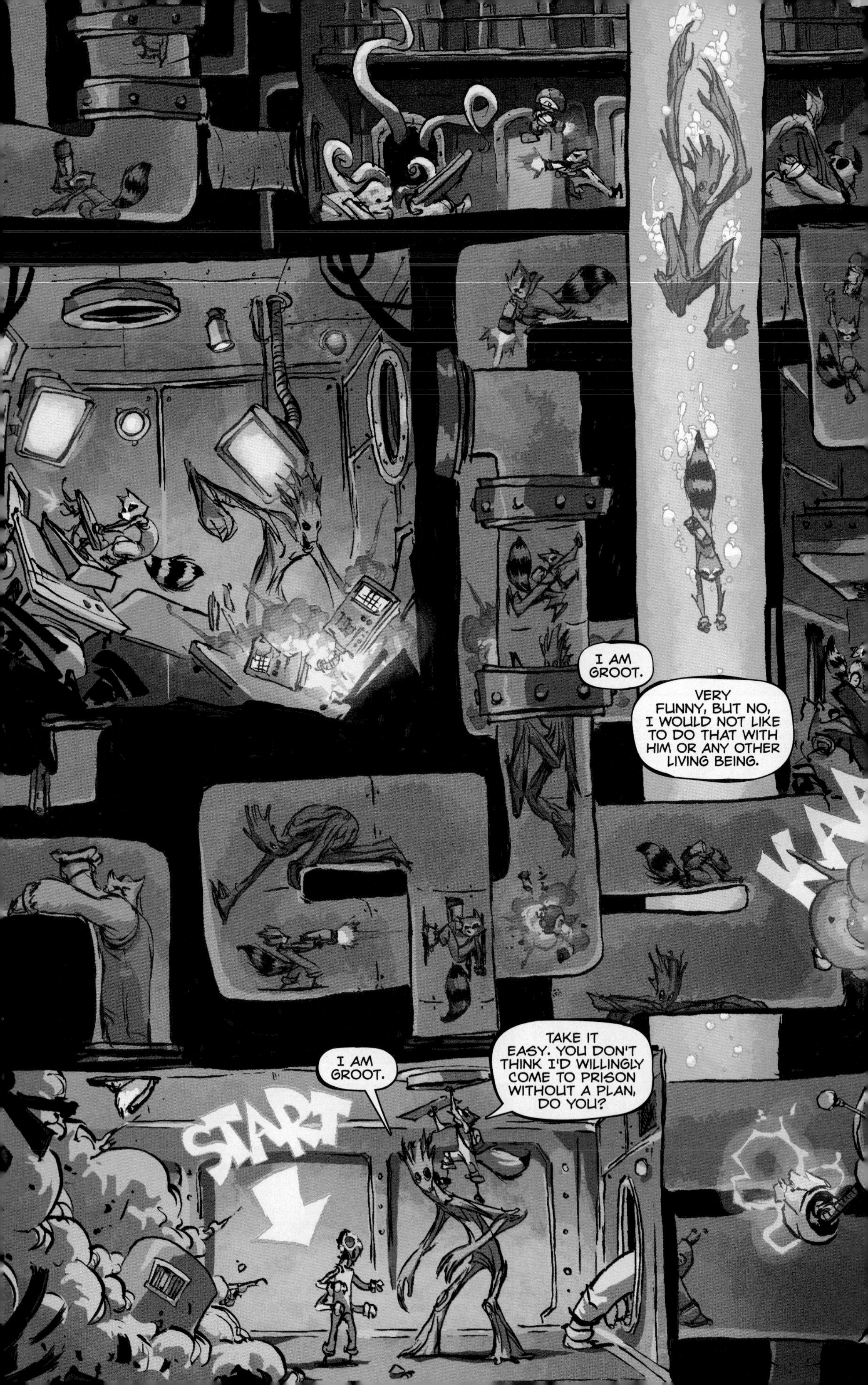
I AM GROOT.
VERY FUNNY, BUT NO, I WOULD NOT LIKE TO DO THAT WITH HIM OR ANY OTHER LIVING BEING.
START
I AM GROOT.
TAKE IT EASY. YOU DON'T THINK I'D WILLINGLY COME TO PRISON WITHOUT A PLAN, DO YOU?

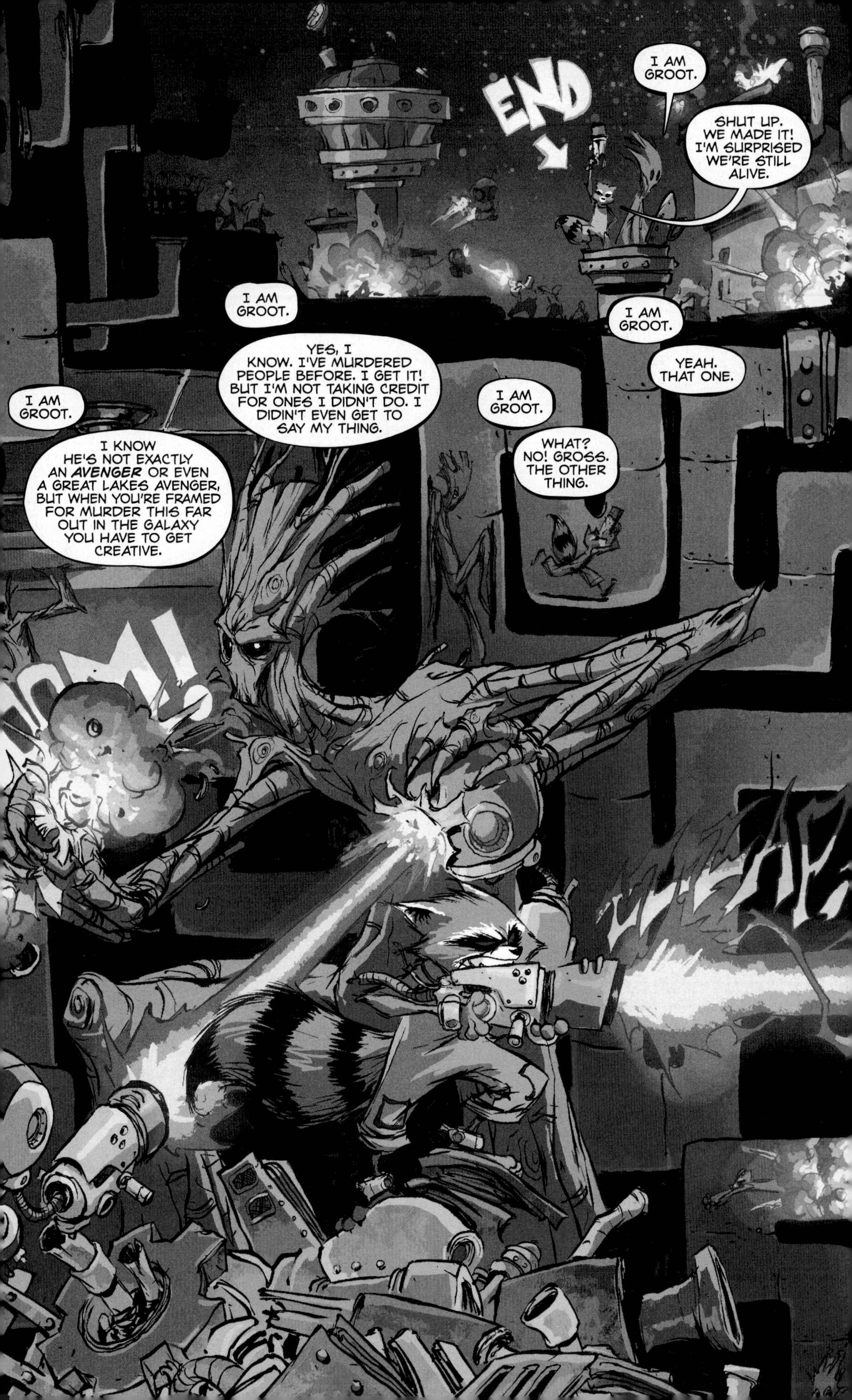
END
I AM GROOT.
SHUT UP. WE MADE IT! I'M SURPRISED WE'RE STILL ALIVE.
I AM GROOT.
I AM GROOT.
I KNOW HE'S NOT EXACTLY AN *AVENGER* OR EVEN A GREAT LAKES AVENGER, BUT WHEN YOU'RE FRAMED FOR MURDER THIS FAR OUT IN THE GALAXY YOU HAVE TO GET CREATIVE.
YES, I KNOW. I'VE MURDERED PEOPLE BEFORE. I GET IT! BUT I'M NOT TAKING CREDIT FOR ONES I DIDN'T DO. I DIDIN'T EVEN GET TO SAY MY THING.
I AM GROOT.
WHAT? NO! GROSS. THE OTHER THING.
I AM GROOT.
YEAH. THAT ONE.

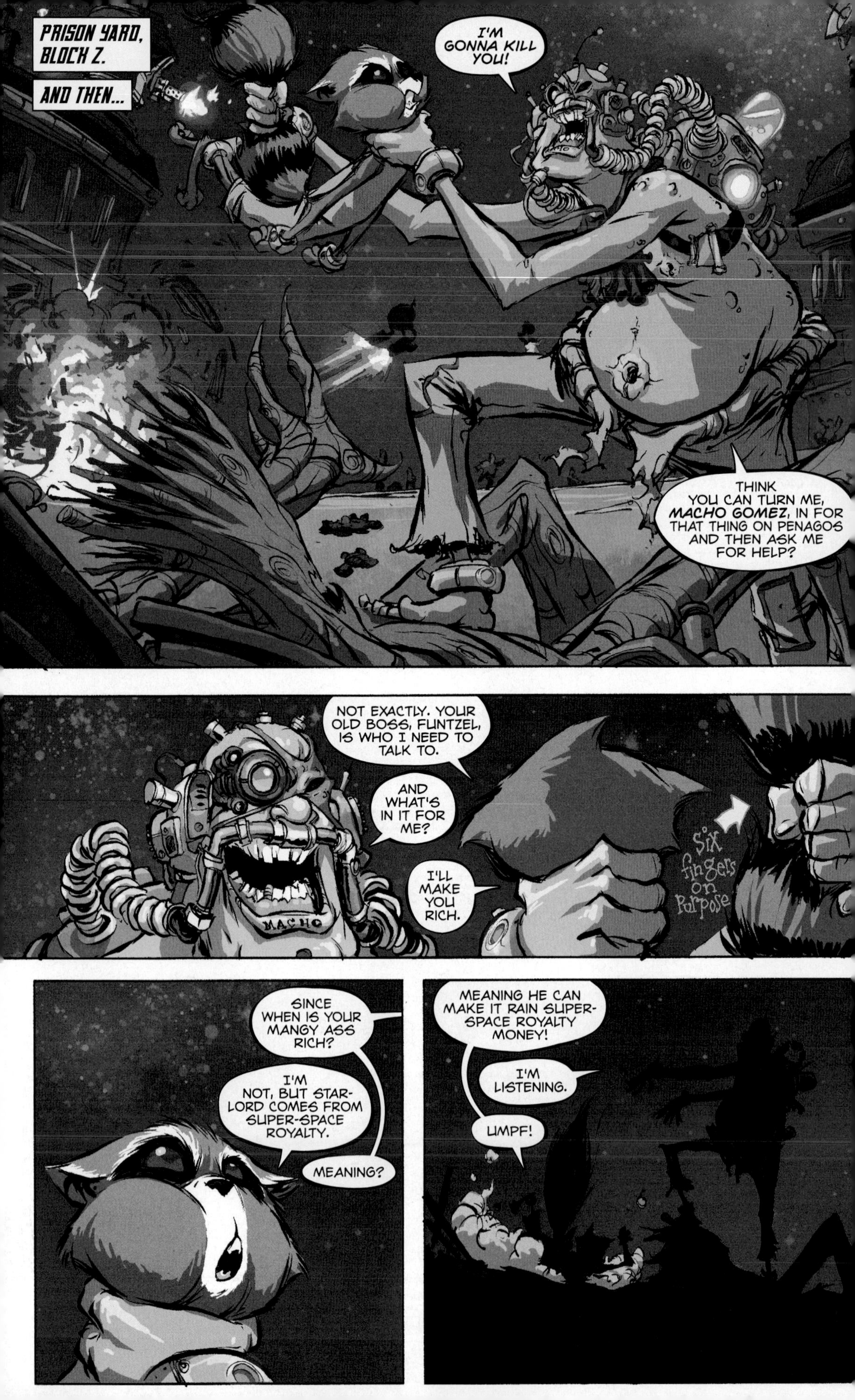
PRISON YARD, BLOCK Z.
AND THEN...
I'M GONNA KILL YOU!
THINK YOU CAN TURN ME, MACHO GOMEZ, IN FOR THAT THING ON PENAGOS AND THEN ASK ME FOR HELP?
NOT EXACTLY. YOUR OLD BOSS, FUNTZEL, IS WHO I NEED TO TALK TO.
AND WHAT'S IN IT FOR ME?
I'LL MAKE YOU RICH.
MACHO
Six fingers on Purpose
SINCE WHEN IS YOUR MANGY ASS RICH?
I'M NOT, BUT STAR-LORD COMES FROM SUPER-SPACE ROYALTY.
MEANING?
MEANING HE CAN MAKE IT RAIN SUPER-SPACE ROYALTY MONEY!
I'M LISTENING.
UMPF!

THANKS FOR THE HELP!

I AM GROOT.

YOU COULDN'T HANDLE MY MOM EVEN IF YOU WANTED TO!

CÁLLATE!!!

A BIT LATER.

I'M BEING SET UP FOR MURDER BY SOMEONE AND I THINK IT'S SOMEONE LIKE ME!

THOUGHT YOU WERE THE ONLY ONE. I REMEMBER YOU SAYING THAT.

LIKE ALL THE TIME.

LOW BLOW.

I KNOW WE'VE HAD OUR SHARE OF RUN-INS, BUT YOU'RE THE ONLY ONE WHO CAN GET ME A SIT-DOWN WITH FLINTZEL.

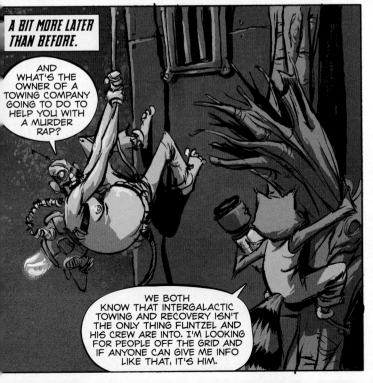

A BIT MORE LATER THAN BEFORE.

AND WHAT'S THE OWNER OF A TOWING COMPANY GOING TO DO TO HELP YOU WITH A MURDER RAP?

WE BOTH KNOW THAT INTERGALACTIC TOWING AND RECOVERY ISN'T THE ONLY THING FLINTZEL AND HIS CREW ARE INTO. I'M LOOKING FOR PEOPLE OFF THE GRID AND IF ANYONE CAN GIVE ME INFO LIKE THAT, IT'S HIM.

HA HA HA. A GUARDIAN OF THE GALAXY SLUMMING IT WITH FLINTZEL. THIS IS TOO GOOD TO PASS UP. I'M GONNA NEED A CHANGE OF CLOTHES AND A RIDE.

WE NEED TO STOP BY THE IMPOUND.

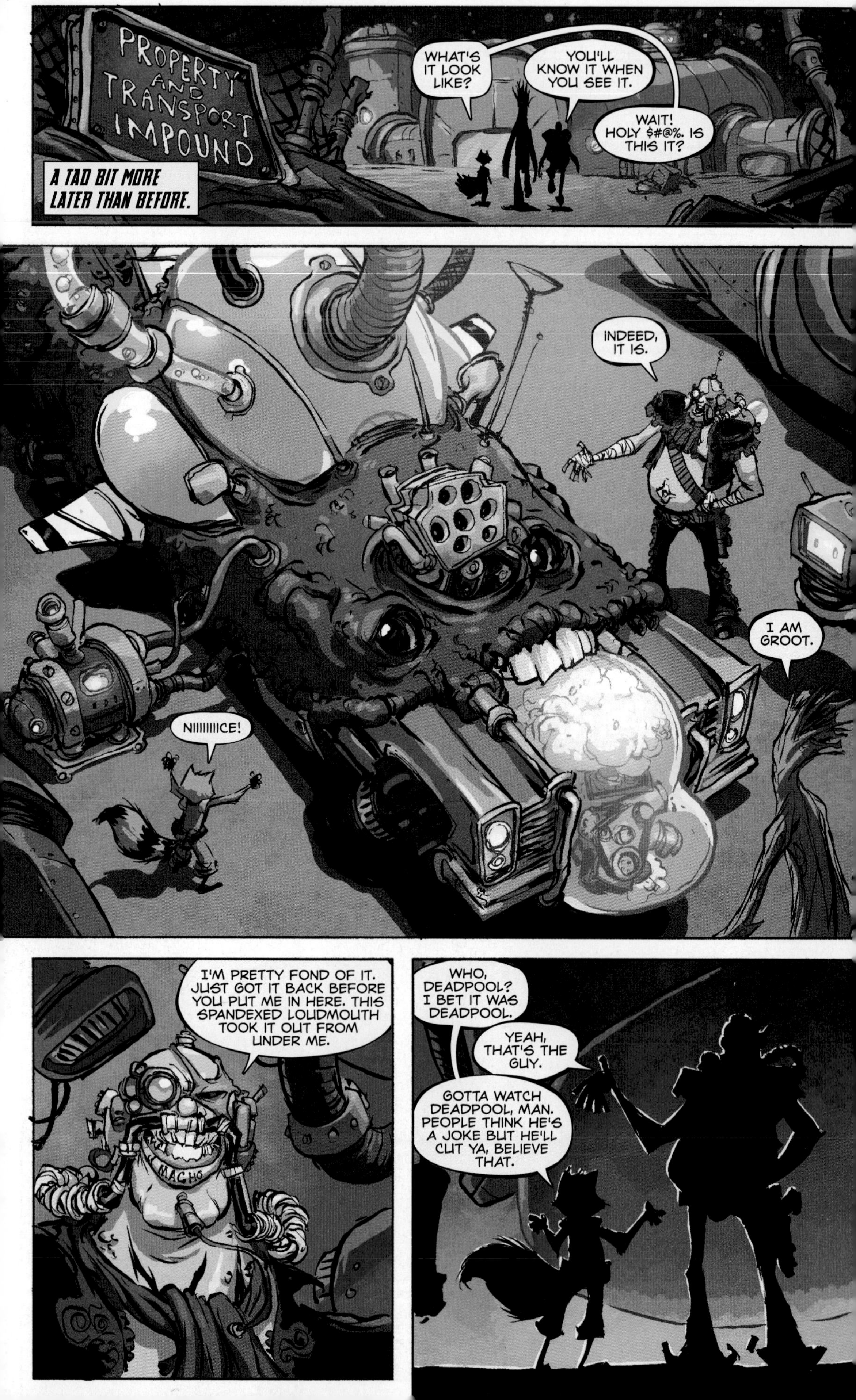
PROPERTY AND TRANSPORT IMPOUND
A TAD BIT MORE LATER THAN BEFORE.
WHAT'S IT LOOK LIKE?
YOU'LL KNOW IT WHEN YOU SEE IT.
WAIT! HOLY $#@%. IS THIS IT?
INDEED, IT IS.
I AM GROOT.
NIIIIIIICE!
I'M PRETTY FOND OF IT. JUST GOT IT BACK BEFORE YOU PUT ME IN HERE. THIS SPANDEXED LOUDMOUTH TOOK IT OUT FROM UNDER ME.
MACHO
WHO, DEADPOOL? I BET IT WAS DEADPOOL.
YEAH, THAT'S THE GUY.
GOTTA WATCH DEADPOOL, MAN. PEOPLE THINK HE'S A JOKE BUT HE'LL CUT YA, BELIEVE THAT.

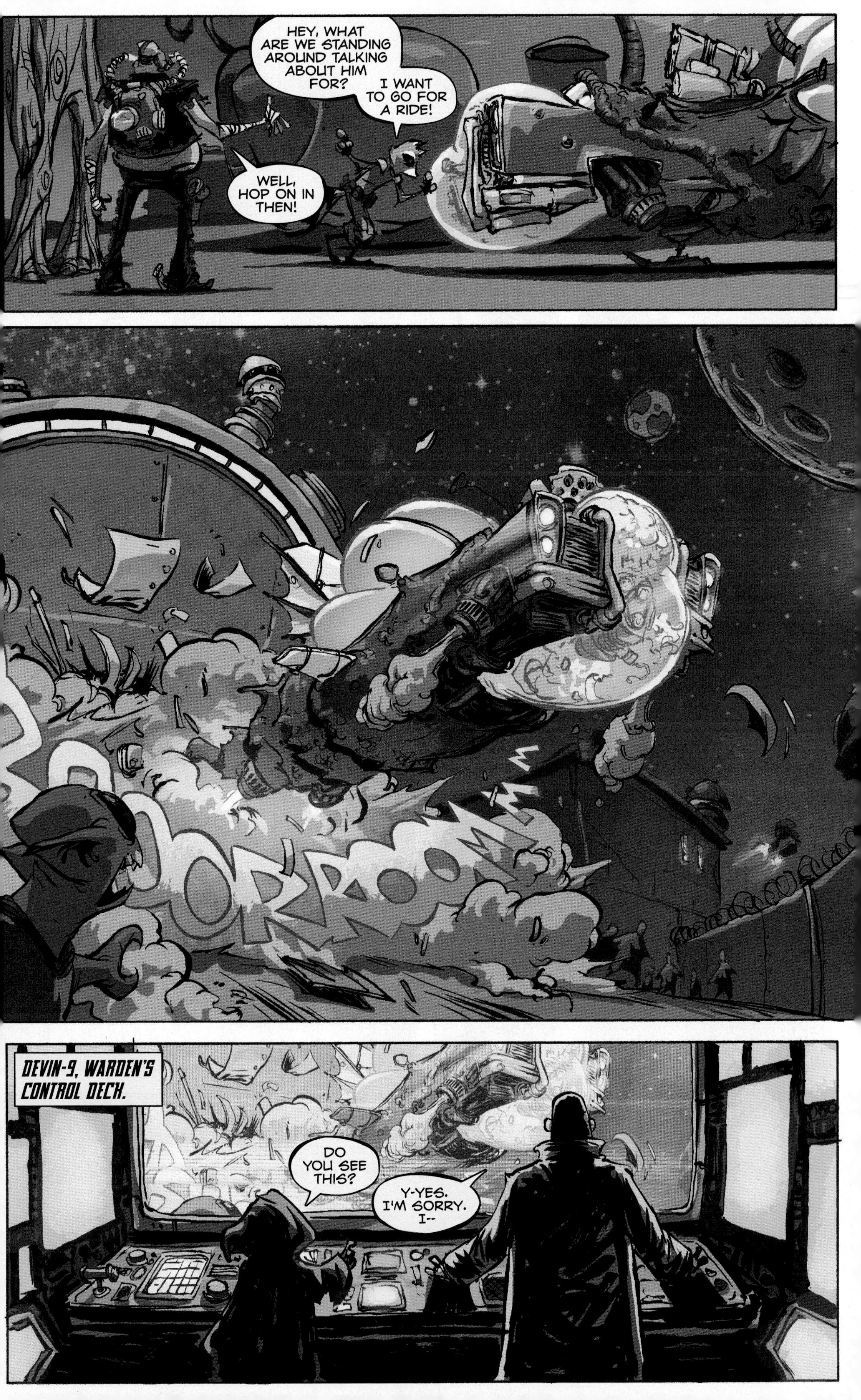
HEY, WHAT ARE WE STANDING AROUND TALKING ABOUT HIM FOR?
I WANT TO GO FOR A RIDE!
WELL, HOP ON IN THEN!
DEVIN-9, WARDEN'S CONTROL DECK.
DO YOU SEE THIS?
Y-YES. I'M SORRY. I--

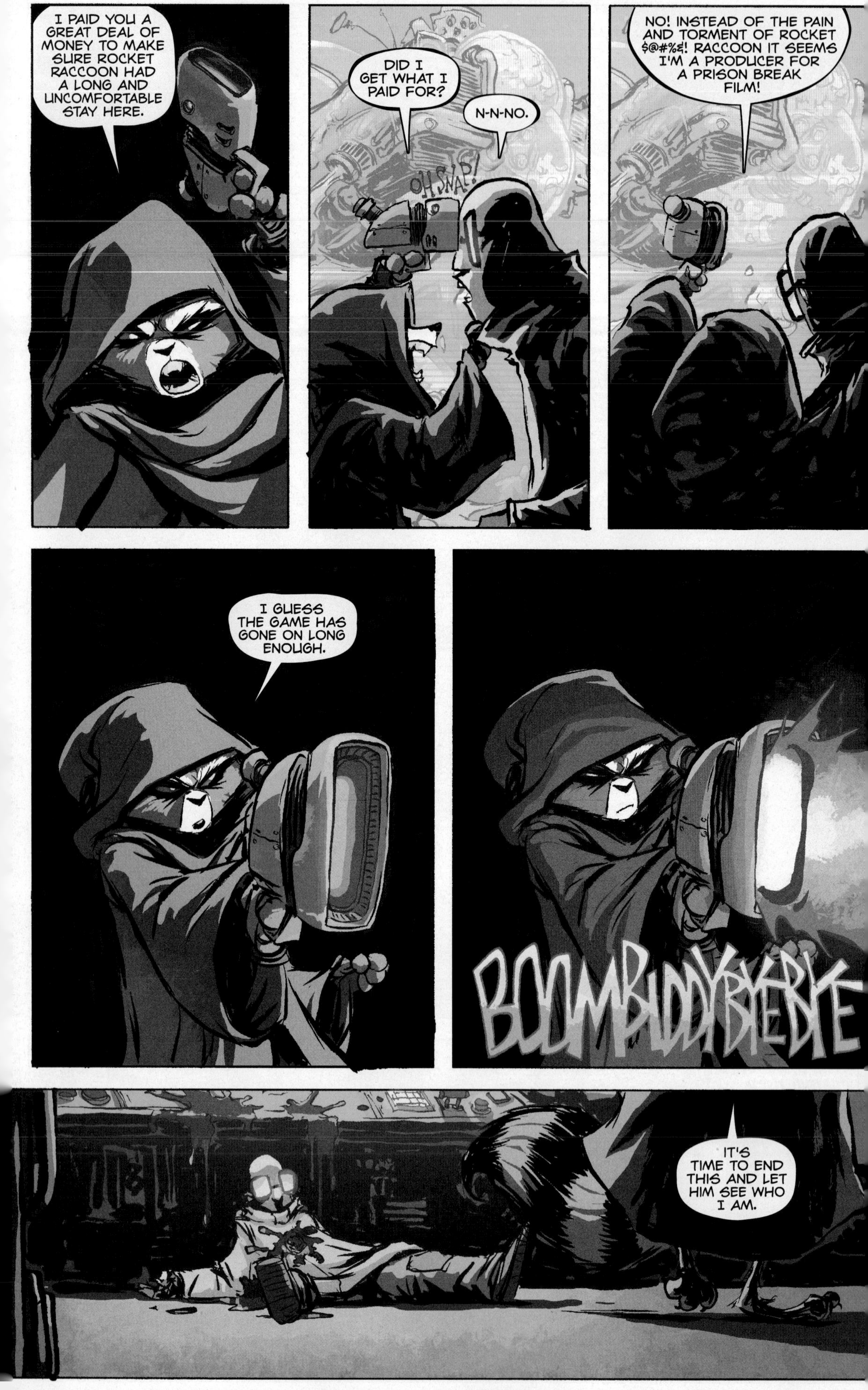
I PAID YOU A GREAT DEAL OF MONEY TO MAKE SURE ROCKET RACCOON HAD A LONG AND UNCOMFORTABLE STAY HERE.
DID I GET WHAT I PAID FOR?
N-N-NO.
OH SNAP!
NO! INSTEAD OF THE PAIN AND TORMENT OF ROCKET $@#%&! RACCOON IT SEEMS I'M A PRODUCER FOR A PRISON BREAK FILM!
I GUESS THE GAME HAS GONE ON LONG ENOUGH.
BOOMBIDDYBYEBYE
IT'S TIME TO END THIS AND LET HIM SEE WHO I AM.

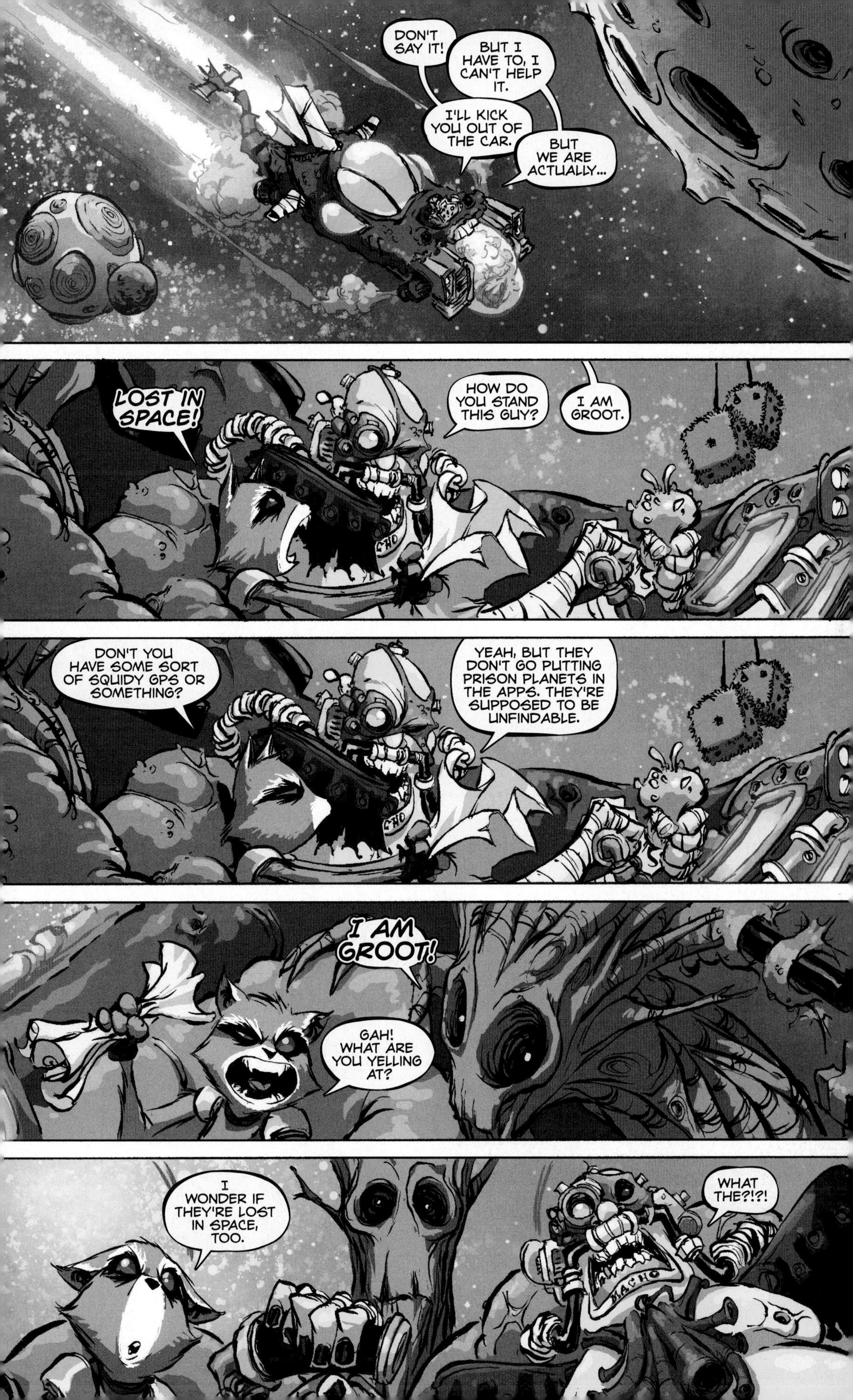
DON'T SAY IT!
BUT I HAVE TO, I CAN'T HELP IT.
I'LL KICK YOU OUT OF THE CAR.
BUT WE ARE ACTUALLY...
LOST IN SPACE!
HOW DO YOU STAND THIS GUY?
I AM GROOT.
DON'T YOU HAVE SOME SORT OF SQUIDY GPS OR SOMETHING?
YEAH, BUT THEY DON'T GO PUTTING PRISON PLANETS IN THE APPS. THEY'RE SUPPOSED TO BE UNFINDABLE.
I AM GROOT!
GAH! WHAT ARE YOU YELLING AT?
I WONDER IF THEY'RE LOST IN SPACE, TOO.
WHAT THE?!?!

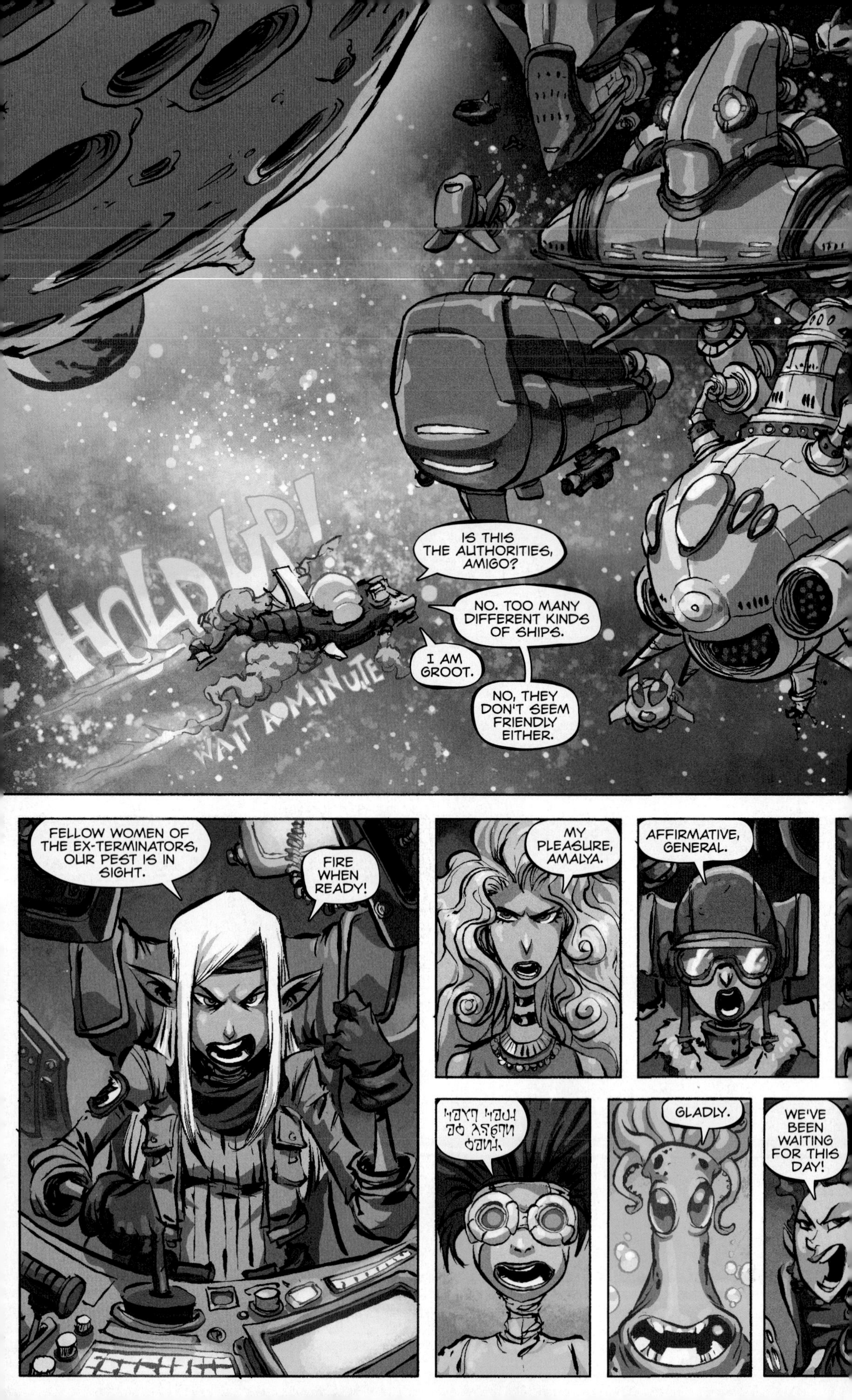
HOLD UP!
WAIT A MINUTE
IS THIS THE AUTHORITIES, AMIGO?
NO. TOO MANY DIFFERENT KINDS OF SHIPS.
I AM GROOT.
NO, THEY DON'T SEEM FRIENDLY EITHER.
FELLOW WOMEN OF THE EX-TERMINATORS, OUR PEST IS IN SIGHT.
FIRE WHEN READY!
MY PLEASURE, AMALYA.
AFFIRMATIVE, GENERAL.
GLADLY.
WE'VE BEEN WAITING FOR THIS DAY!

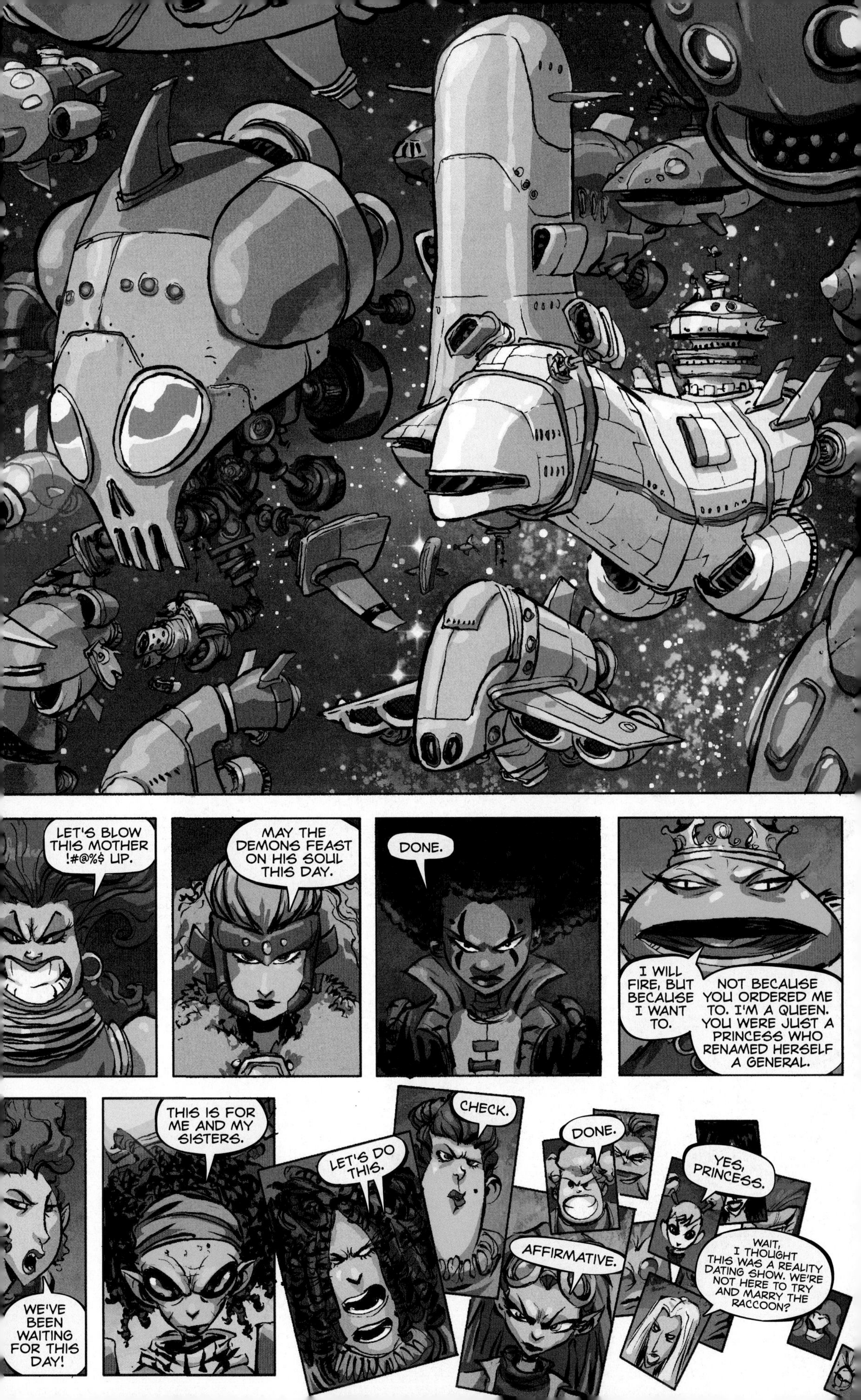
LET'S BLOW THIS MOTHER !#@%$ UP.
MAY THE DEMONS FEAST ON HIS SOUL THIS DAY.
DONE.
I WILL FIRE, BUT BECAUSE I WANT TO.
NOT BECAUSE YOU ORDERED ME TO. I'M A QUEEN. YOU WERE JUST A PRINCESS WHO RENAMED HERSELF A GENERAL.
WE'VE BEEN WAITING FOR THIS DAY!
THIS IS FOR ME AND MY SISTERS.
LET'S DO THIS.
CHECK.
DONE.
AFFIRMATIVE.
YES, PRINCESS.
WAIT, I THOUGHT THIS WAS A REALITY DATING SHOW. WE'RE NOT HERE TO TRY AND MARRY THE RACCOON?

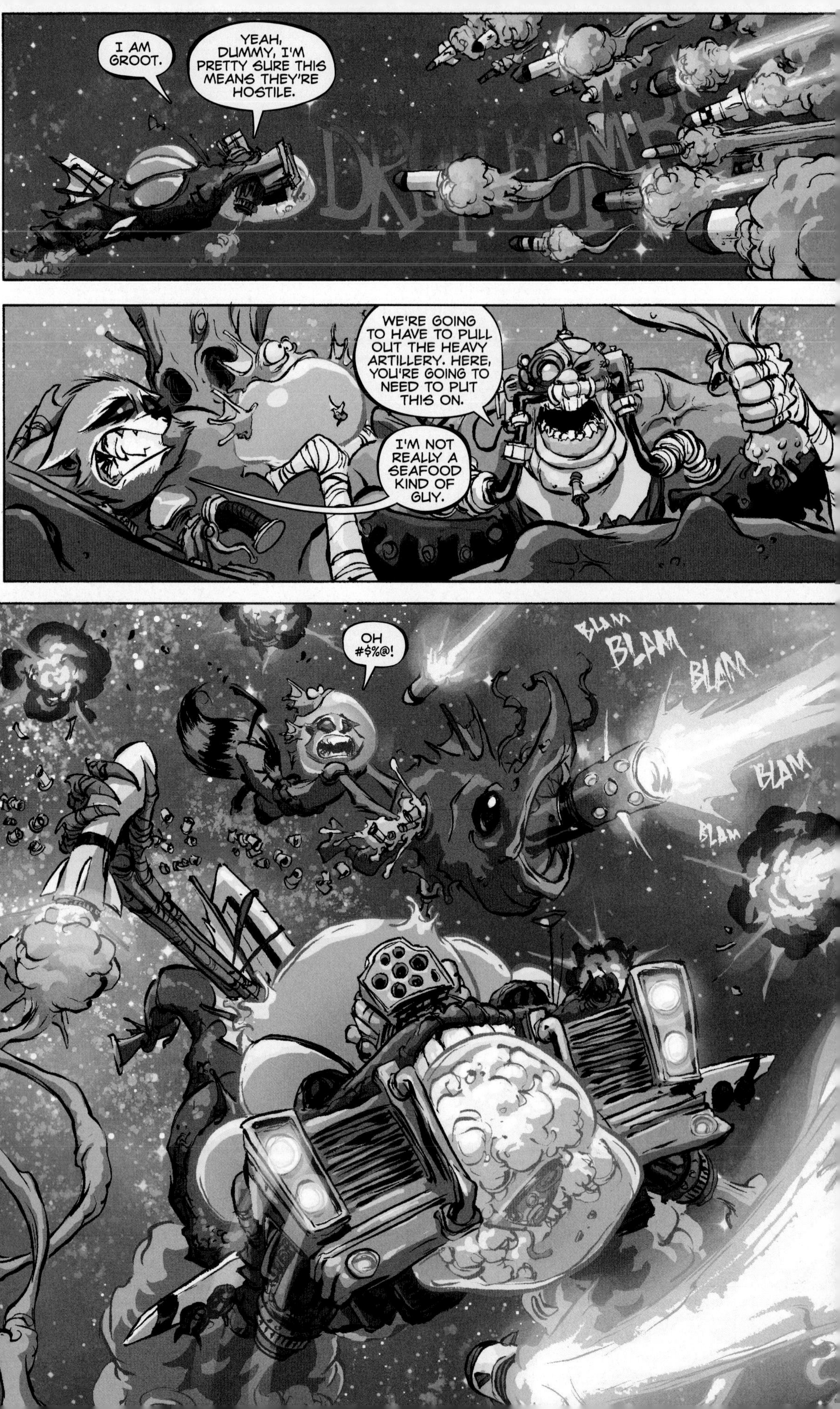
I AM GROOT.
YEAH, DUMMY, I'M PRETTY SURE THIS MEANS THEY'RE HOSTILE.
WE'RE GOING TO HAVE TO PULL OUT THE HEAVY ARTILLERY. HERE, YOU'RE GOING TO NEED TO PUT THIS ON.
I'M NOT REALLY A SEAFOOD KIND OF GUY.
OH #$%@!
BLAM
BLAM
BLAM
BLAM
BLAM

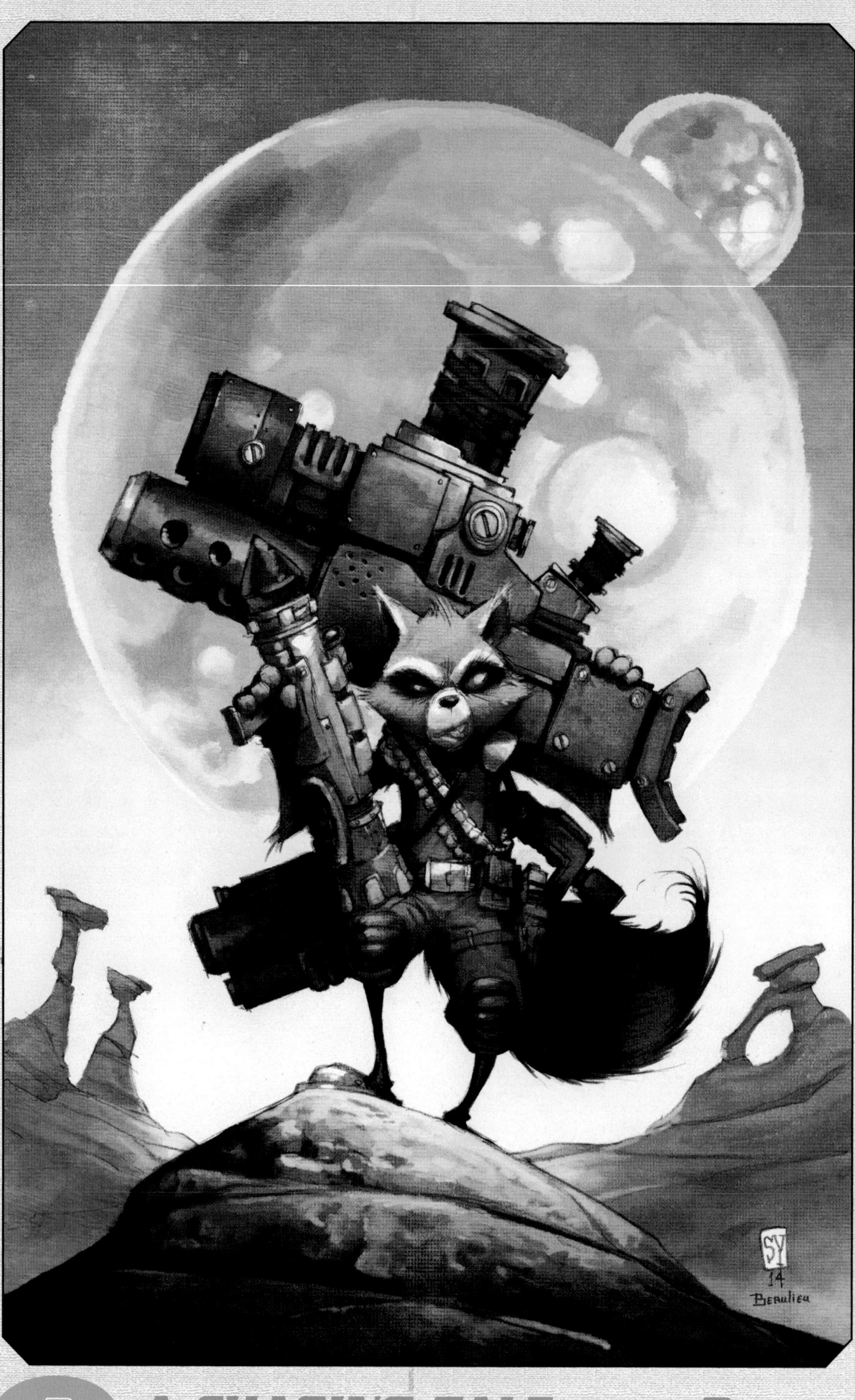
SY
14
Beaulieu

3 A CHASING TALE part 3

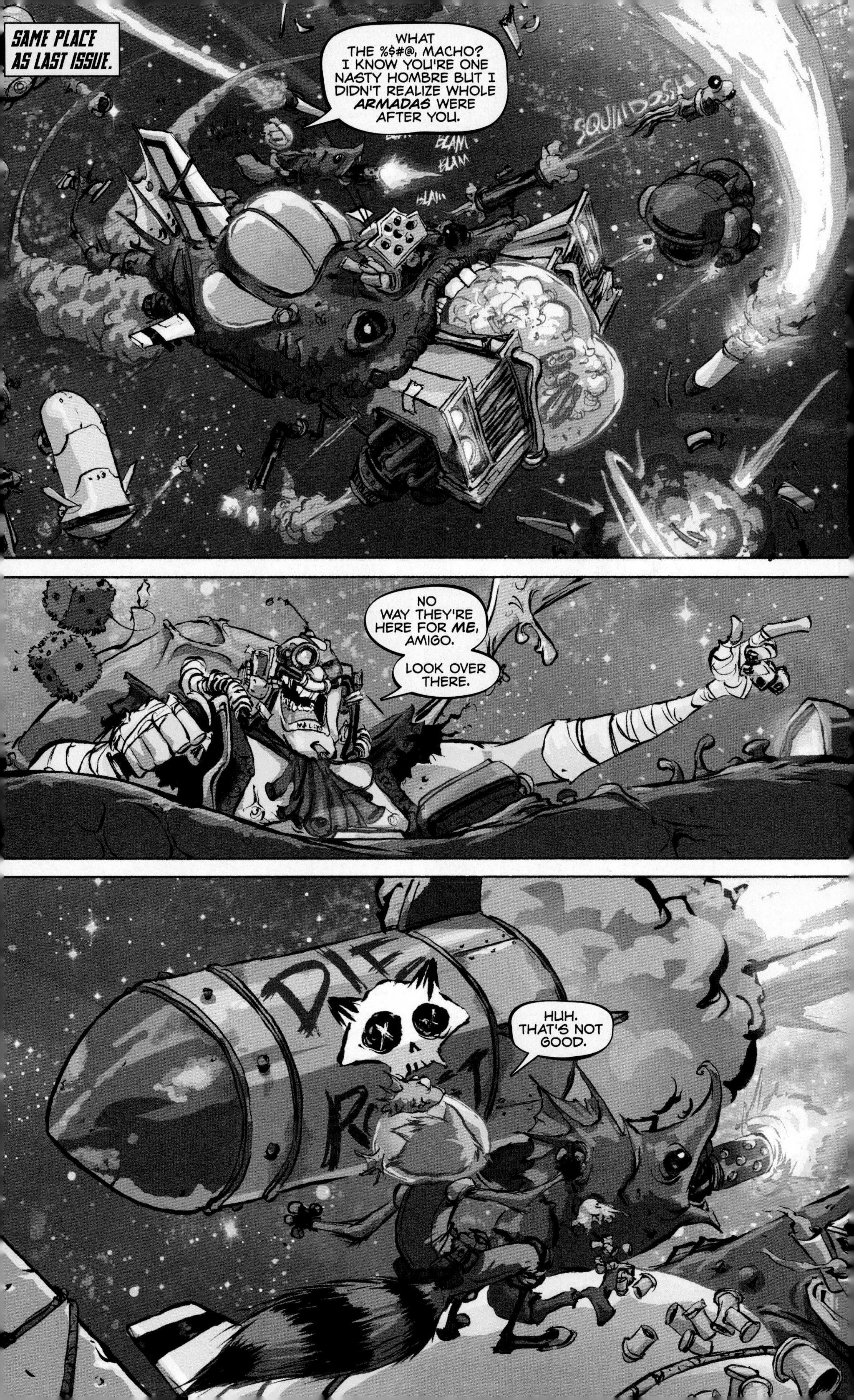
SAME PLACE AS LAST ISSUE.
WHAT THE %$#@, MACHO? I KNOW YOU'RE ONE NASTY HOMBRE BUT I DIDN'T REALIZE WHOLE ARMADAS WERE AFTER YOU.
BLAM
BLAM
BLAM
NO WAY THEY'RE HERE FOR ME, AMIGO.
LOOK OVER THERE.
HUH. THAT'S NOT GOOD.

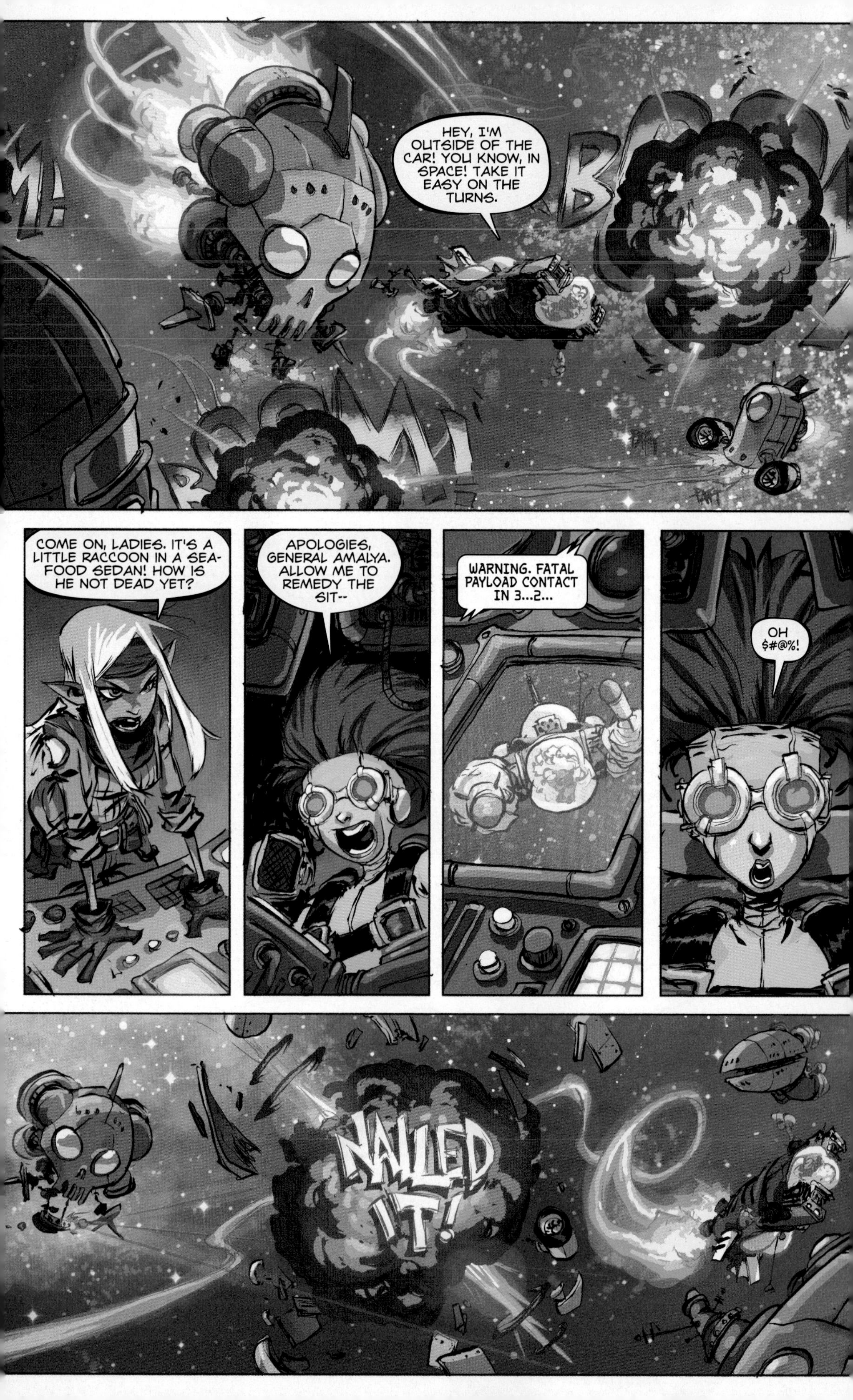
HEY, I'M OUTSIDE OF THE CAR! YOU KNOW, IN SPACE! TAKE IT EASY ON THE TURNS.
COME ON, LADIES. IT'S A LITTLE RACCOON IN A SEA-FOOD SEDAN! HOW IS HE NOT DEAD YET?
APOLOGIES, GENERAL AMALYA. ALLOW ME TO REMEDY THE SIT--
WARNING. FATAL PAYLOAD CONTACT IN 3...2...
OH $#@%!
NAILED IT!

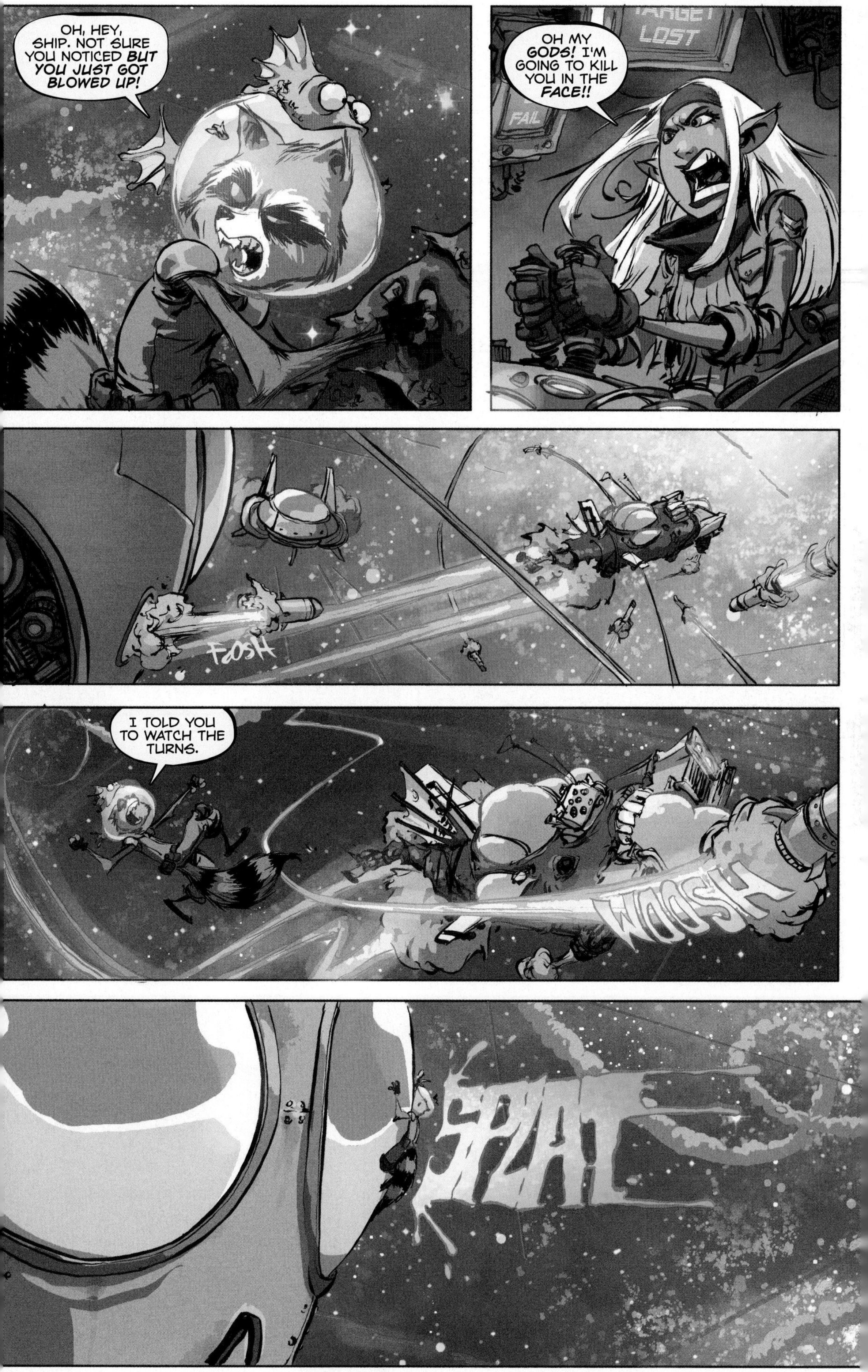
OH, HEY, SHIP. NOT SURE YOU NOTICED BUT YOU JUST GOT BLOWED UP!
LOST
FAIL
OH MY GODS! I'M GOING TO KILL YOU IN THE FACE!!
FOOSH
I TOLD YOU TO WATCH THE TURNS.
WOOSH
SPLAT

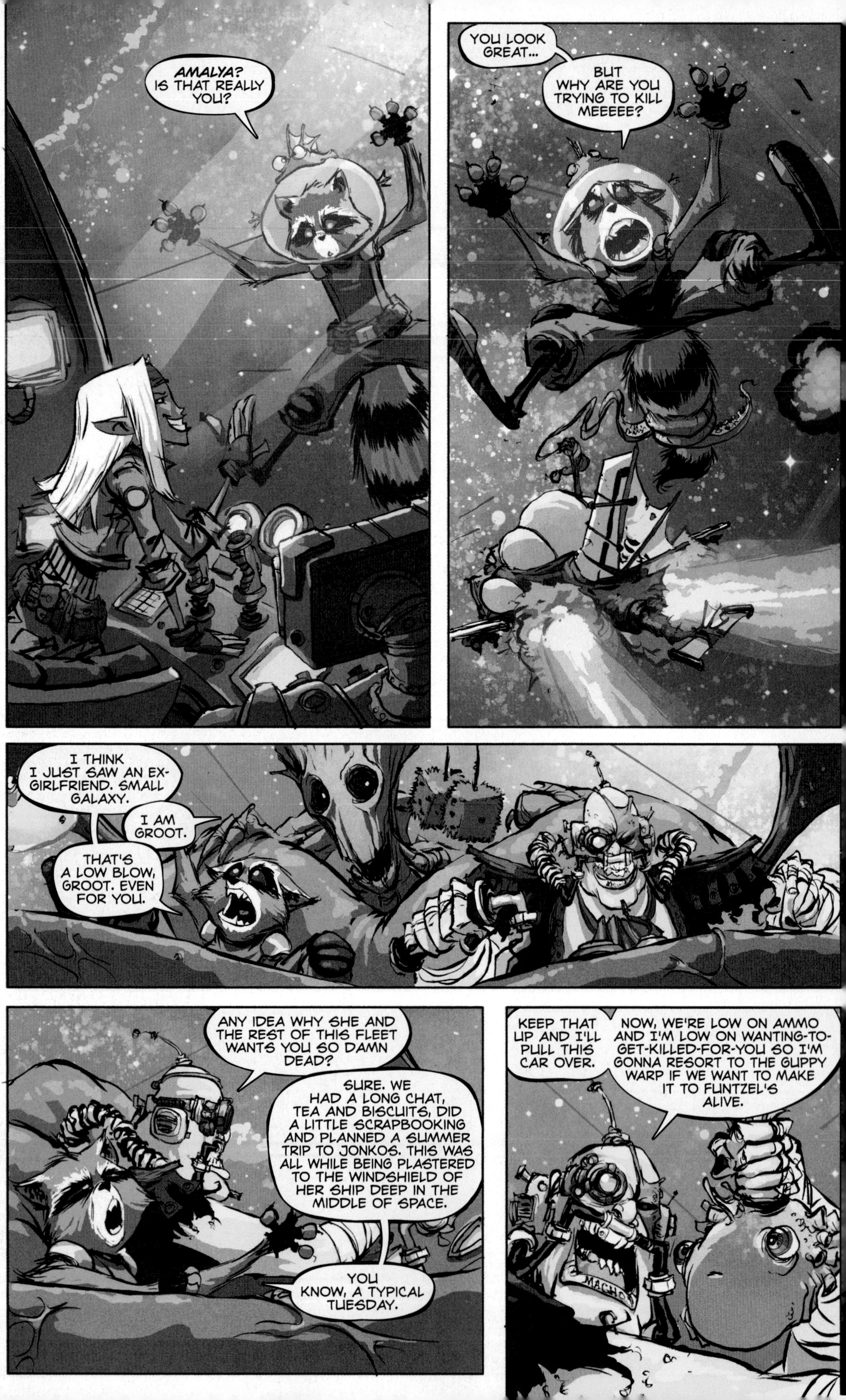
AMALYA? IS THAT REALLY YOU?
YOU LOOK GREAT...
BUT WHY ARE YOU TRYING TO KILL MEEEEE?
I THINK I JUST SAW AN EX-GIRLFRIEND. SMALL GALAXY.
I AM GROOT.
THAT'S A LOW BLOW, GROOT. EVEN FOR YOU.
ANY IDEA WHY SHE AND THE REST OF THIS FLEET WANTS YOU SO DAMN DEAD?
SURE. WE HAD A LONG CHAT, TEA AND BISCUITS, DID A LITTLE SCRAPBOOKING AND PLANNED A SUMMER TRIP TO JONKOS. THIS WAS ALL WHILE BEING PLASTERED TO THE WINDSHIELD OF HER SHIP DEEP IN THE MIDDLE OF SPACE.
YOU KNOW, A TYPICAL TUESDAY.
KEEP THAT UP AND I'LL PULL THIS CAR OVER.
NOW, WE'RE LOW ON AMMO AND I'M LOW ON WANTING-TO-GET-KILLED-FOR-YOU SO I'M GONNA RESORT TO THE GUPPY WARP IF WE WANT TO MAKE IT TO FLINTZEL'S ALIVE.
MACHO

I'VE ALWAYS WANTED TO SEE HOW THESE THINGS WORKED.

HKSOOOOSH

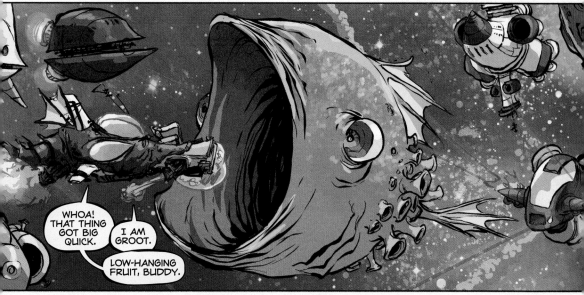

WHOA! THAT THING GOT BIG QUICK.

I AM GROOT.

LOW-HANGING FRUIT, BUDDY.

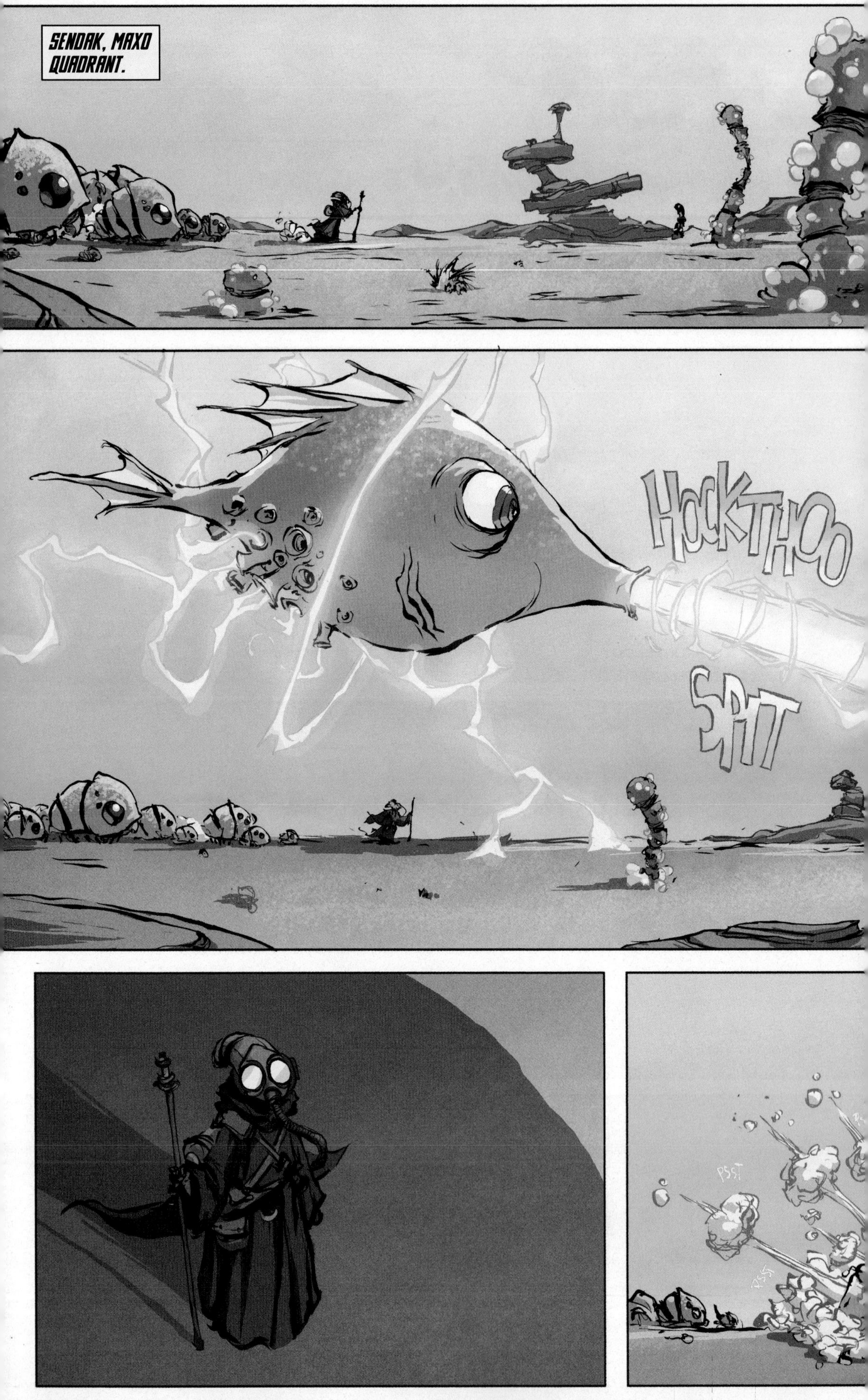
SENDAK, MAXO QUADRANT.
HOCKTHOO
SPIT
PSST
PSST

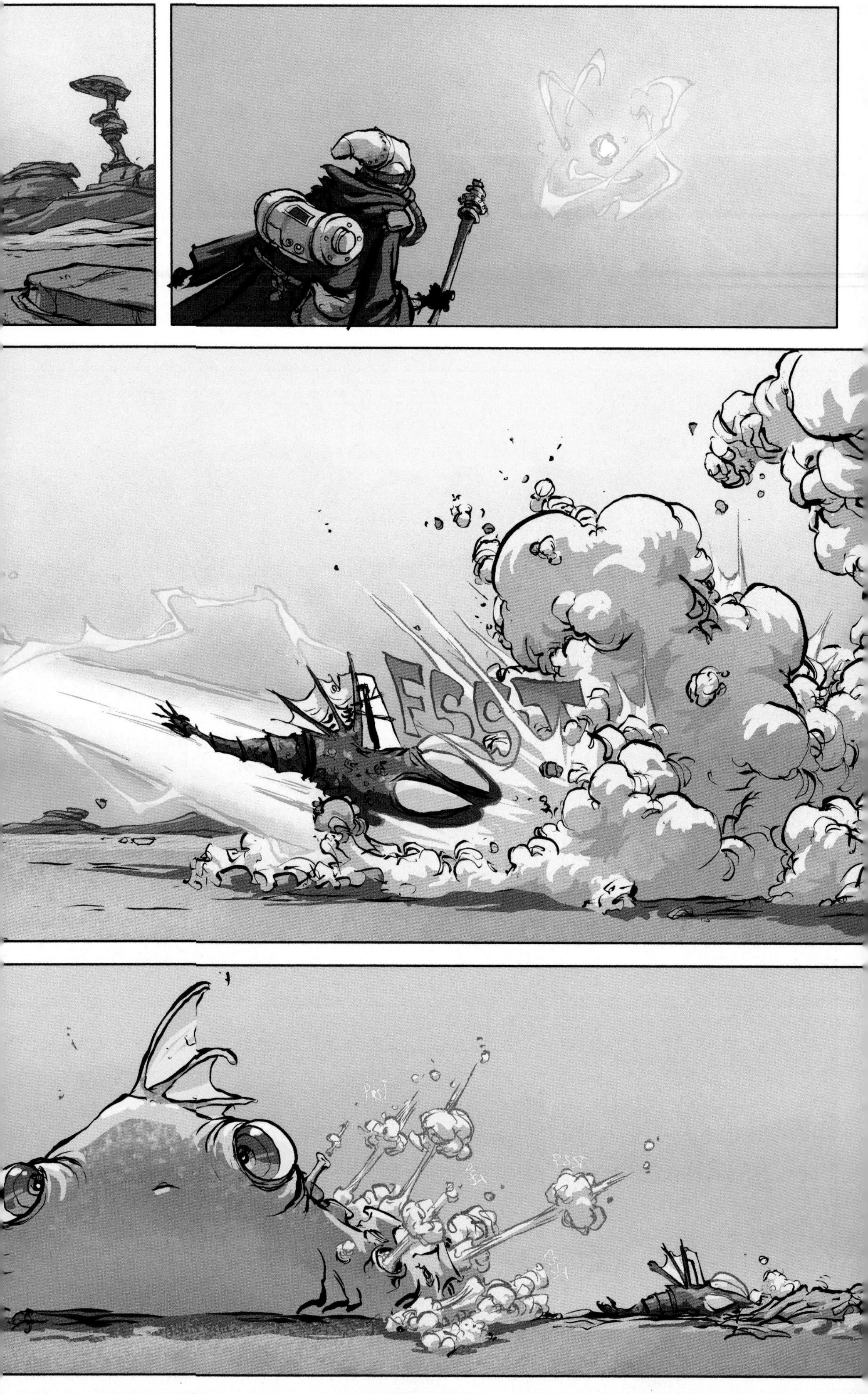
FSST
PSST
PSST
PSST
PSST

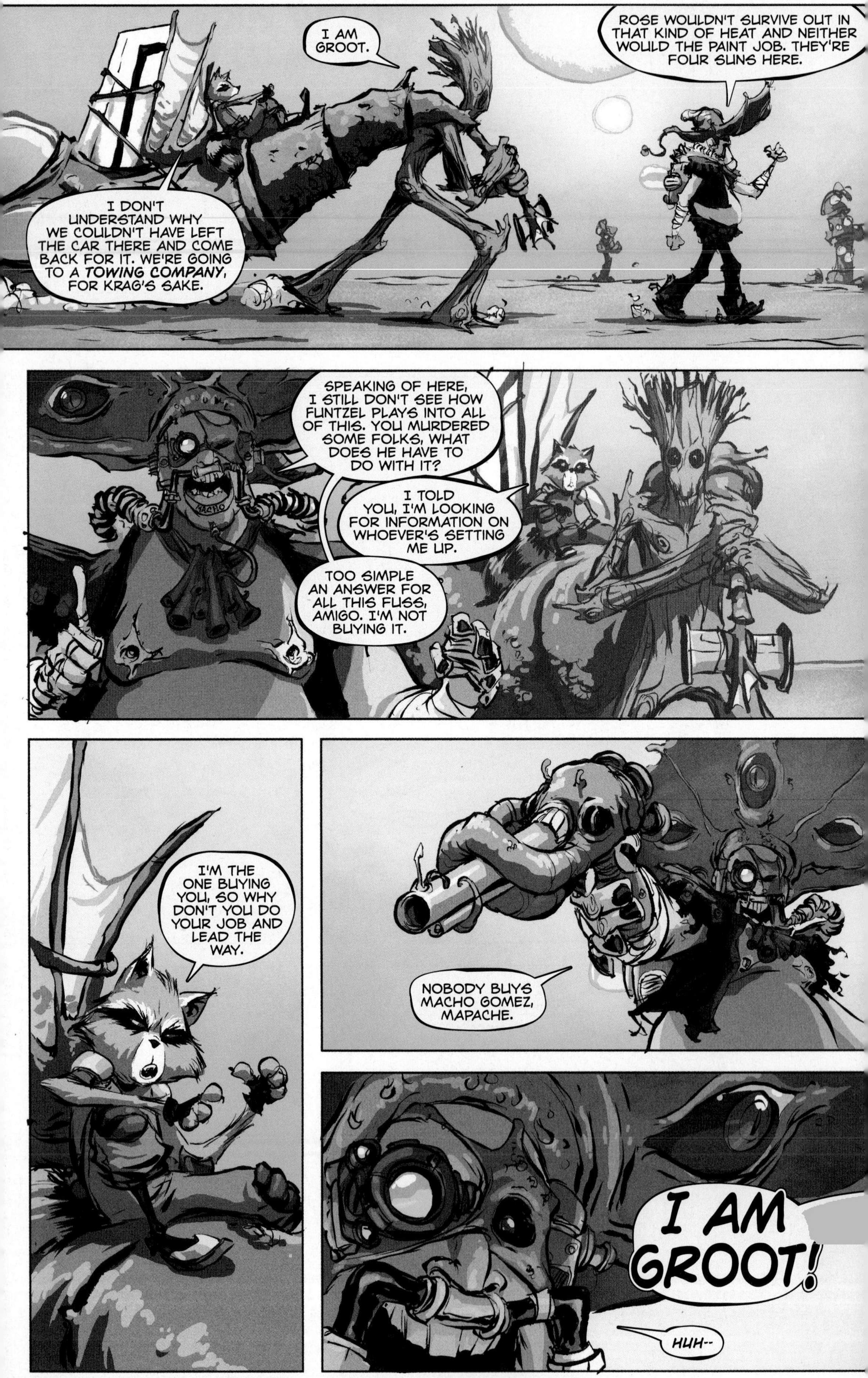
I AM GROOT.
ROSE WOULDN'T SURVIVE OUT IN THAT KIND OF HEAT AND NEITHER WOULD THE PAINT JOB. THEY'RE FOUR SUNS HERE.
I DON'T UNDERSTAND WHY WE COULDN'T HAVE LEFT THE CAR THERE AND COME BACK FOR IT. WE'RE GOING TO A *TOWING COMPANY*, FOR KRAG'S SAKE.
SPEAKING OF HERE, I STILL DON'T SEE HOW FUNTZEL PLAYS INTO ALL OF THIS. YOU MURDERED SOME FOLKS, WHAT DOES HE HAVE TO DO WITH IT?
I TOLD YOU, I'M LOOKING FOR INFORMATION ON WHOEVER'S SETTING ME UP.
TOO SIMPLE AN ANSWER FOR ALL THIS FUSS, AMIGO. I'M NOT BUYING IT.
MACHO
I'M THE ONE BUYING YOU, SO WHY DON'T YOU DO YOUR JOB AND LEAD THE WAY.
NOBODY BUYS MACHO GOMEZ, MAPACHE.
I AM GROOT!
HUH--

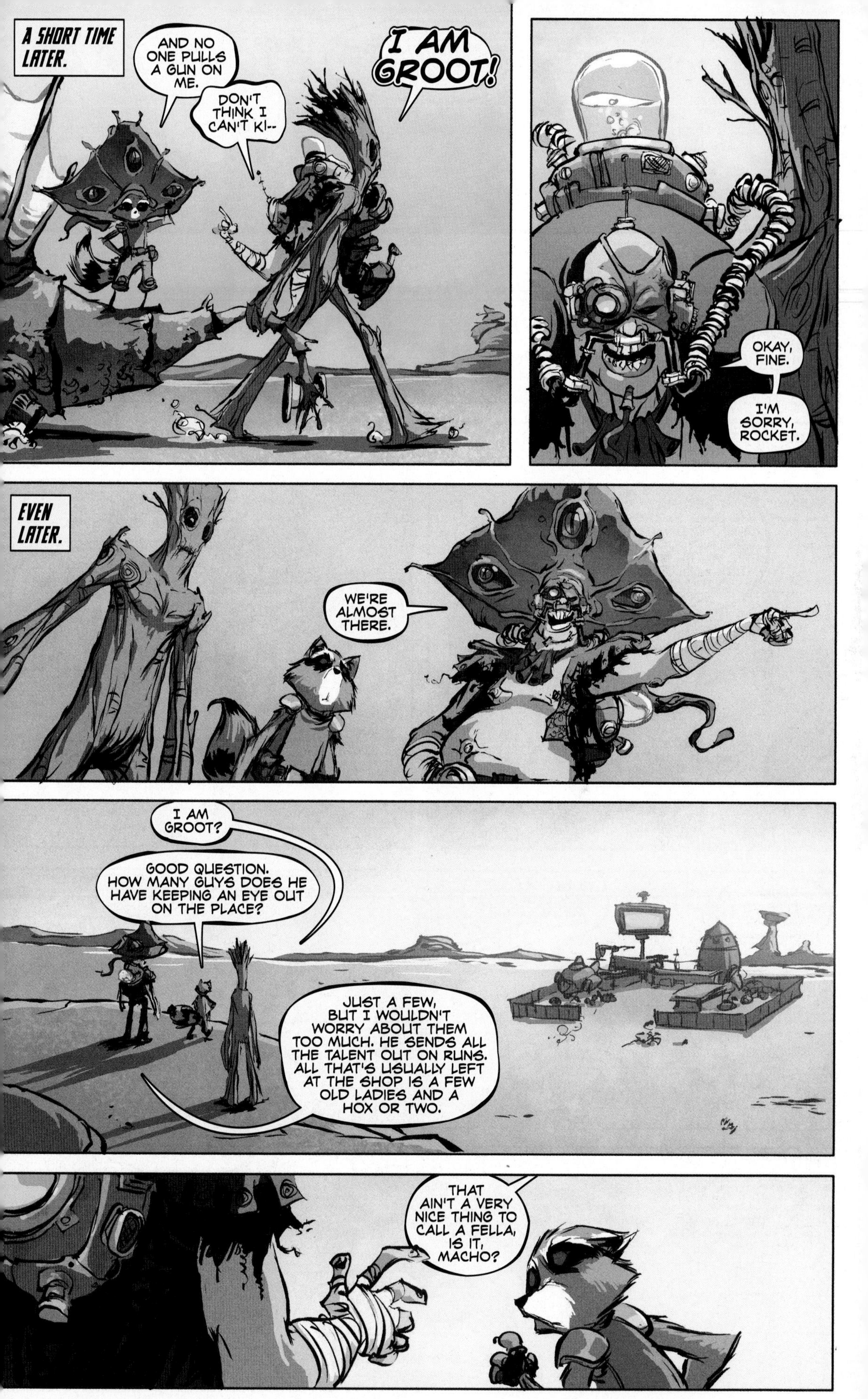
A SHORT TIME LATER.
AND NO ONE PULLS A GUN ON ME.
DON'T THINK I CAN'T KI--
I AM GROOT!
OKAY, FINE.
I'M SORRY, ROCKET.
EVEN LATER.
WE'RE ALMOST THERE.
I AM GROOT?
GOOD QUESTION. HOW MANY GUYS DOES HE HAVE KEEPING AN EYE OUT ON THE PLACE?
JUST A FEW, BUT I WOULDN'T WORRY ABOUT THEM TOO MUCH. HE SENDS ALL THE TALENT OUT ON RUNS. ALL THAT'S USUALLY LEFT AT THE SHOP IS A FEW OLD LADIES AND A HOX OR TWO.
THAT AIN'T A VERY NICE THING TO CALL A FELLA, IS IT, MACHO?

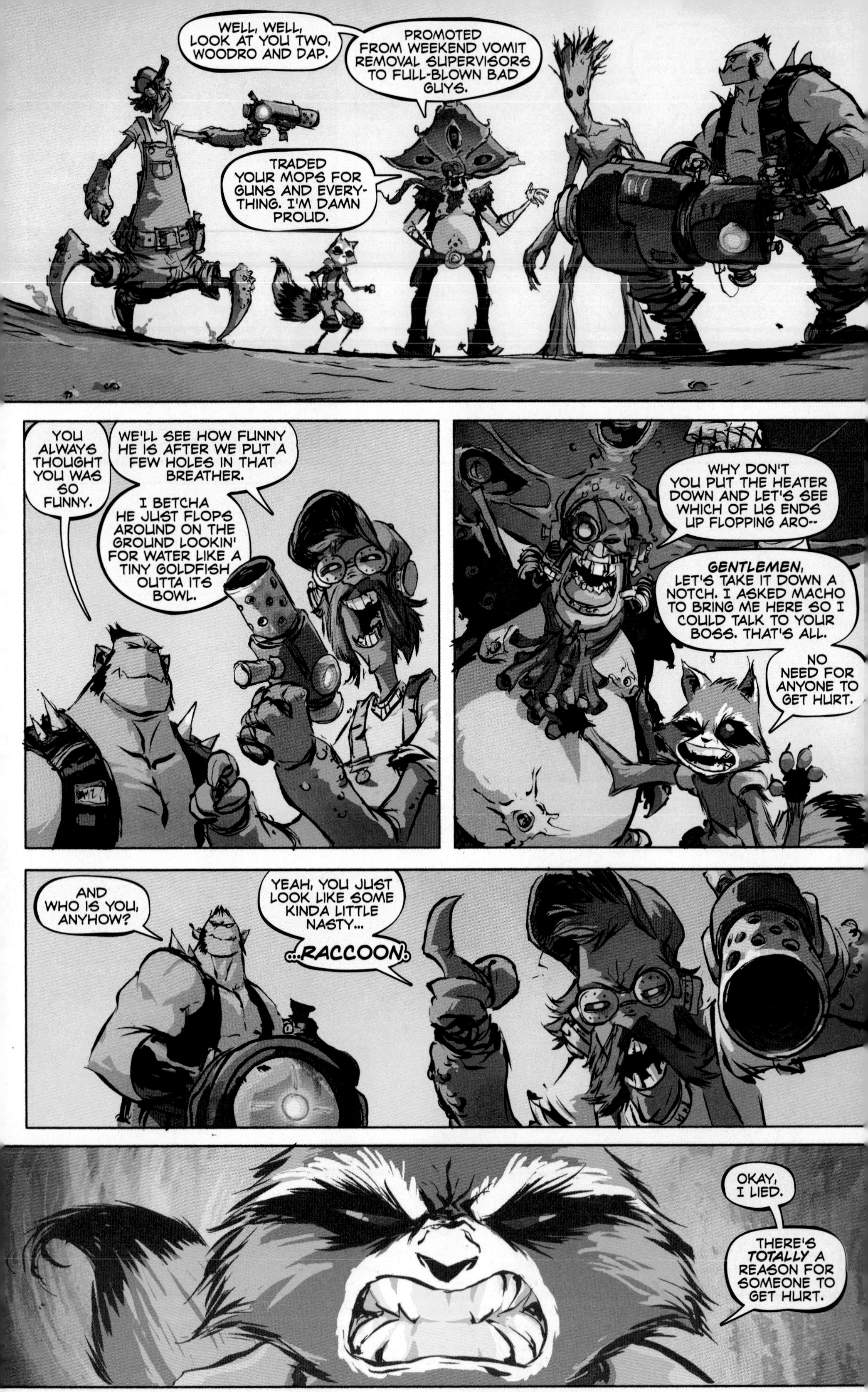
WELL, WELL, LOOK AT YOU TWO, WOODRO AND DAP.
PROMOTED FROM WEEKEND VOMIT REMOVAL SUPERVISORS TO FULL-BLOWN BAD GUYS.
TRADED YOUR MOPS FOR GUNS AND EVERYTHING. I'M DAMN PROUD.
YOU ALWAYS THOUGHT YOU WAS SO FUNNY.
WE'LL SEE HOW FUNNY HE IS AFTER WE PUT A FEW HOLES IN THAT BREATHER.
I BETCHA HE JUST FLOPS AROUND ON THE GROUND LOOKIN' FOR WATER LIKE A TINY GOLDFISH OUTTA ITS BOWL.
WHY DON'T YOU PUT THE HEATER DOWN AND LET'S SEE WHICH OF US ENDS UP FLOPPING ARO--
GENTLEMEN, LET'S TAKE IT DOWN A NOTCH. I ASKED MACHO TO BRING ME HERE SO I COULD TALK TO YOUR BOSS. THAT'S ALL.
NO NEED FOR ANYONE TO GET HURT.
AND WHO IS YOU, ANYHOW?
YEAH, YOU JUST LOOK LIKE SOME KINDA LITTLE NASTY...
...RACCOON.
OKAY, I LIED.
THERE'S TOTALLY A REASON FOR SOMEONE TO GET HURT.

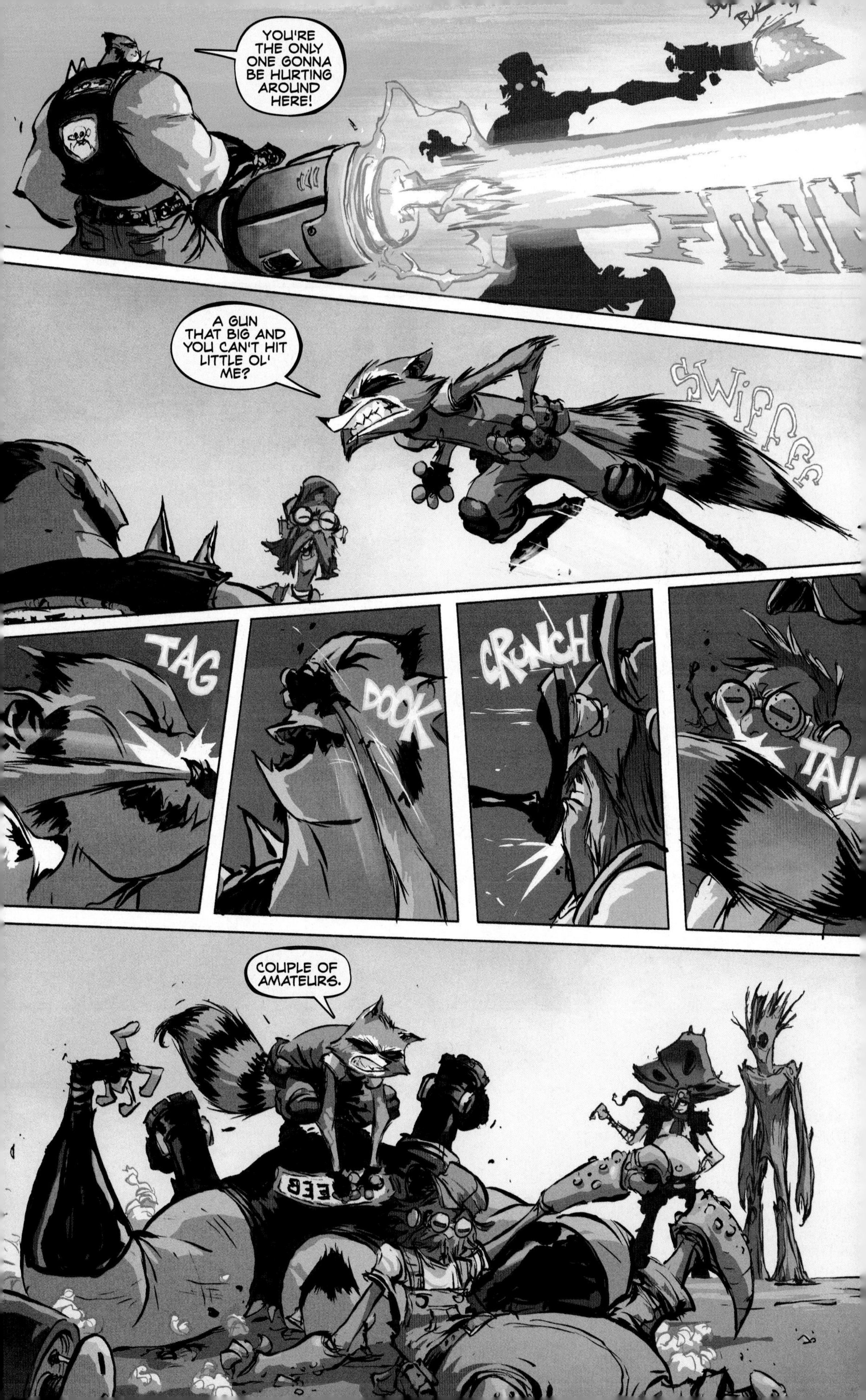
YOU'RE THE ONLY ONE GONNA BE HURTING AROUND HERE!
A GUN THAT BIG AND YOU CAN'T HIT LITTLE OL' ME?
SWIFFFF
TAG
DOOK
CRUNCH
COUPLE OF AMATEURS.

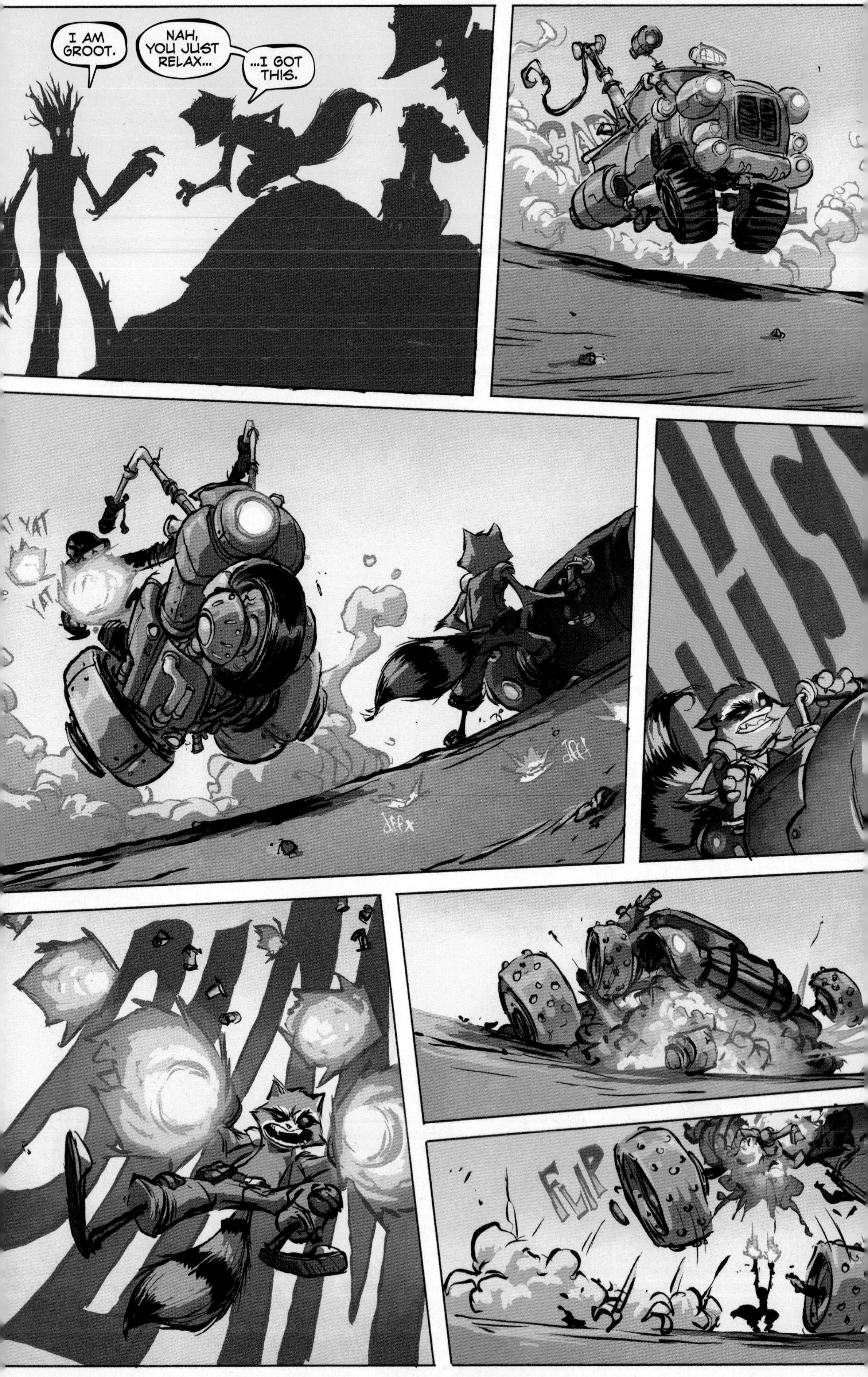
I AM GROOT.
NAH, YOU JUST RELAX...
...I GOT THIS.
FLIP

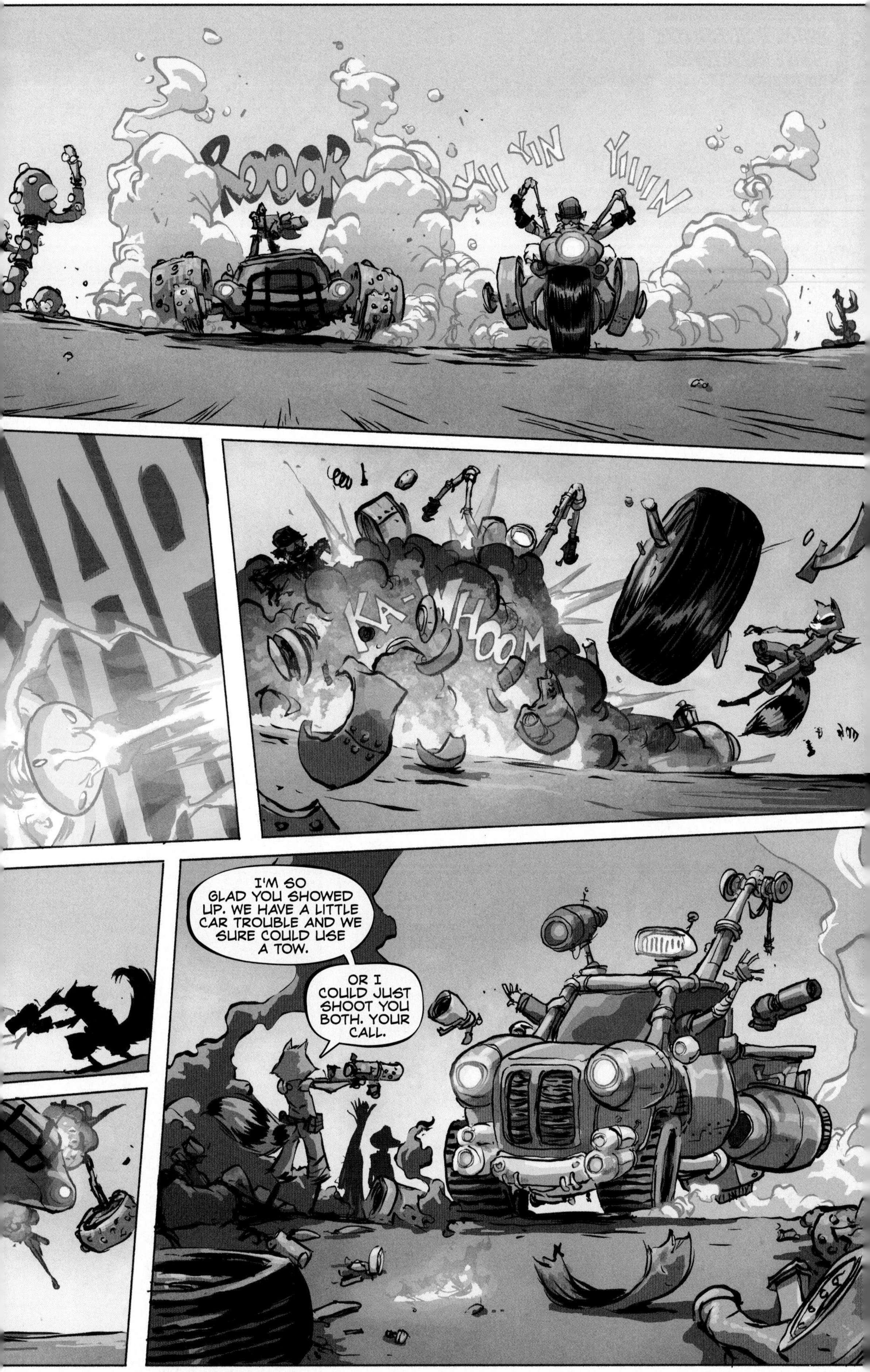
ROOOR
YIII YIN
YIIIIN
KA-WHOOM
I'M SO GLAD YOU SHOWED UP. WE HAVE A LITTLE CAR TROUBLE AND WE SURE COULD USE A TOW.
OR I COULD JUST SHOOT YOU BOTH. YOUR CALL.

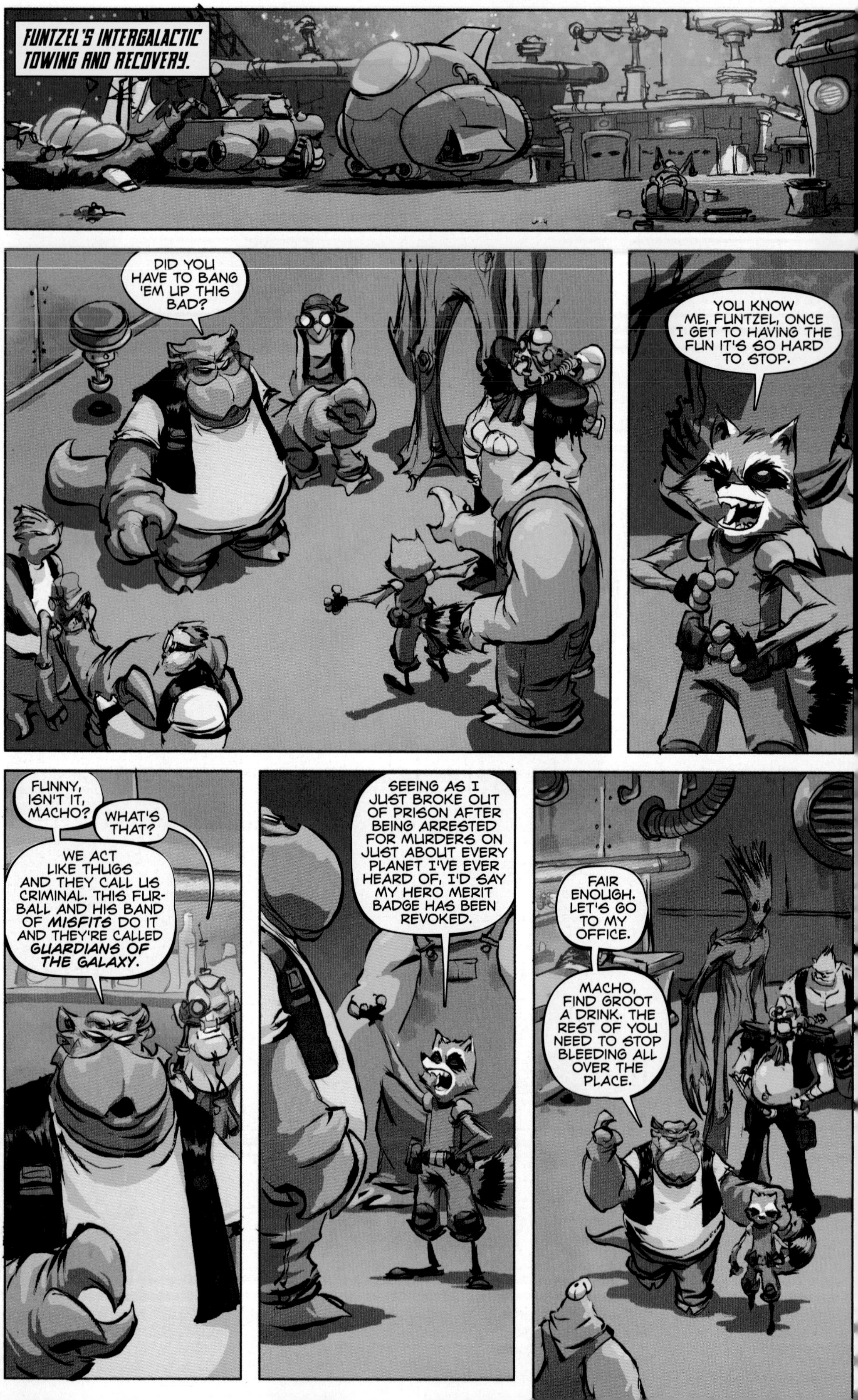

FUNTZEL'S INTERGALACTIC TOWING AND RECOVERY.
DID YOU HAVE TO BANG 'EM UP THIS BAD?
YOU KNOW ME, FUNTZEL, ONCE I GET TO HAVING THE FUN IT'S SO HARD TO STOP.
FUNNY, ISN'T IT, MACHO?
WHAT'S THAT?
WE ACT LIKE THUGS AND THEY CALL US CRIMINAL. THIS FUR-BALL AND HIS BAND OF MISFITS DO IT AND THEY'RE CALLED GUARDIANS OF THE GALAXY.
SEEING AS I JUST BROKE OUT OF PRISON AFTER BEING ARRESTED FOR MURDERS ON JUST ABOUT EVERY PLANET I'VE EVER HEARD OF, I'D SAY MY HERO MERIT BADGE HAS BEEN REVOKED.
FAIR ENOUGH. LET'S GO TO MY OFFICE.
MACHO, FIND GROOT A DRINK. THE REST OF YOU NEED TO STOP BLEEDING ALL OVER THE PLACE.

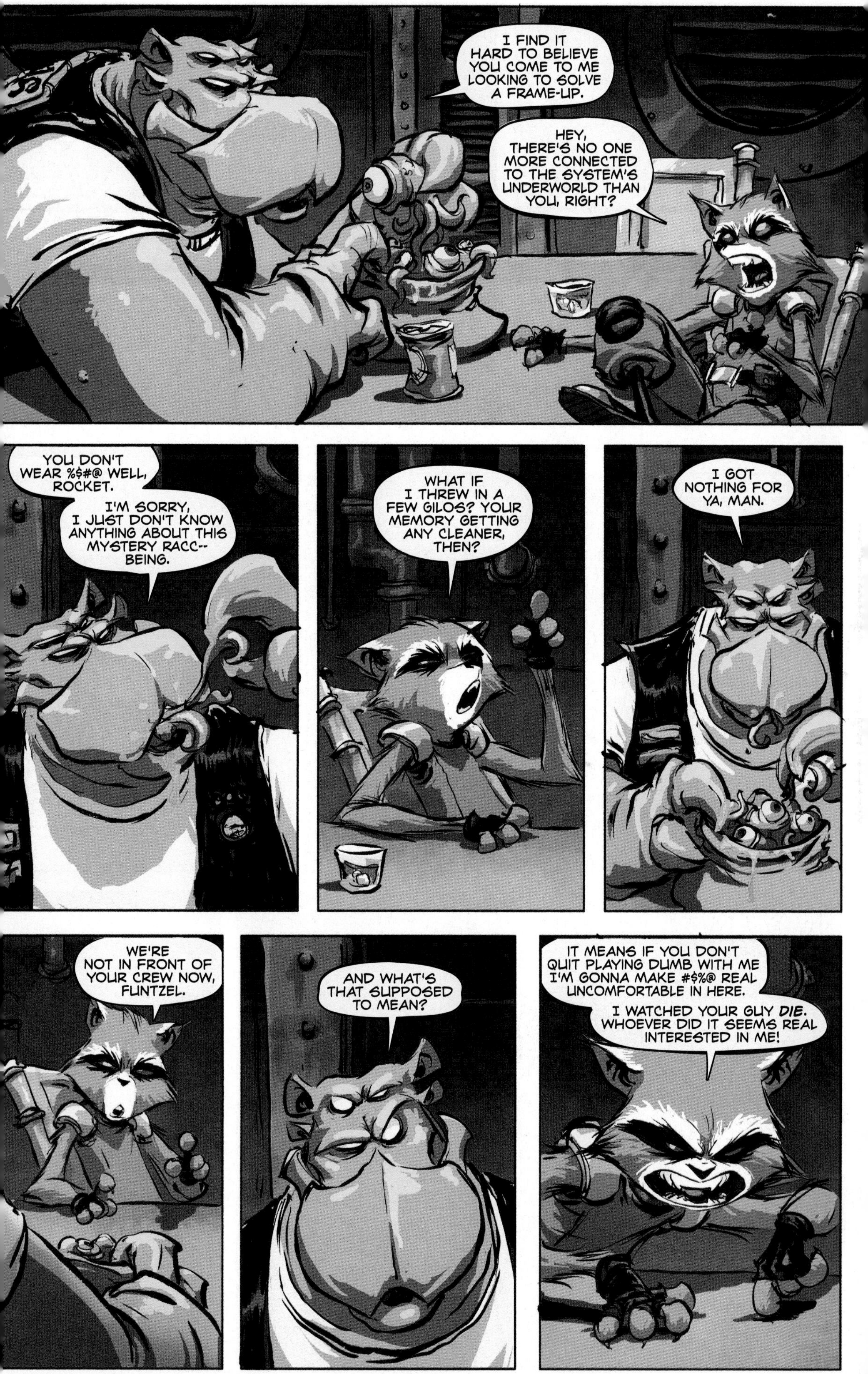
I FIND IT HARD TO BELIEVE YOU COME TO ME LOOKING TO SOLVE A FRAME-UP.
HEY, THERE'S NO ONE MORE CONNECTED TO THE SYSTEM'S UNDERWORLD THAN YOU, RIGHT?
YOU DON'T WEAR %$#@ WELL, ROCKET.
I'M SORRY, I JUST DON'T KNOW ANYTHING ABOUT THIS MYSTERY RACC-- BEING.
WHAT IF I THREW IN A FEW GILOS? YOUR MEMORY GETTING ANY CLEANER, THEN?
I GOT NOTHING FOR YA, MAN.
WE'RE NOT IN FRONT OF YOUR CREW NOW, FUNTZEL.
AND WHAT'S THAT SUPPOSED TO MEAN?
IT MEANS IF YOU DON'T QUIT PLAYING DUMB WITH ME I'M GONNA MAKE #$%@ REAL UNCOMFORTABLE IN HERE.
I WATCHED YOUR GUY *DIE*. WHOEVER DID IT SEEMS REAL INTERESTED IN ME!

YOU KNOW ABOUT WHEEZEY?

YEAH, YOUR GUY WITH THE HOLE IN HIM ON RIGEL SEVEN. HE TOLD ME HE SAW ME, OR SOMEONE *LIKE* ME BEFORE. AND THEN HE WAS CAPPED.

CEEBS

AND I KNOW YOU'RE NOT THE TYPE TO LET THAT GO. MAKES YOU LOOK WEAK. MAKES THIS WHOLE THING YOU GOT GOING OUT THERE FALL APART.

WATCH YOUR MOUTH, LITTLE THING. FLINTZEL'S *NOT* WEAK.

THEN I FIGURE YOU'D BE LOOKING TO RETURN THE FAVOR WITH A HOLE OR TWO IN WHOEVER'S RESPONSIBLE.

AND WHAT IF I DID THAT ALREADY?

CEET

THEN THEY'D BE DEAD AND NOT OUT THERE LOOKING LIKE ME WHILE KILLING ALL THESE POOR BASTARDS.

OKAY, FINE. I DID SOME SNIFFING AROUND BUT COULDN'T FIND ANYTHING SOLID.

MY PEOPLE JUST CAME BACK TO ME WITH A BUNCH OF MUMBO JUMBO ABOUT SOME CRAZY PEOPLE OFF IN SOME TOWER.

WHAT'S THAT SUPPOSED TO MEAN?

LOOK, I DON'T KNOW. THEY CALL THEM LOONIES OR SOMETHING. THAT AND SOME GIBBERISH ABOUT SOME *HALF-BOOK.* JUST DEAD ENDS.

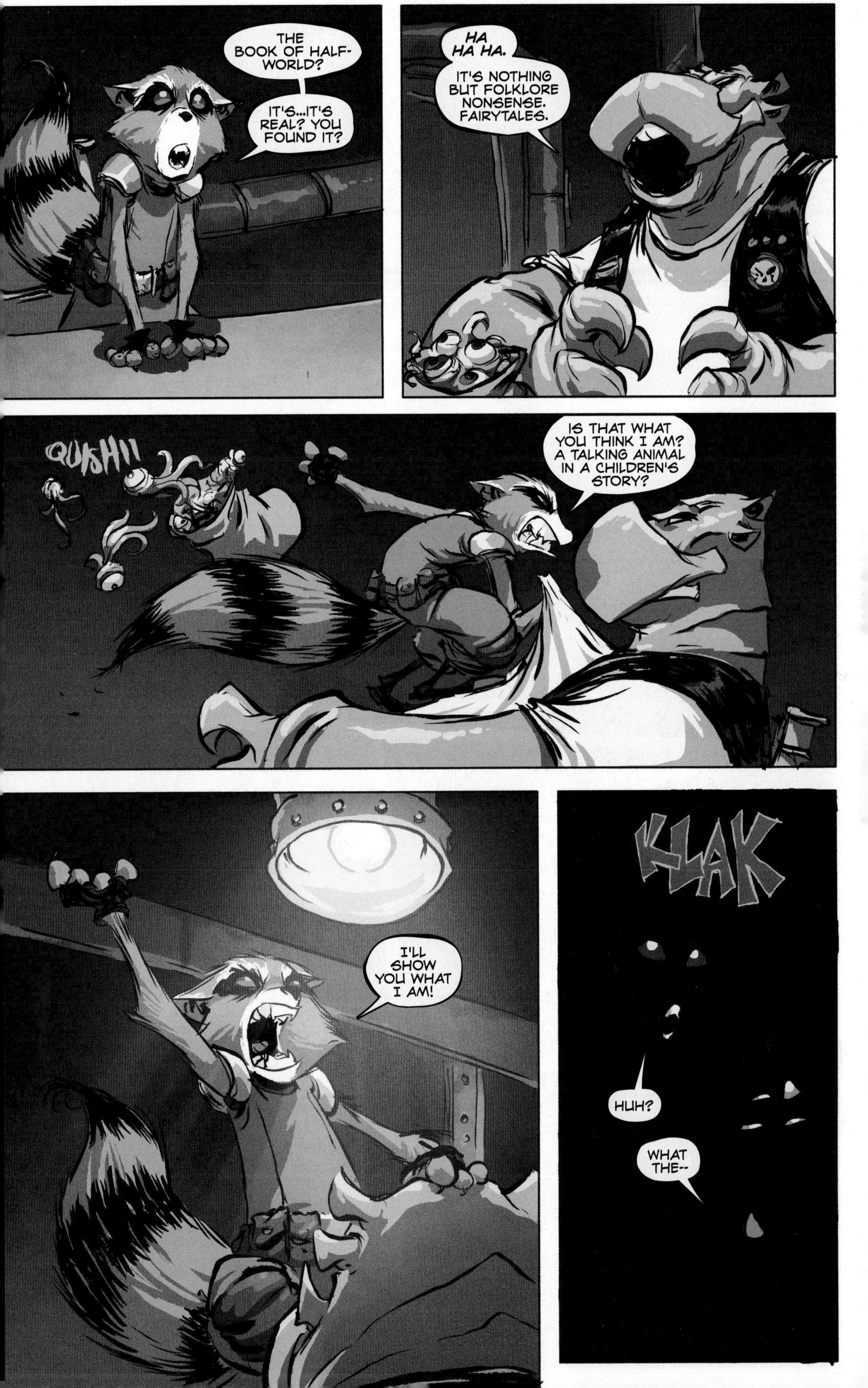
THE BOOK OF HALF-WORLD?
IT'S...IT'S REAL? YOU FOUND IT?
HA HA HA.
IT'S NOTHING BUT FOLKLORE NONSENSE. FAIRYTALES.
QUISH!!
IS THAT WHAT YOU THINK I AM? A TALKING ANIMAL IN A CHILDREN'S STORY?
I'LL SHOW YOU WHAT I AM!
KLAK
HUH?
WHAT THE--

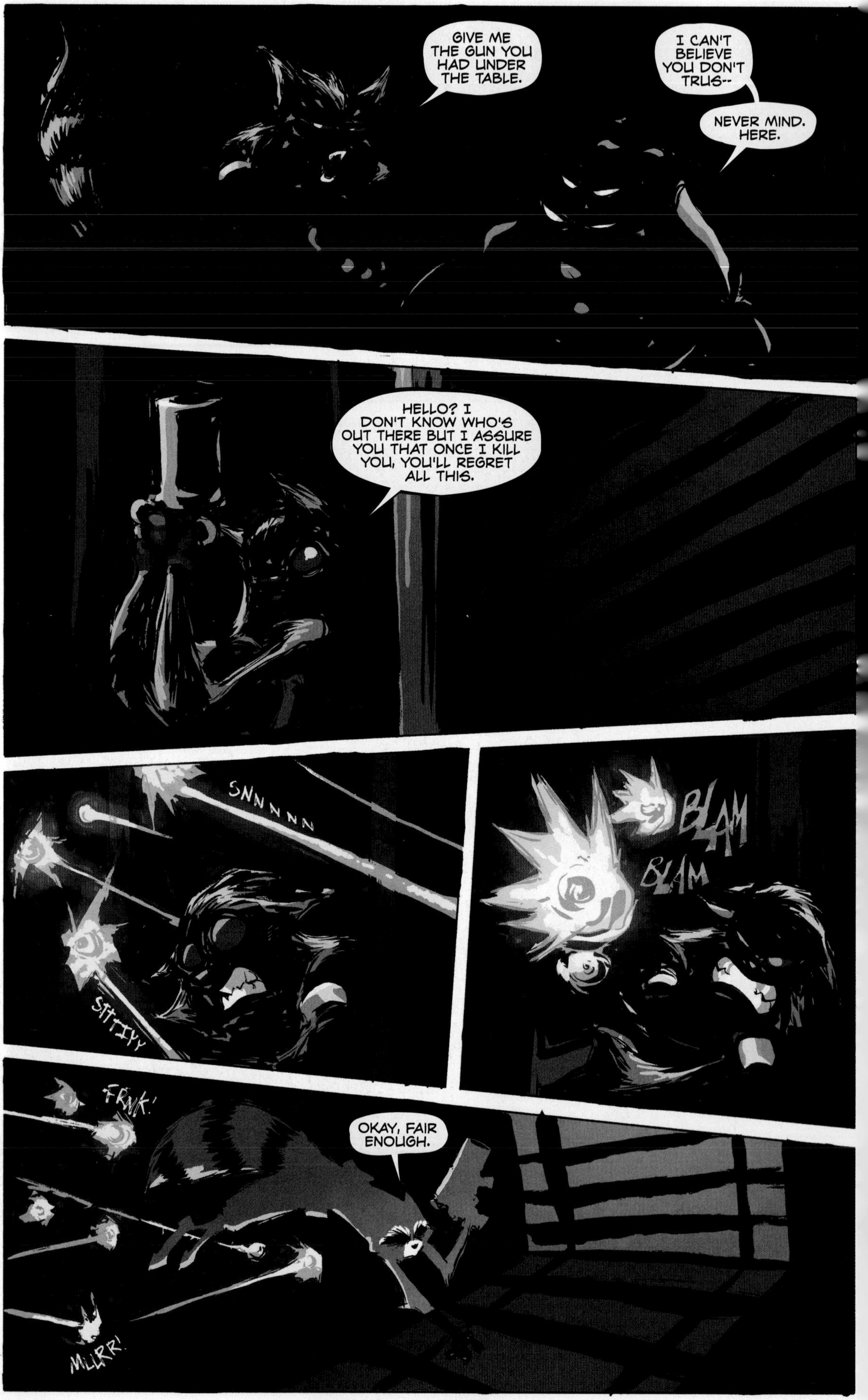
GIVE ME THE GUN YOU HAD UNDER THE TABLE.
I CAN'T BELIEVE YOU DON'T TRUS--
NEVER MIND. HERE.
HELLO? I DON'T KNOW WHO'S OUT THERE BUT I ASSURE YOU THAT ONCE I KILL YOU, YOU'LL REGRET ALL THIS.
SNNNNN
BLAM
BLAM
OKAY, FAIR ENOUGH.
MLRR!

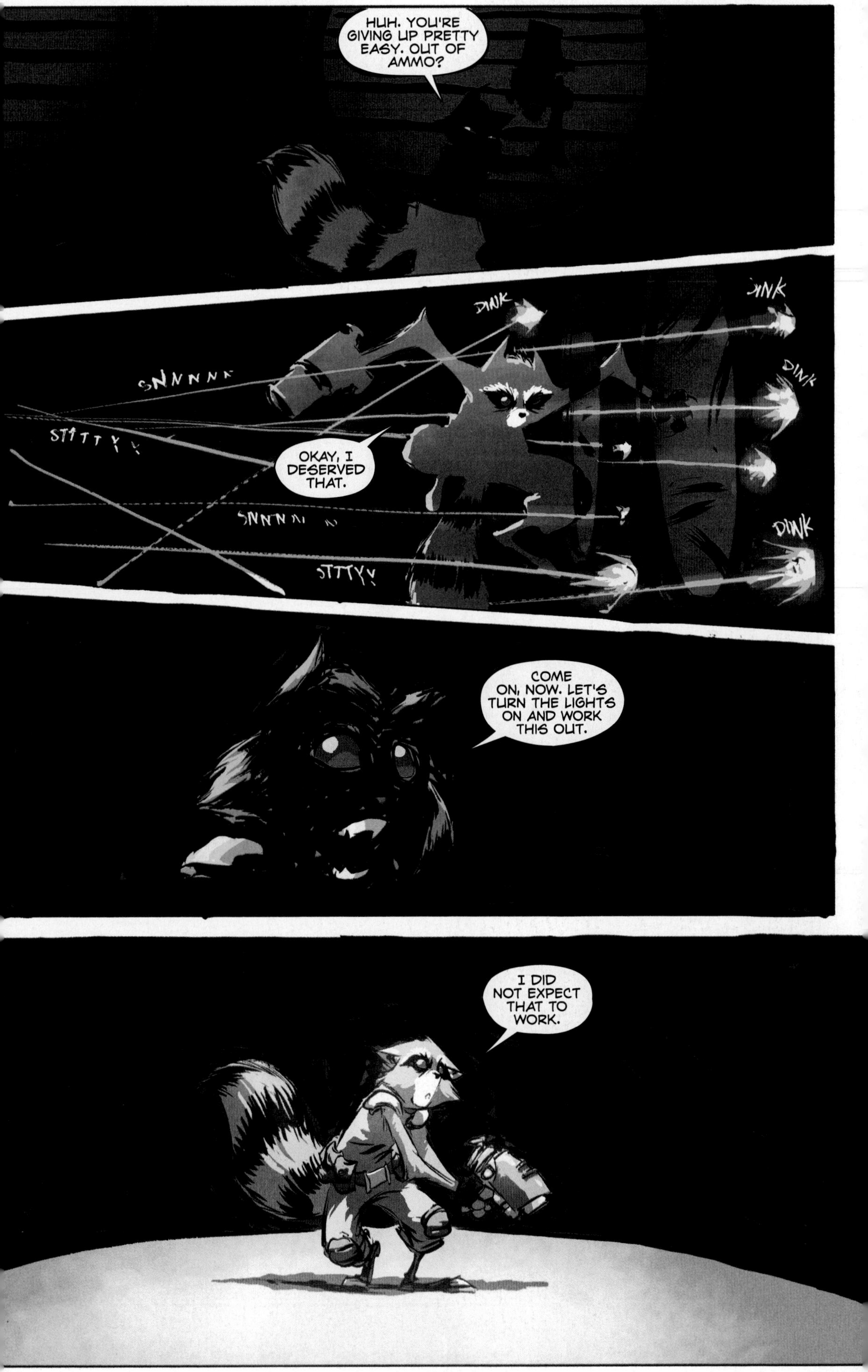
HUH. YOU'RE GIVING UP PRETTY EASY. OUT OF AMMO?
DINK
DINK
SNNNNK
DINK
STTTYK
OKAY, I DESERVED THAT.
SNNNN
DINK
STTTYK
COME ON, NOW. LET'S TURN THE LIGHTS ON AND WORK THIS OUT.
I DID NOT EXPECT THAT TO WORK.

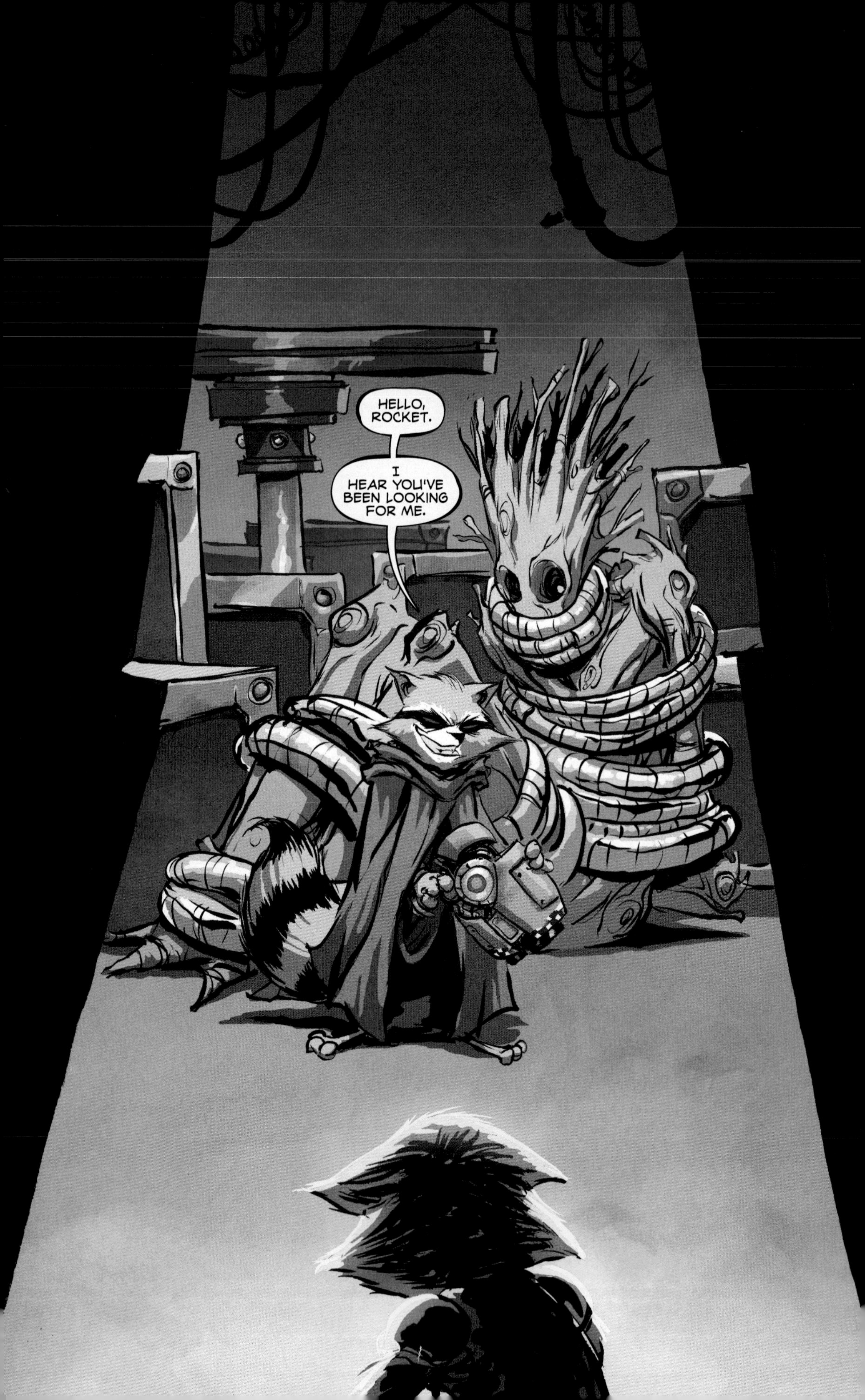
HELLO, ROCKET.
I HEAR YOU'VE BEEN LOOKING FOR ME.

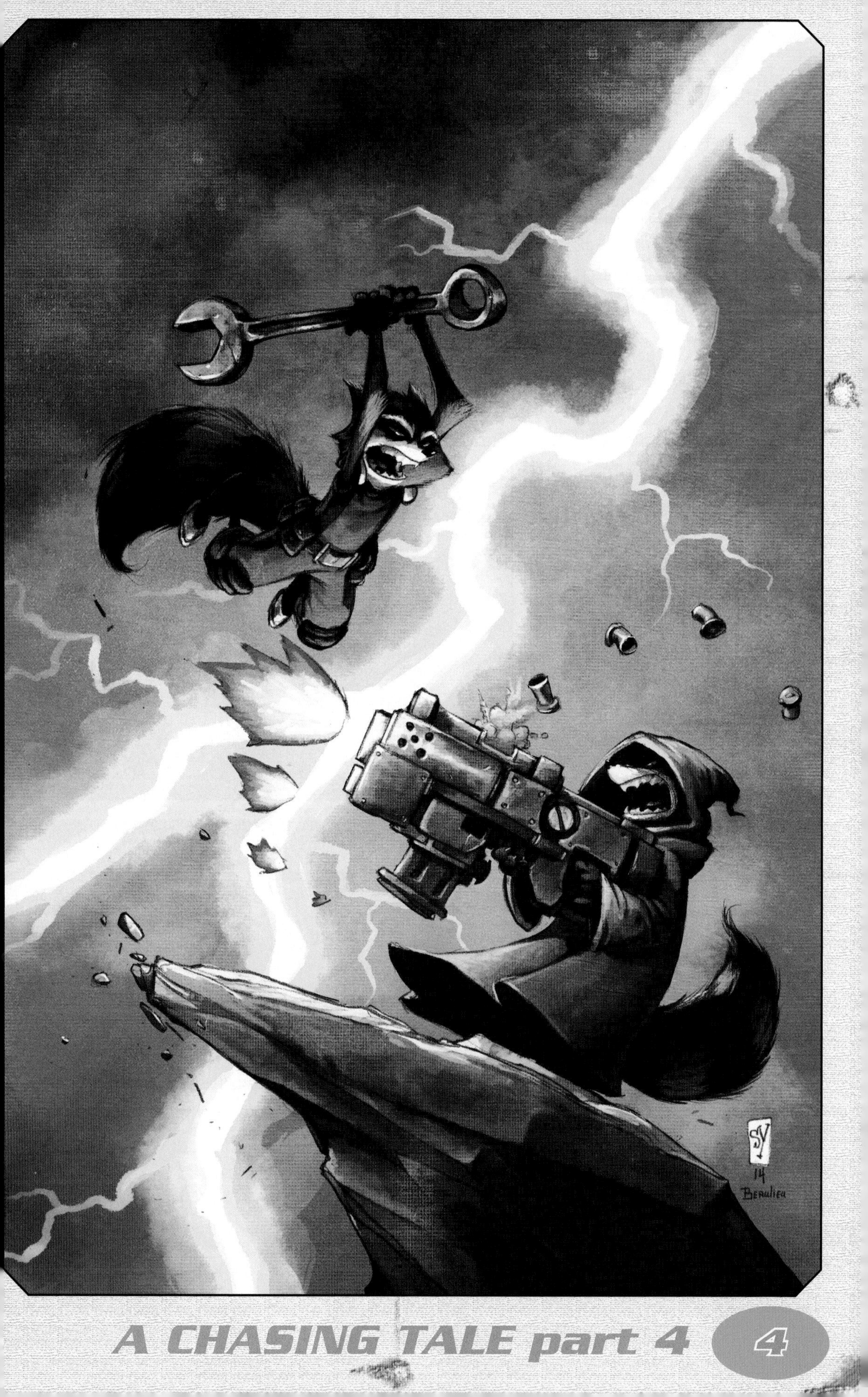

A CHASING TALE part 4

4

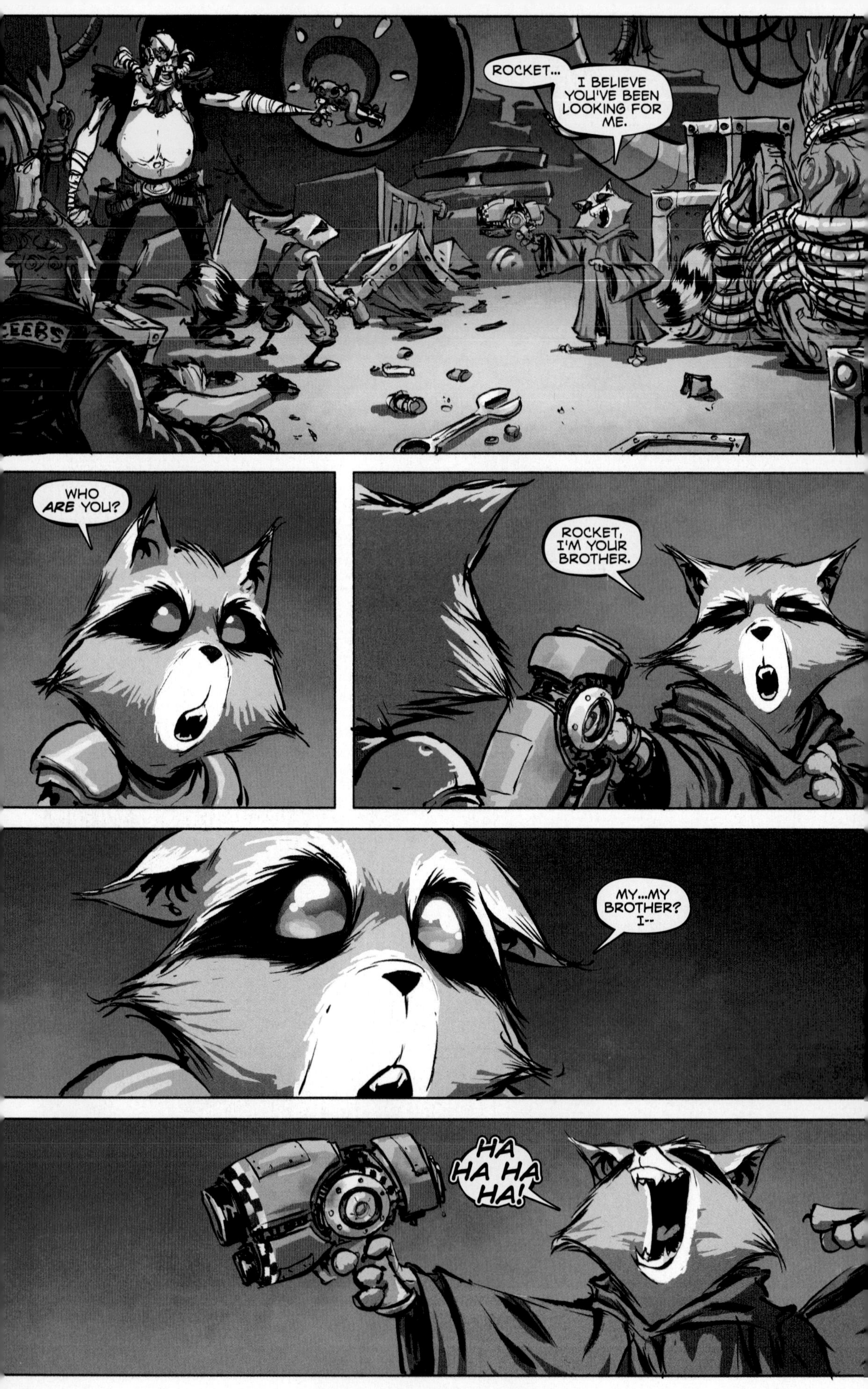
ROCKET... I BELIEVE YOU'VE BEEN LOOKING FOR ME.
WHO *ARE* YOU?
ROCKET, I'M YOUR BROTHER.
MY...MY BROTHER? I--
HA HA HA HA HA!

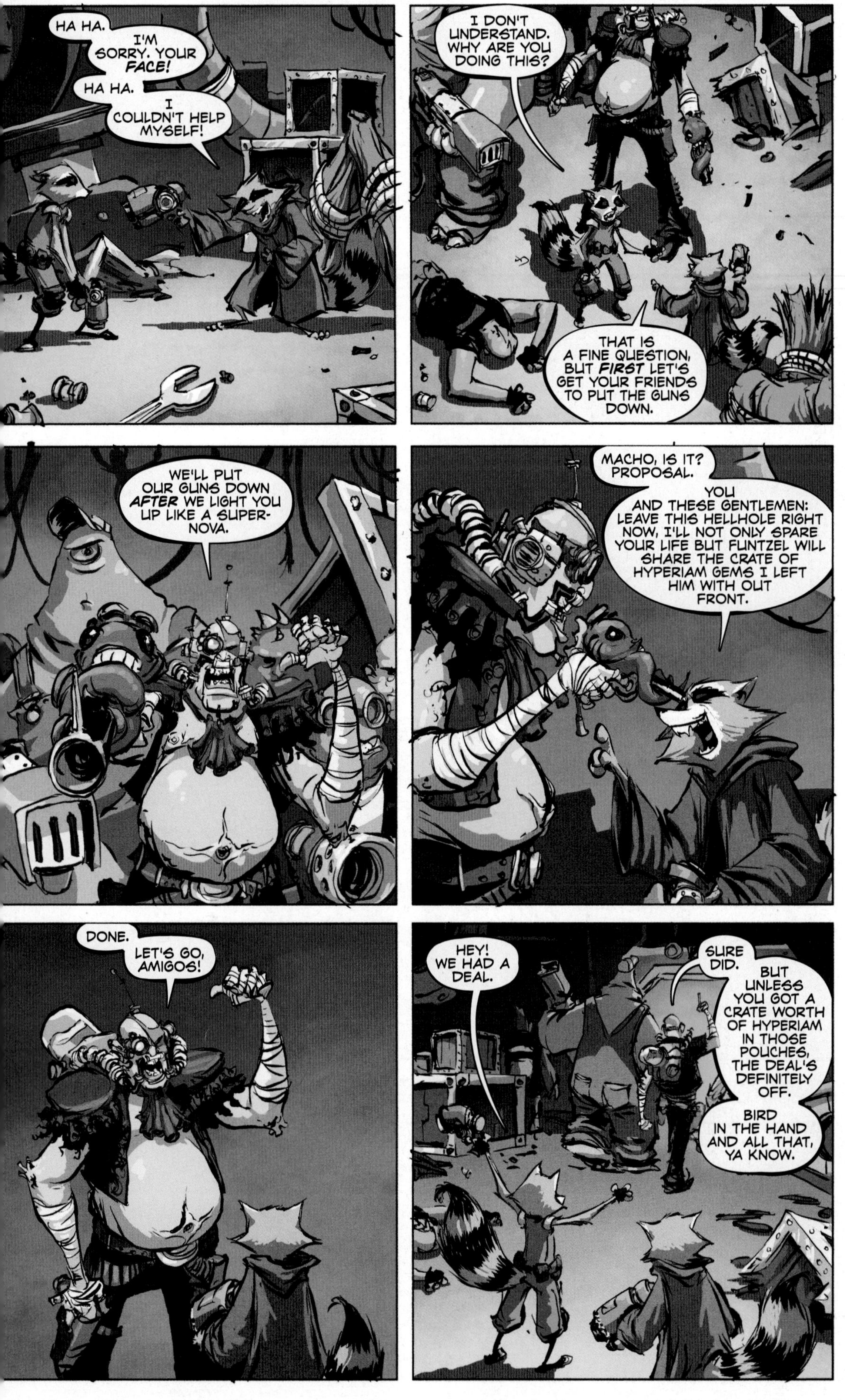
HA HA.
I'M SORRY. YOUR FACE!
HA HA.
I COULDN'T HELP MYSELF!
I DON'T UNDERSTAND. WHY ARE YOU DOING THIS?
THAT IS A FINE QUESTION, BUT FIRST LET'S GET YOUR FRIENDS TO PUT THE GUNS DOWN.
WE'LL PUT OUR GUNS DOWN AFTER WE LIGHT YOU UP LIKE A SUPER-NOVA.
MACHO, IS IT? PROPOSAL.
YOU AND THESE GENTLEMEN: LEAVE THIS HELLHOLE RIGHT NOW, I'LL NOT ONLY SPARE YOUR LIFE BUT FUNTZEL WILL SHARE THE CRATE OF HYPERIAM GEMS I LEFT HIM WITH OUT FRONT.
DONE.
LET'S GO, AMIGOS!
HEY! WE HAD A DEAL.
SURE DID.
BUT UNLESS YOU GOT A CRATE WORTH OF HYPERIAM IN THOSE POUCHES, THE DEAL'S DEFINITELY OFF.
BIRD IN THE HAND AND ALL THAT, YA KNOW.

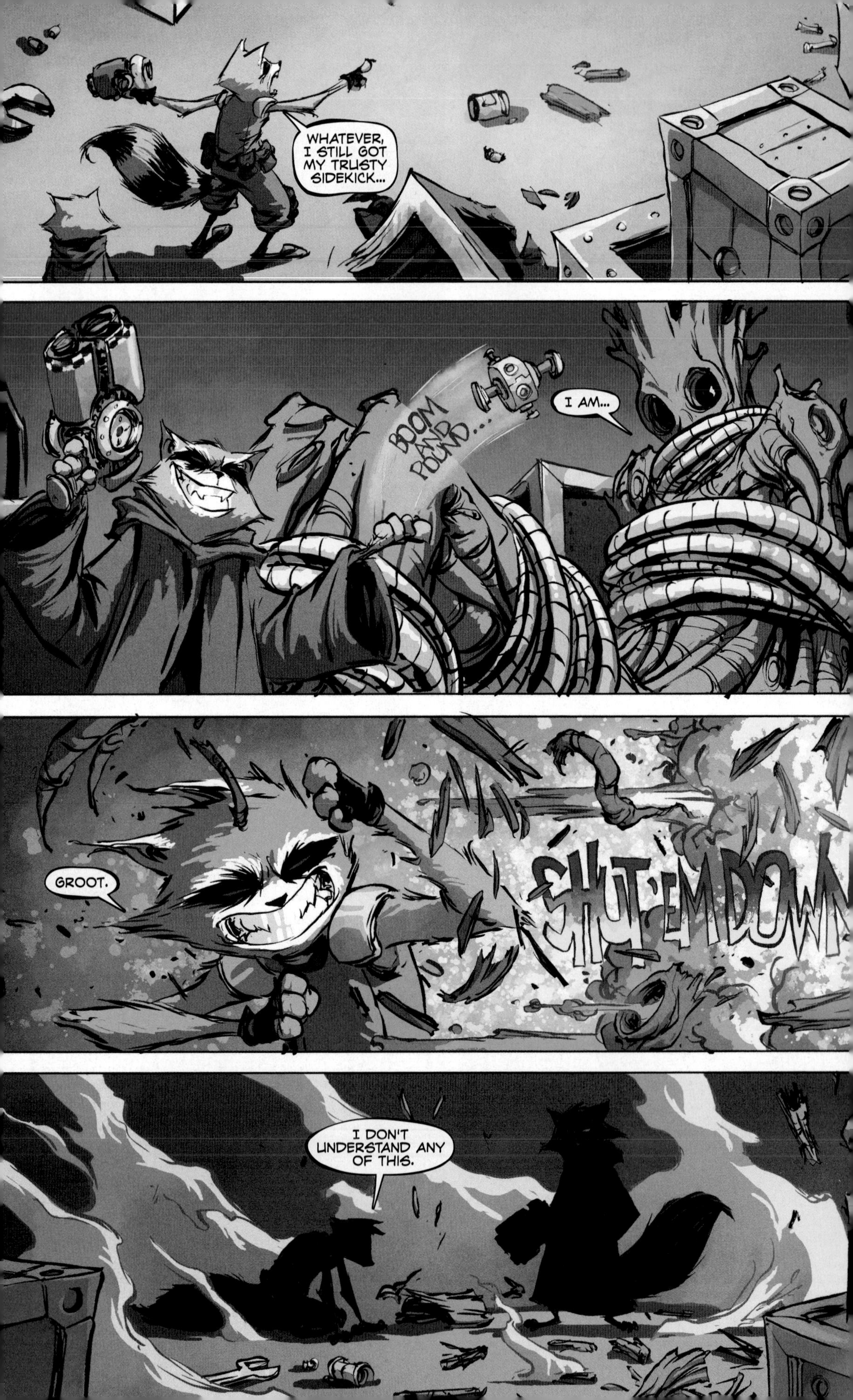
WHATEVER, I STILL GOT MY TRUSTY SIDEKICK...
BOOM AND POUND...
I AM...
GROOT.
SHUT'EM DOWN
I DON'T UNDERSTAND ANY OF THIS.

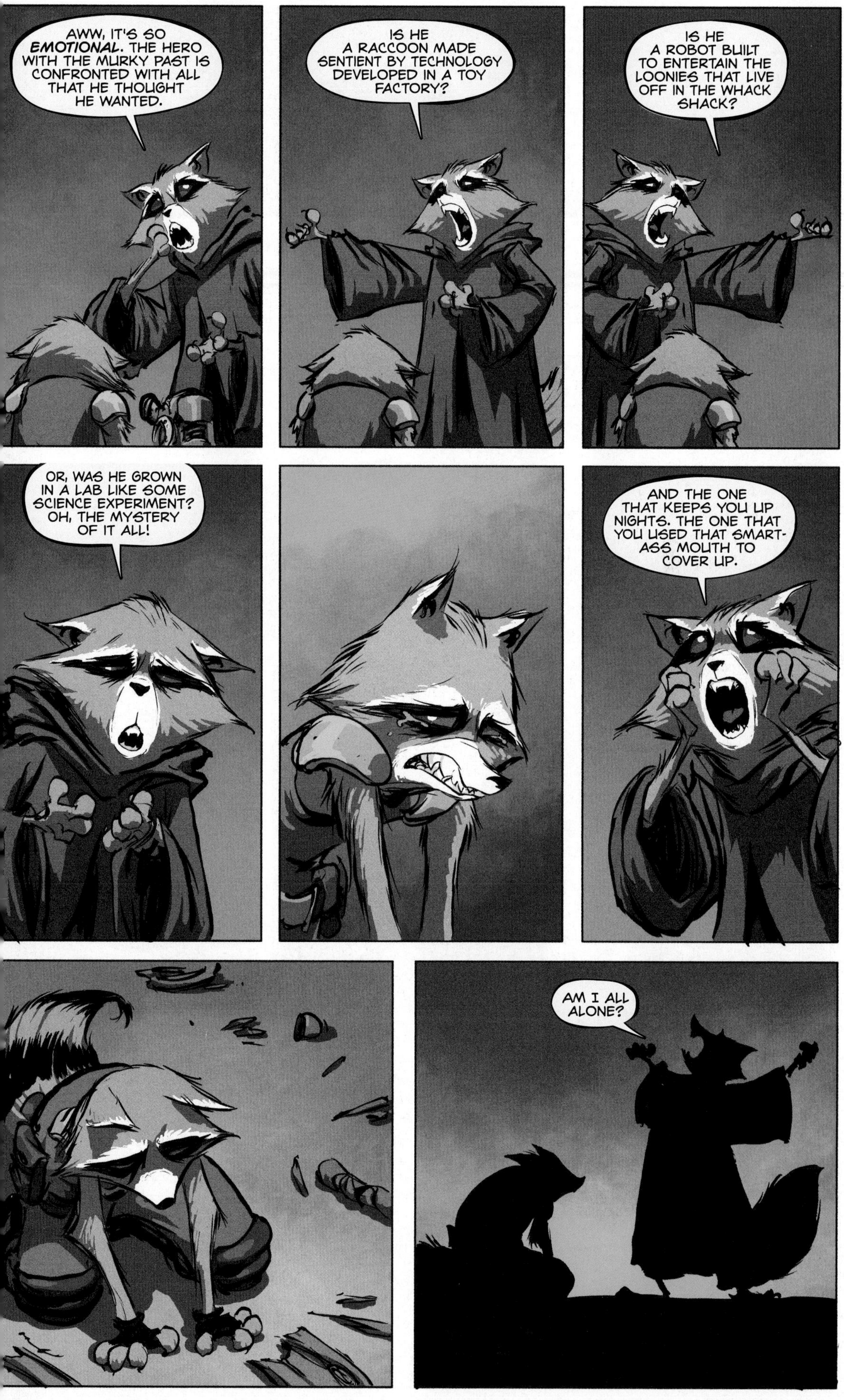
AWW, IT'S SO *EMOTIONAL*. THE HERO WITH THE MURKY PAST IS CONFRONTED WITH ALL THAT HE THOUGHT HE WANTED.
IS HE A RACCOON MADE SENTIENT BY TECHNOLOGY DEVELOPED IN A TOY FACTORY?
IS HE A ROBOT BUILT TO ENTERTAIN THE LOONIES THAT LIVE OFF IN THE WHACK SHACK?
OR, WAS HE GROWN IN A LAB LIKE SOME SCIENCE EXPERIMENT? OH, THE MYSTERY OF IT ALL!
AND THE ONE THAT KEEPS YOU UP NIGHTS. THE ONE THAT YOU USED THAT SMART-ASS MOUTH TO COVER UP.
AM I ALL ALONE?

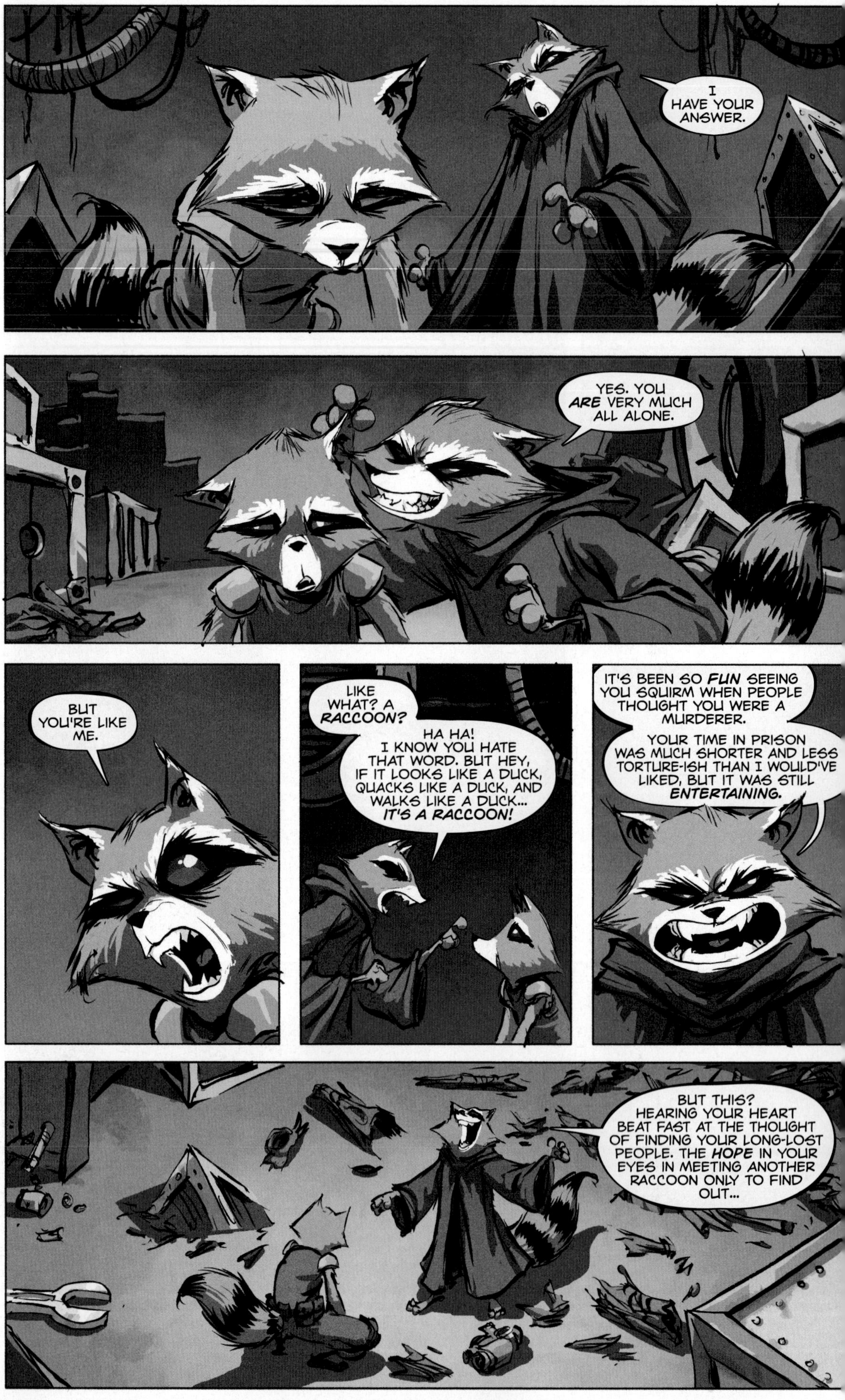
I HAVE YOUR ANSWER.
YES. YOU ARE VERY MUCH ALL ALONE.
BUT YOU'RE LIKE ME.
LIKE WHAT? A RACCOON?
HA HA! I KNOW YOU HATE THAT WORD. BUT HEY, IF IT LOOKS LIKE A DUCK, QUACKS LIKE A DUCK, AND WALKS LIKE A DUCK... IT'S A RACCOON!
IT'S BEEN SO FUN SEEING YOU SQUIRM WHEN PEOPLE THOUGHT YOU WERE A MURDERER.
YOUR TIME IN PRISON WAS MUCH SHORTER AND LESS TORTURE-ISH THAN I WOULD'VE LIKED, BUT IT WAS STILL ENTERTAINING.
BUT THIS? HEARING YOUR HEART BEAT FAST AT THE THOUGHT OF FINDING YOUR LONG-LOST PEOPLE. THE HOPE IN YOUR EYES IN MEETING ANOTHER RACCOON ONLY TO FIND OUT...

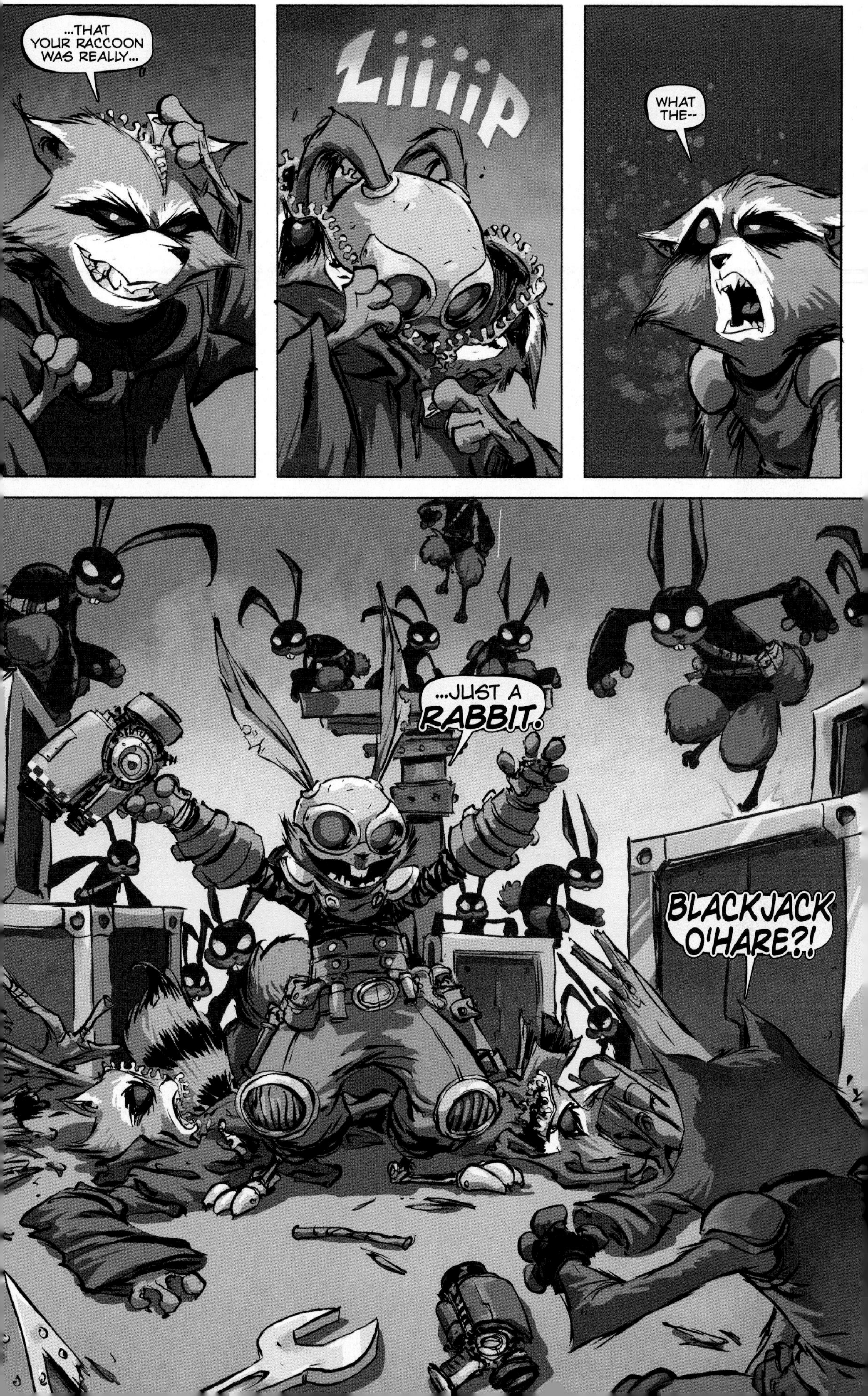
...THAT YOUR RACCOON WAS REALLY...
LIIIIP
WHAT THE--
...JUST A RABBIT.
BLACKJACK O'HARE?!

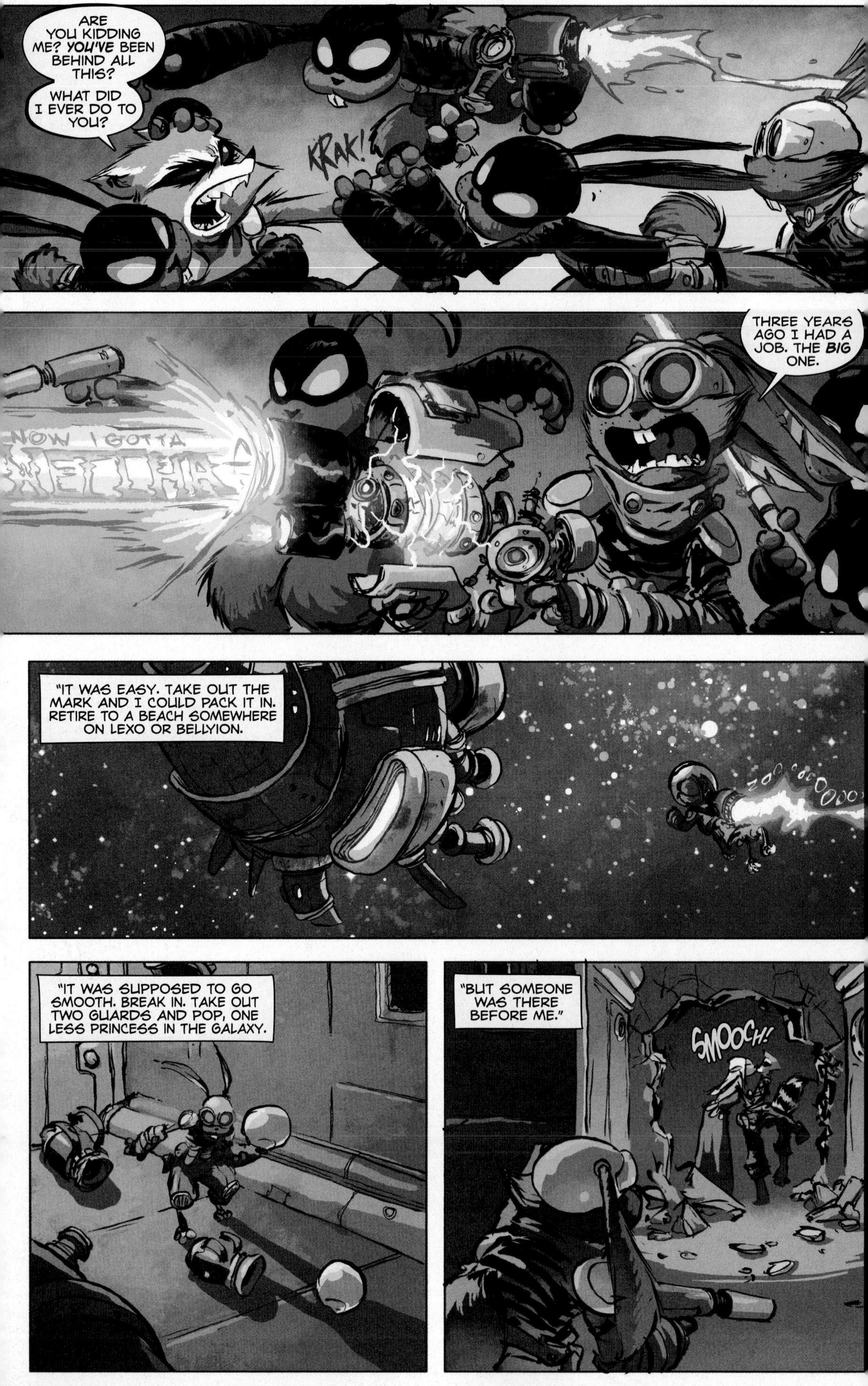
ARE YOU KIDDING ME? YOU'VE BEEN BEHIND ALL THIS?
WHAT DID I EVER DO TO YOU?
KRAK!
THREE YEARS AGO I HAD A JOB. THE BIG ONE.
NOW I GOTTA
"IT WAS EASY. TAKE OUT THE MARK AND I COULD PACK IT IN. RETIRE TO A BEACH SOMEWHERE ON LEXO OR BELLYION.
"IT WAS SUPPOSED TO GO SMOOTH. BREAK IN. TAKE OUT TWO GUARDS AND POP, ONE LESS PRINCESS IN THE GALAXY.
"BUT SOMEONE WAS THERE BEFORE ME."
SMOOCH!

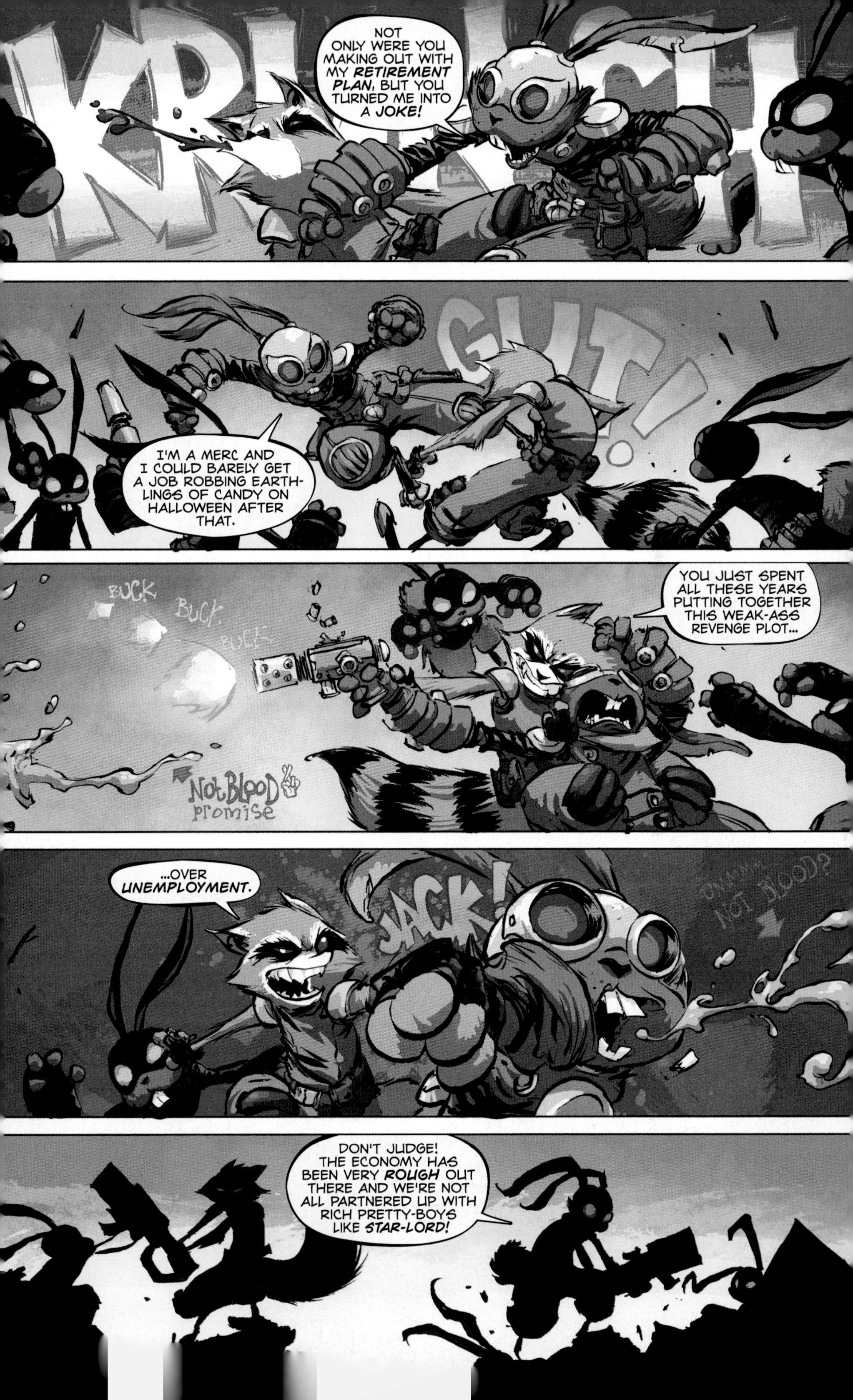
NOT ONLY WERE YOU MAKING OUT WITH MY RETIREMENT PLAN, BUT YOU TURNED ME INTO A JOKE!
GUT!
I'M A MERC AND I COULD BARELY GET A JOB ROBBING EARTH-LINGS OF CANDY ON HALLOWEEN AFTER THAT.
BUCK BUCK BUCK
YOU JUST SPENT ALL THESE YEARS PUTTING TOGETHER THIS WEAK-ASS REVENGE PLOT...
NotBlood promise
...OVER UNEMPLOYMENT.
JACK!
NOT BLOOD?
DON'T JUDGE! THE ECONOMY HAS BEEN VERY ROUGH OUT THERE AND WE'RE NOT ALL PARTNERED UP WITH RICH PRETTY-BOYS LIKE STAR-LORD!

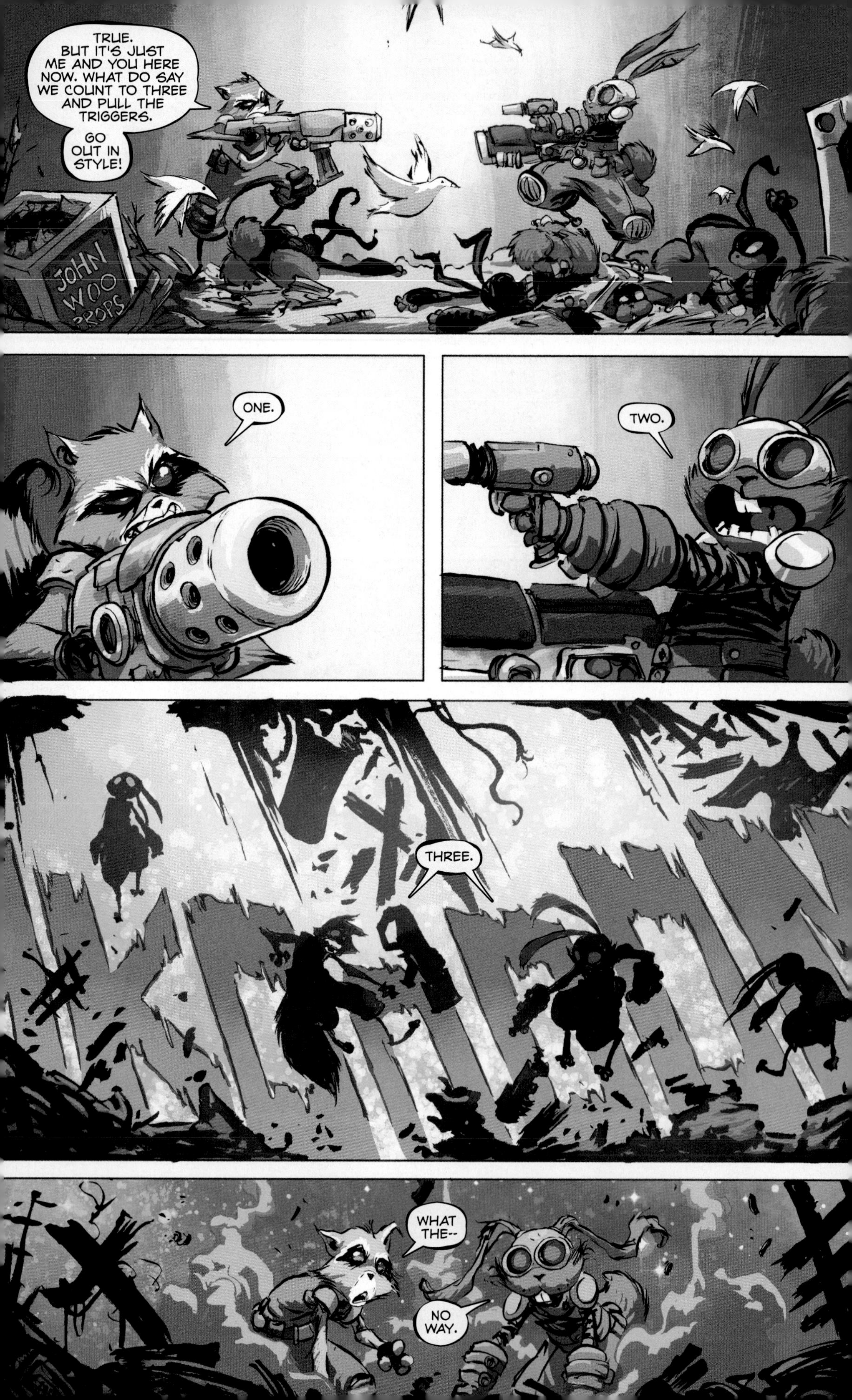
TRUE. BUT IT'S JUST ME AND YOU HERE NOW. WHAT DO SAY WE COUNT TO THREE AND PULL THE TRIGGERS.
GO OUT IN STYLE!
JOHN WOO PROPS
ONE.
TWO.
THREE.
WHAT THE--
NO WAY.

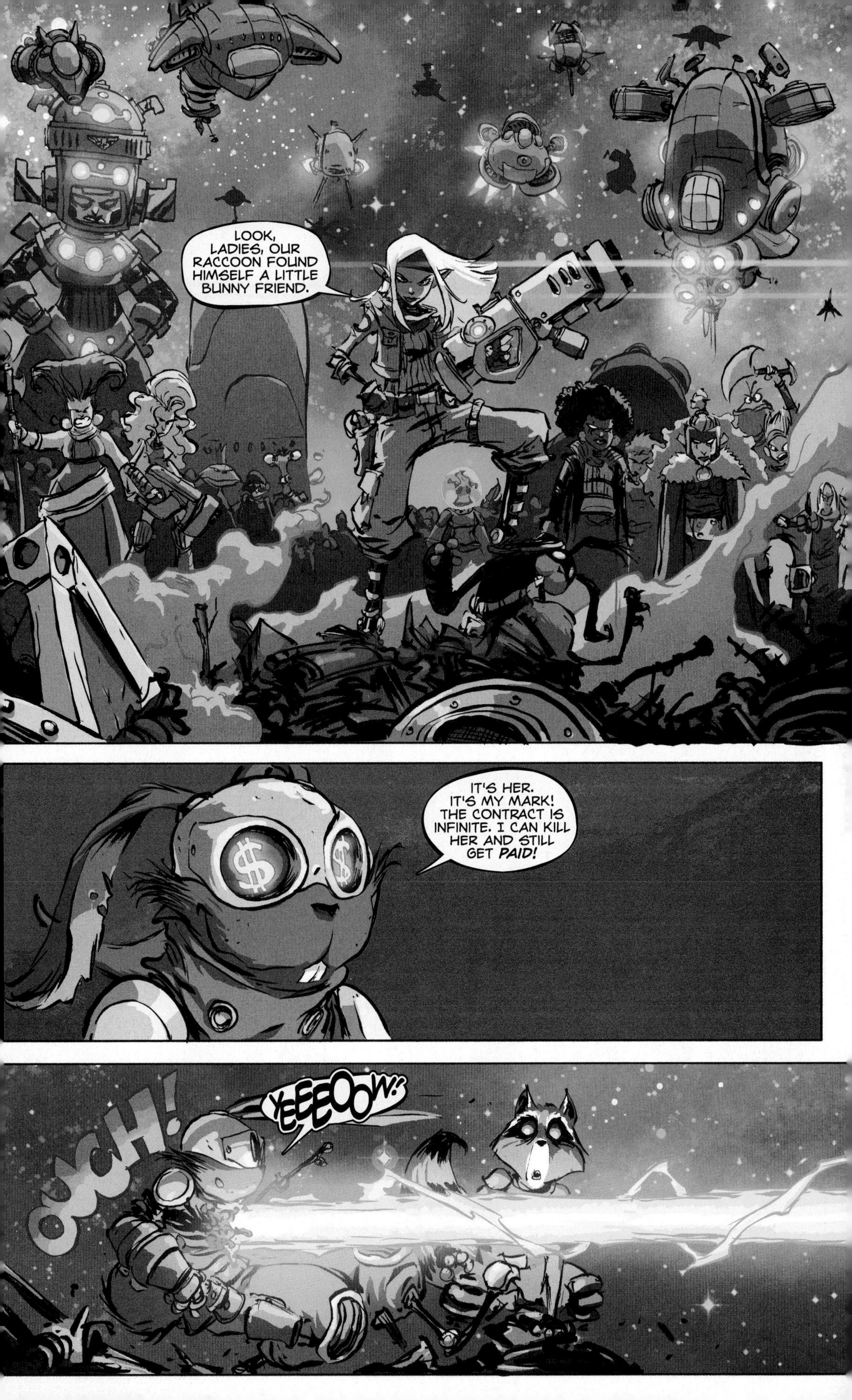
LOOK, LADIES, OUR RACCOON FOUND HIMSELF A LITTLE BUNNY FRIEND.
IT'S HER. IT'S MY MARK! THE CONTRACT IS INFINITE. I CAN KILL HER AND STILL GET *PAID!*
OUCH!
YEEEEOOOW!

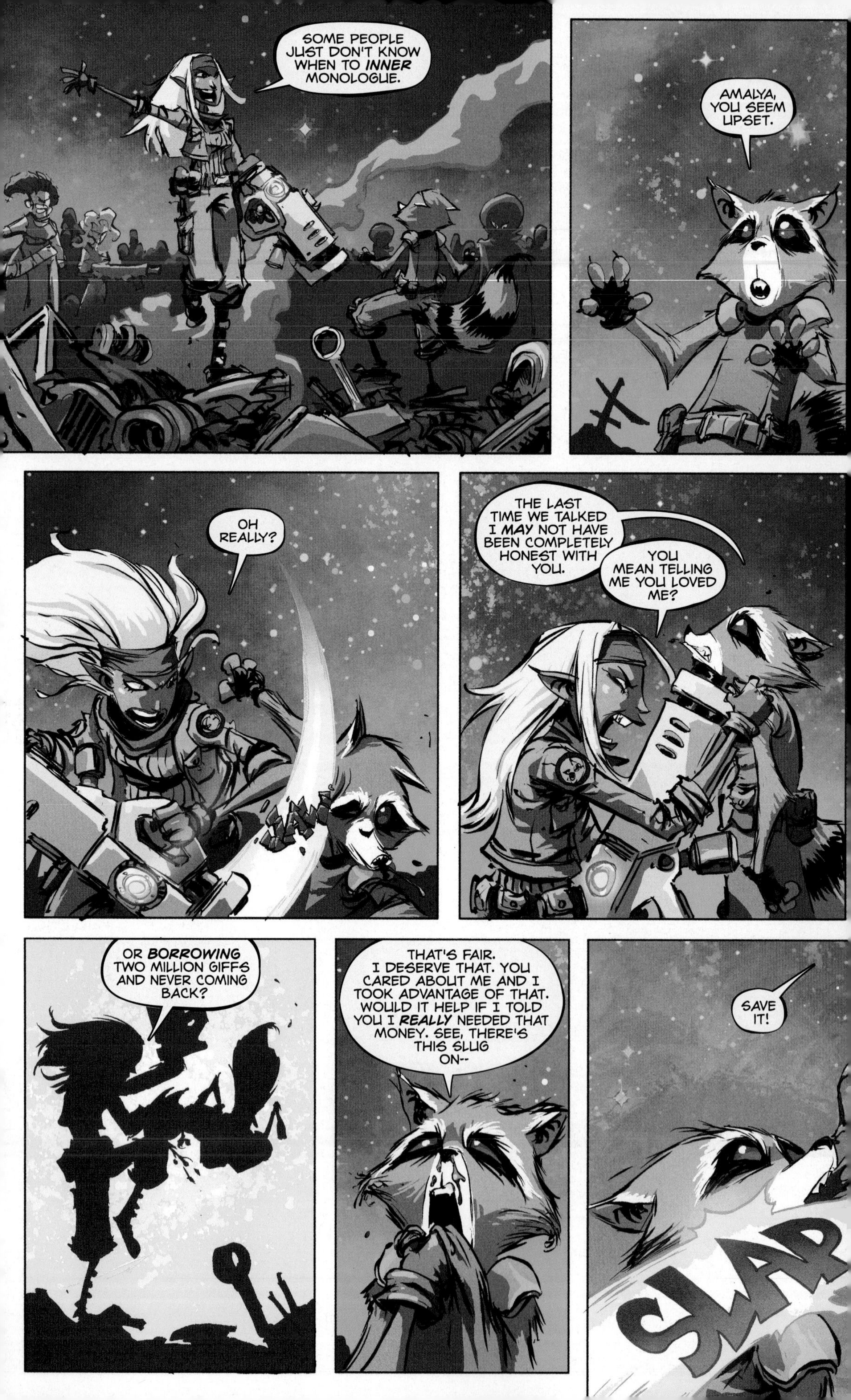
SOME PEOPLE JUST DON'T KNOW WHEN TO *INNER* MONOLOGUE.
AMALYA, YOU SEEM UPSET.
OH REALLY?
THE LAST TIME WE TALKED I *MAY* NOT HAVE BEEN COMPLETELY HONEST WITH YOU.
YOU MEAN TELLING ME YOU LOVED ME?
OR *BORROWING* TWO MILLION GIFFS AND NEVER COMING BACK?
THAT'S FAIR. I DESERVE THAT. YOU CARED ABOUT ME AND I TOOK ADVANTAGE OF THAT. WOULD IT HELP IF I TOLD YOU I *REALLY* NEEDED THAT MONEY. SEE, THERE'S THIS SLUG ON--
SAVE IT!
SLAP

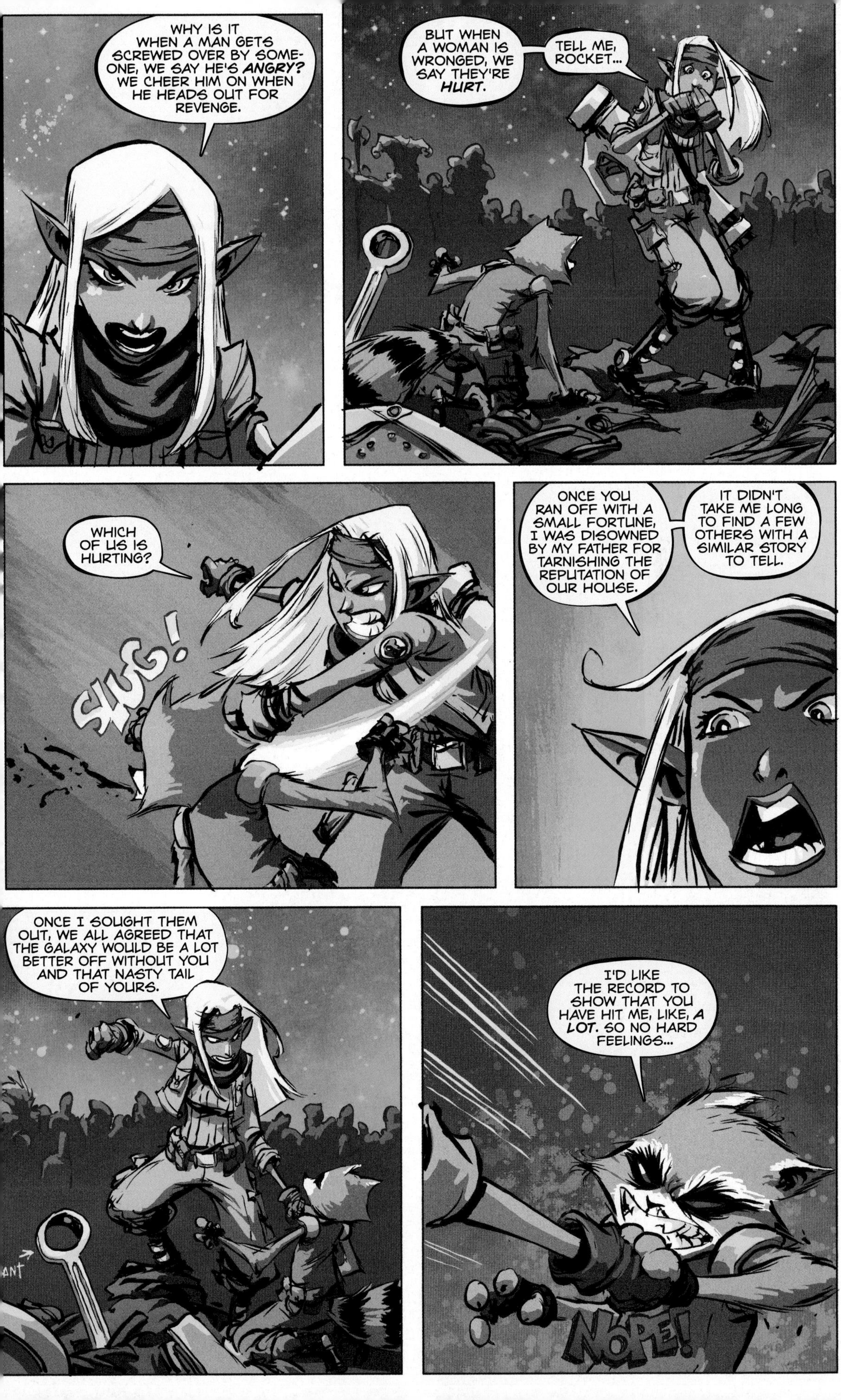

WHY IS IT WHEN A MAN GETS SCREWED OVER BY SOMEONE, WE SAY HE'S ANGRY? WE CHEER HIM ON WHEN HE HEADS OUT FOR REVENGE.
BUT WHEN A WOMAN IS WRONGED, WE SAY THEY'RE HURT.
TELL ME, ROCKET...
WHICH OF US IS HURTING?
SLUG!
ONCE YOU RAN OFF WITH A SMALL FORTUNE, I WAS DISOWNED BY MY FATHER FOR TARNISHING THE REPUTATION OF OUR HOUSE.
IT DIDN'T TAKE ME LONG TO FIND A FEW OTHERS WITH A SIMILAR STORY TO TELL.
ONCE I SOUGHT THEM OUT, WE ALL AGREED THAT THE GALAXY WOULD BE A LOT BETTER OFF WITHOUT YOU AND THAT NASTY TAIL OF YOURS.
I'D LIKE THE RECORD TO SHOW THAT YOU HAVE HIT ME, LIKE, A LOT. SO NO HARD FEELINGS...
NOPE!

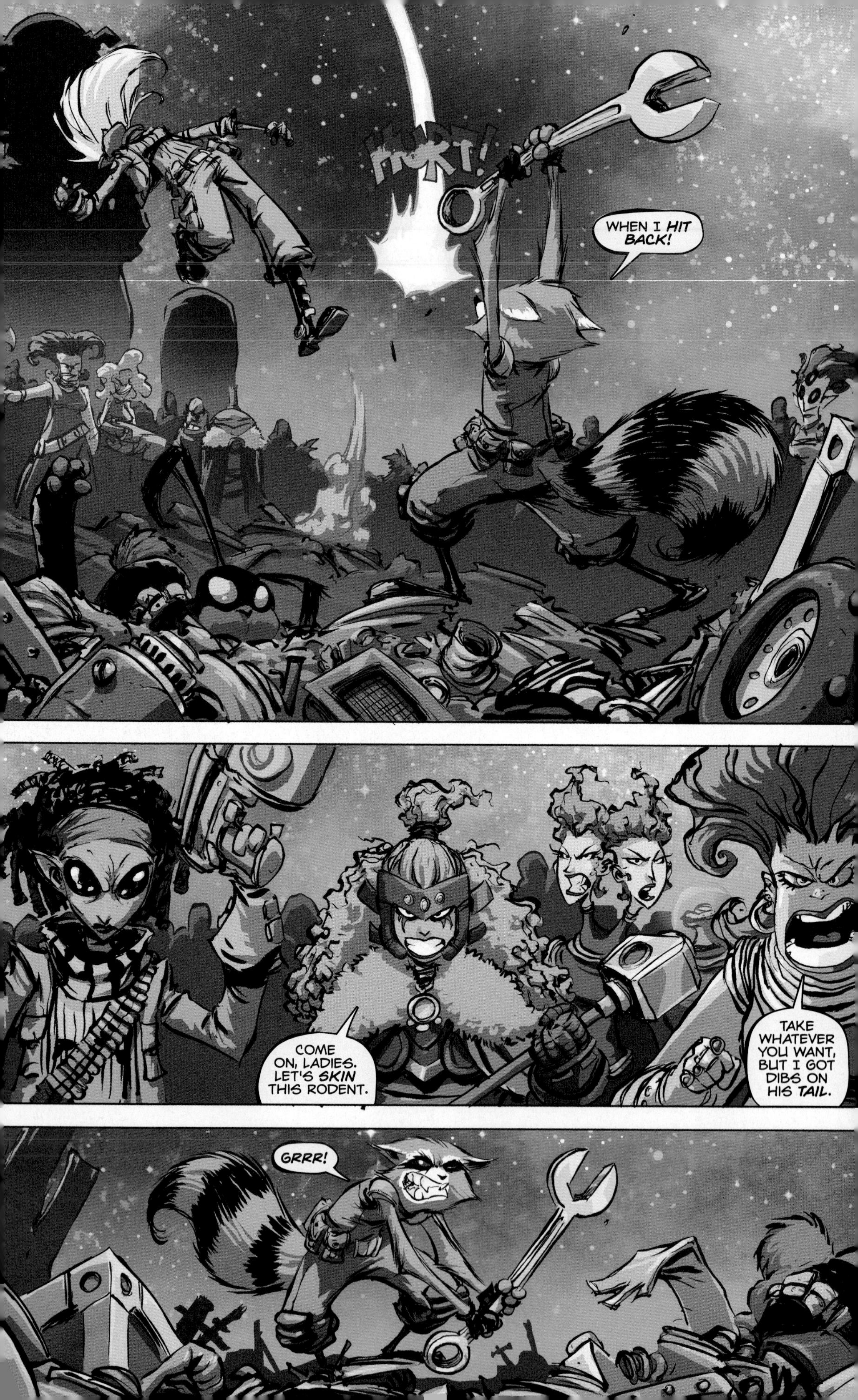
HURT!
WHEN I HIT BACK!
COME ON, LADIES. LET'S SKIN THIS RODENT.
TAKE WHATEVER YOU WANT, BUT I GOT DIBS ON HIS TAIL.
GRRR!

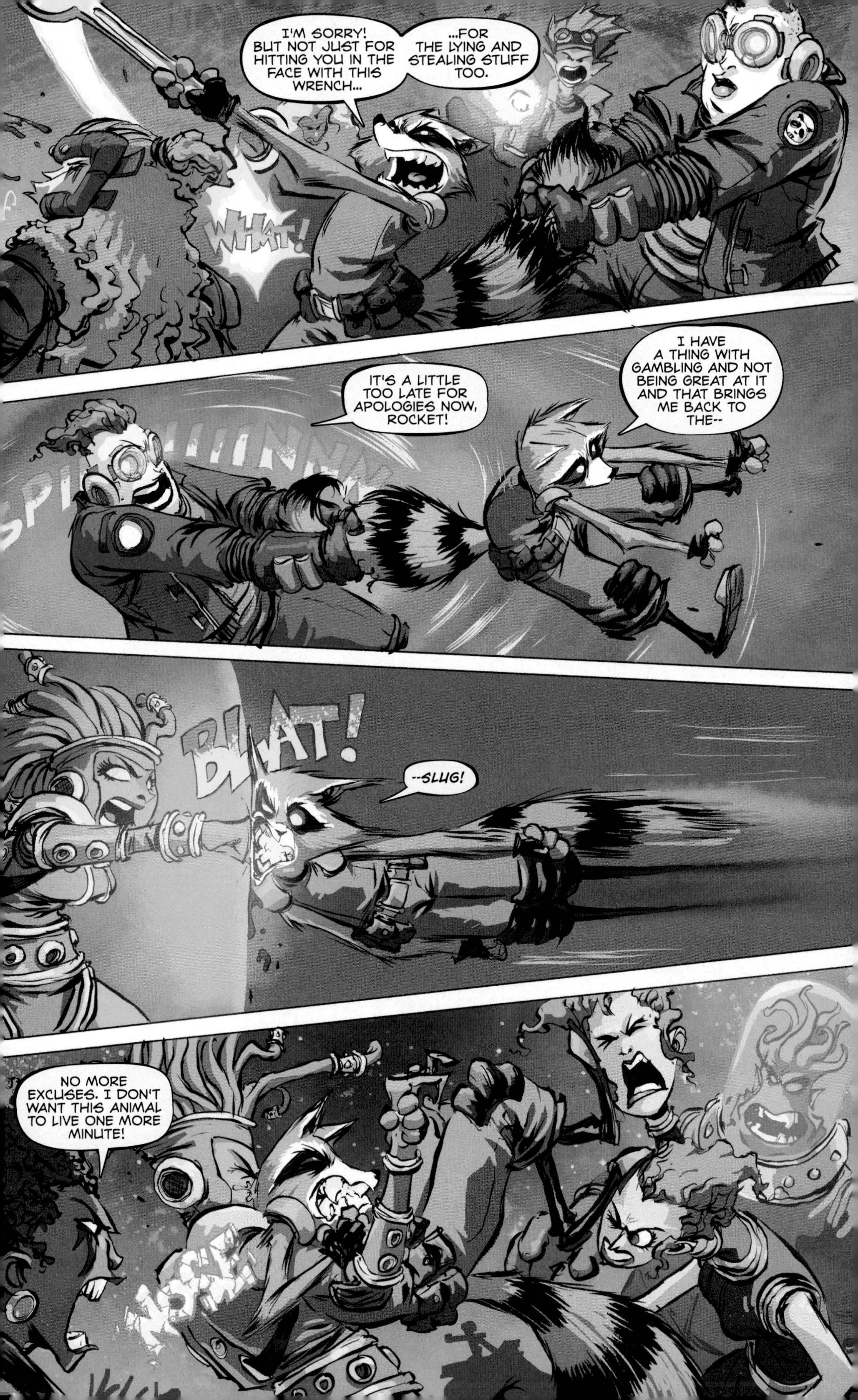
I'M SORRY! BUT NOT JUST FOR HITTING YOU IN THE FACE WITH THIS WRENCH...
...FOR THE LYING AND STEALING STUFF TOO.
WHAM!
IT'S A LITTLE TOO LATE FOR APOLOGIES NOW, ROCKET!
I HAVE A THING WITH GAMBLING AND NOT BEING GREAT AT IT AND THAT BRINGS ME BACK TO THE--
SPIIIIINNNN
BLAT!
--SLUG!
NO MORE EXCUSES. I DON'T WANT THIS ANIMAL TO LIVE ONE MORE MINUTE!

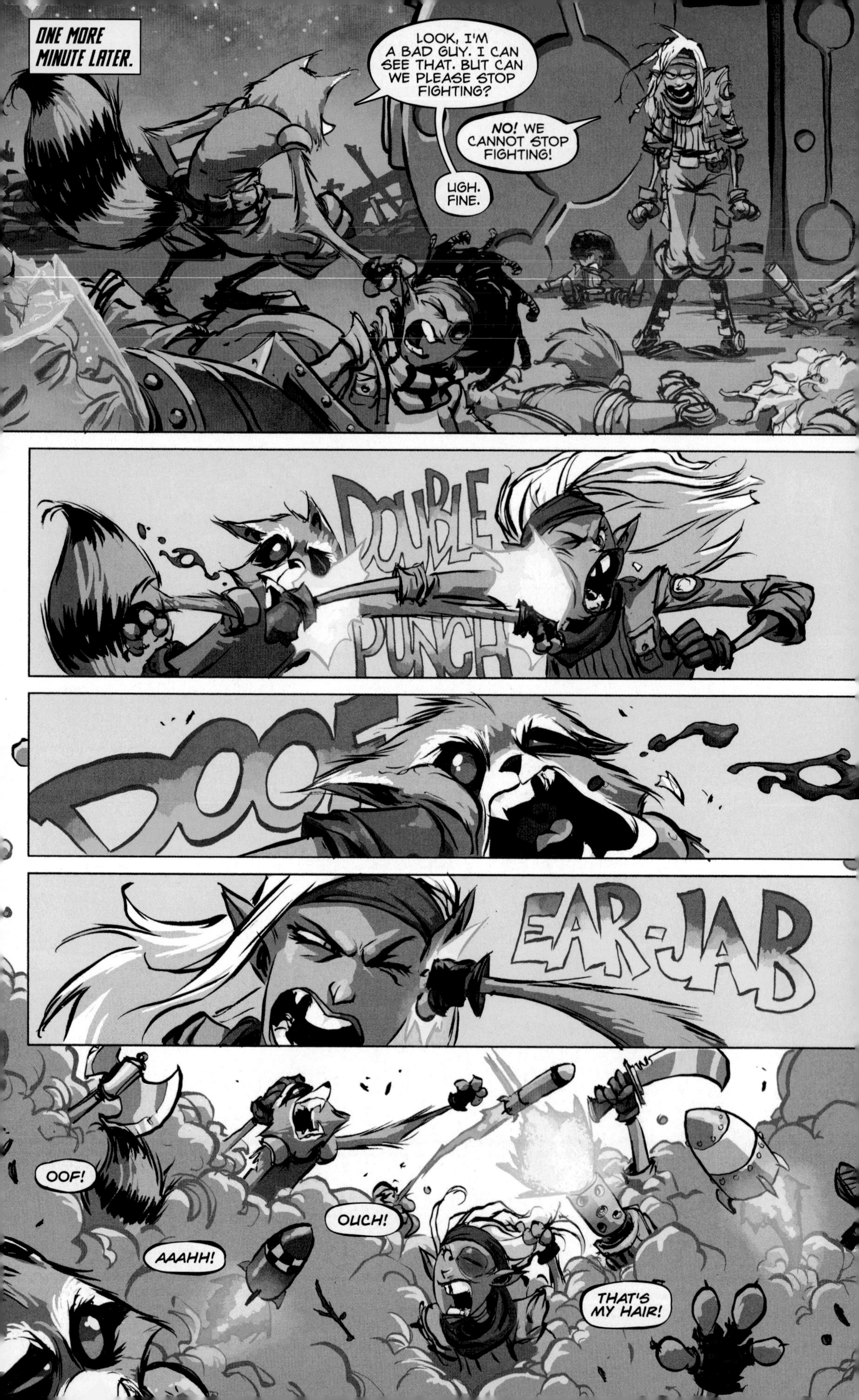
ONE MORE MINUTE LATER.
LOOK, I'M A BAD GUY. I CAN SEE THAT. BUT CAN WE PLEASE STOP FIGHTING?
NO! WE CANNOT STOP FIGHTING!
UGH. FINE.
DOUBLE PUNCH
DOOOOF
EAR-JAB
OOF!
OUCH!
AAAHH!
THAT'S MY HAIR!

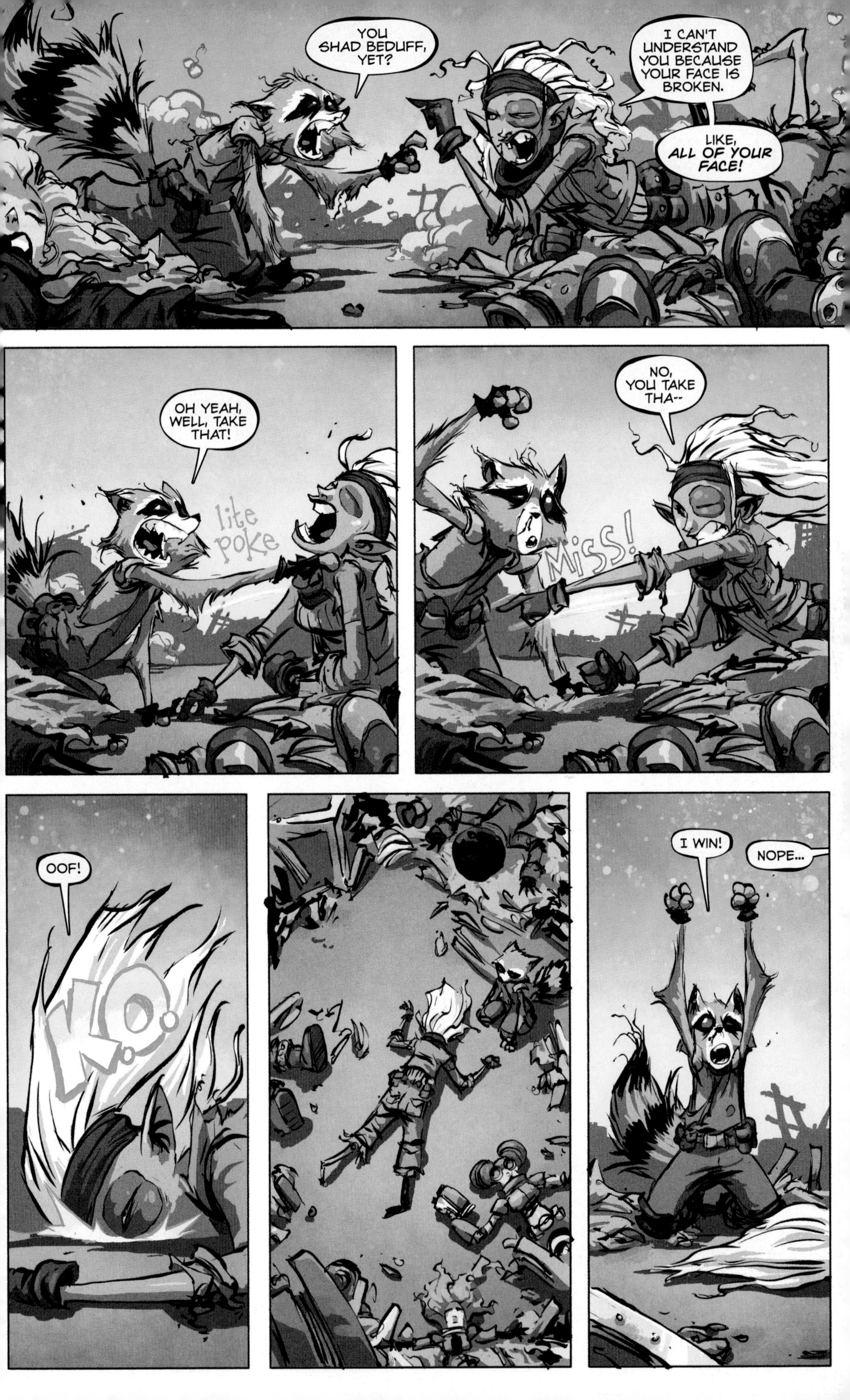
YOU SHAD BEDUFF, YET?
I CAN'T UNDERSTAND YOU BECAUSE YOUR FACE IS BROKEN.
LIKE, ALL OF YOUR FACE!
OH YEAH, WELL, TAKE THAT!
lite poke
NO, YOU TAKE THA--
MISS!
OOF!
I WIN!
NOPE...

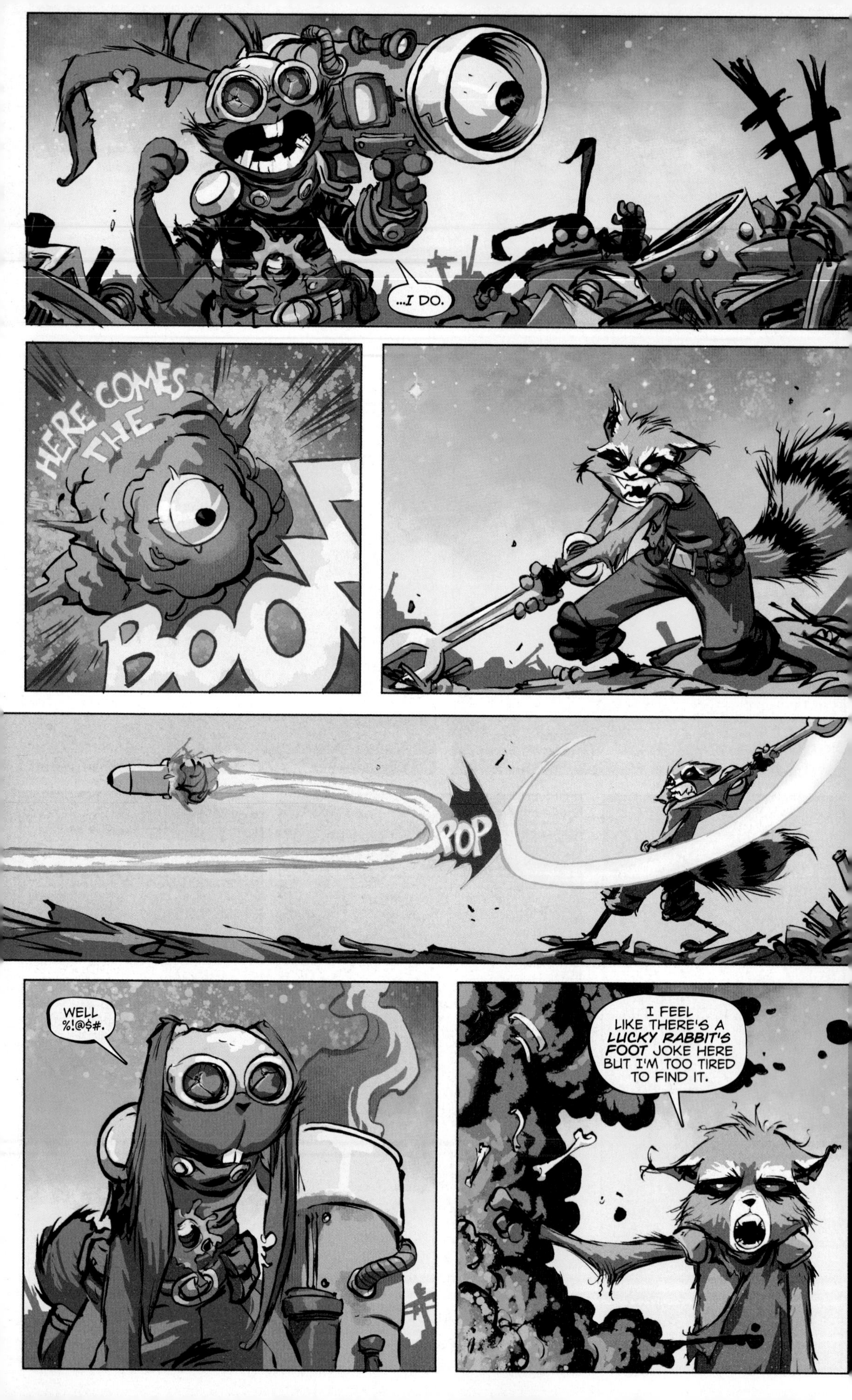
...I DO.
HERE COMES THE
BOOM
POP
WELL %!@$#.
I FEEL LIKE THERE'S A LUCKY RABBIT'S FOOT JOKE HERE BUT I'M TOO TIRED TO FIND IT.

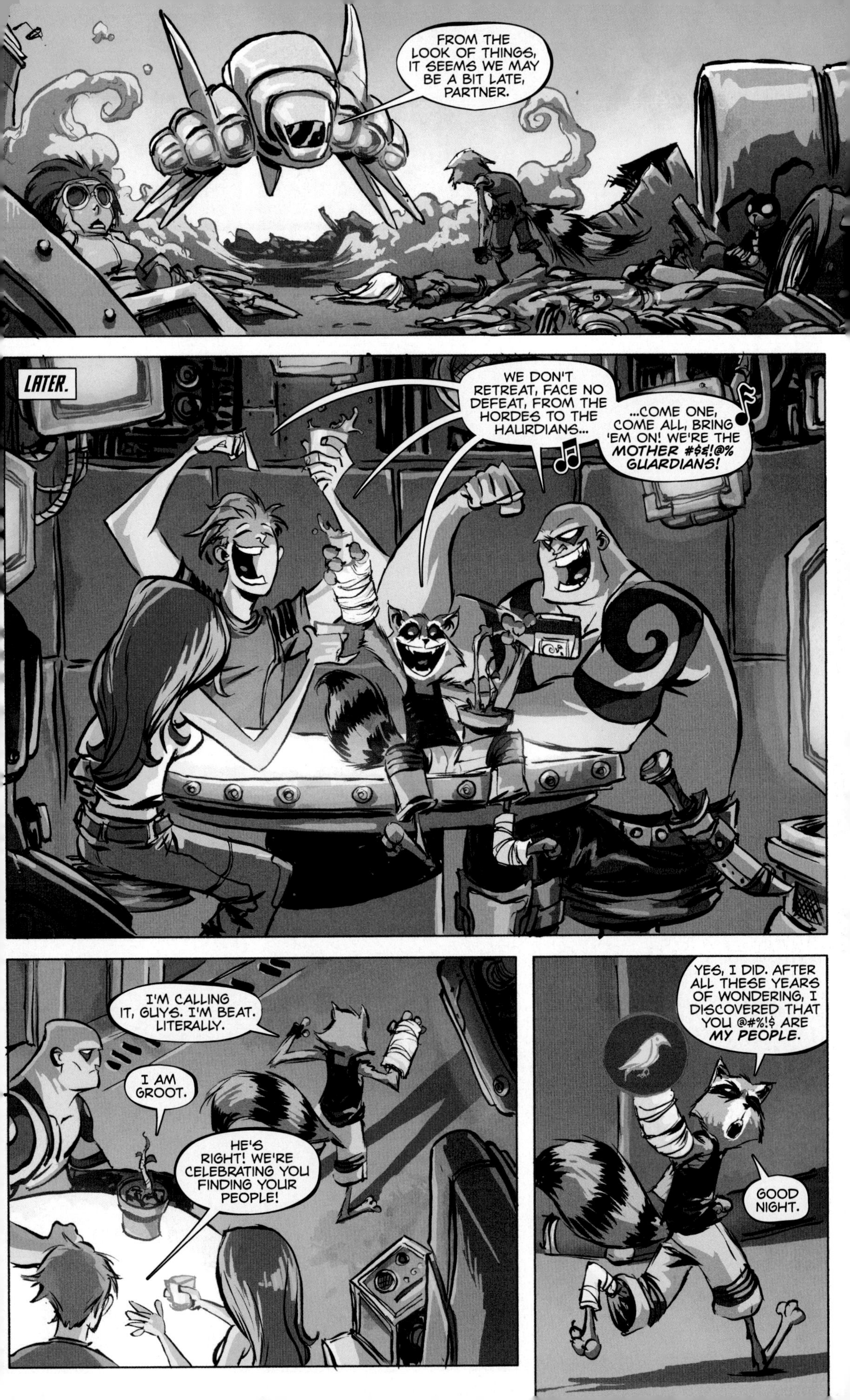
FROM THE LOOK OF THINGS, IT SEEMS WE MAY BE A BIT LATE, PARTNER.
LATER.
WE DON'T RETREAT, FACE NO DEFEAT, FROM THE HORDES TO THE HAURDIANS...
...COME ONE, COME ALL, BRING 'EM ON! WE'RE THE *MOTHER #$&!@% GUARDIANS!*
I'M CALLING IT, GUYS. I'M BEAT. LITERALLY.
I AM GROOT.
HE'S RIGHT! WE'RE CELEBRATING YOU FINDING YOUR PEOPLE!
YES, I DID. AFTER ALL THESE YEARS OF WONDERING, I DISCOVERED THAT YOU @#%!$ ARE *MY PEOPLE*.
GOOD NIGHT.

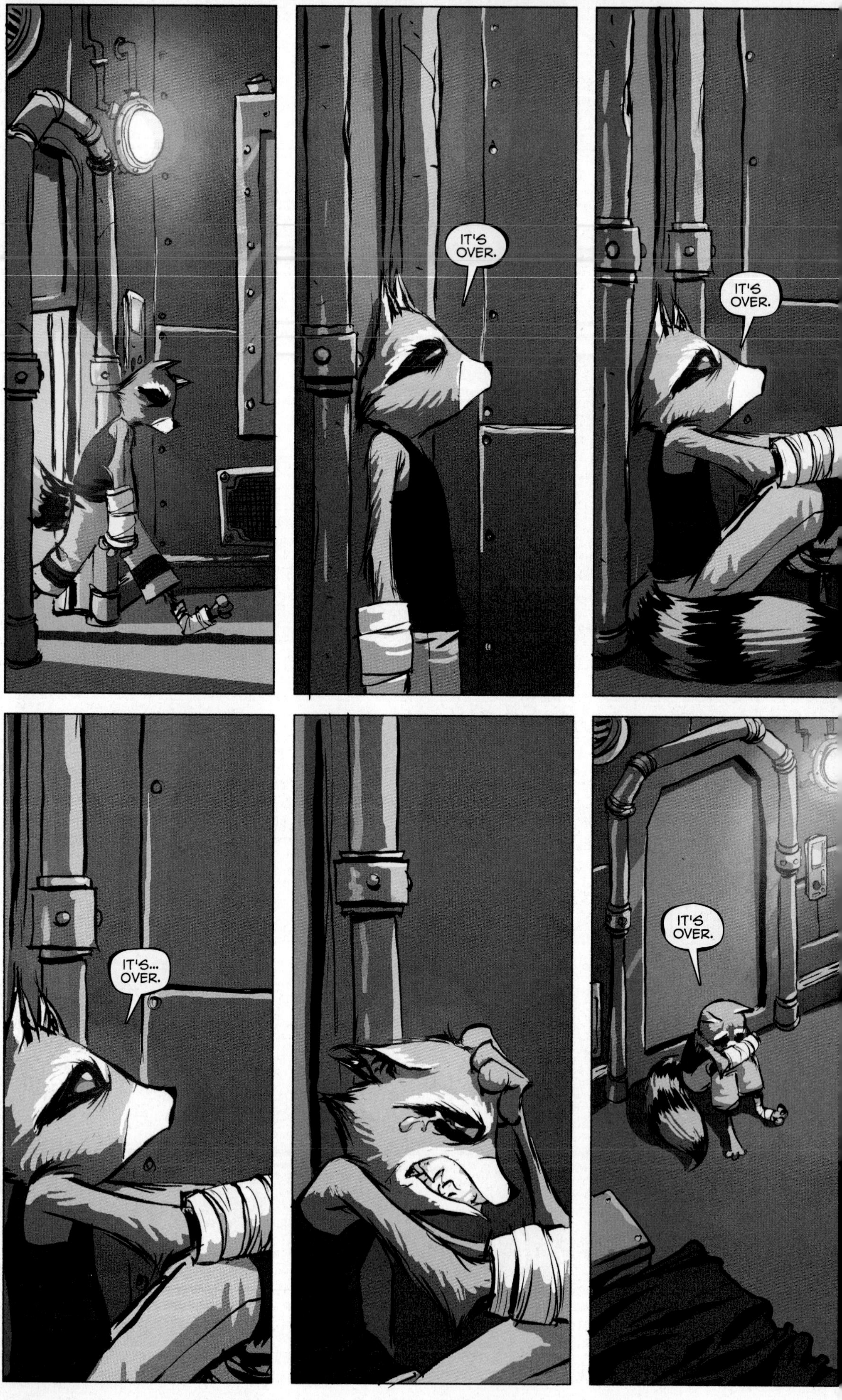
IT'S OVER.
IT'S OVER.
IT'S... OVER.
IT'S OVER.

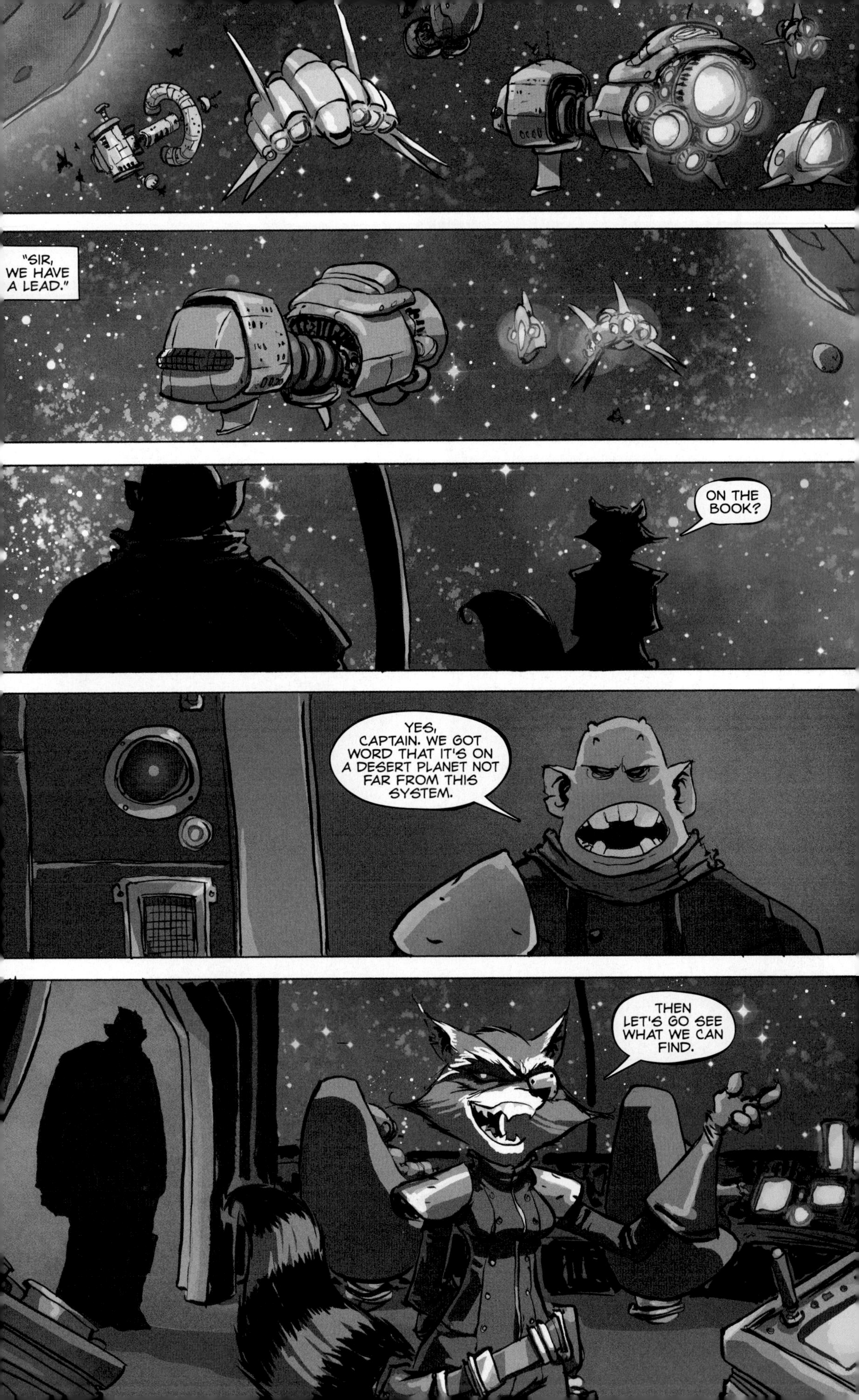
"SIR, WE HAVE A LEAD."
ON THE BOOK?
YES, CAPTAIN. WE GOT WORD THAT IT'S ON A DESERT PLANET NOT FAR FROM THIS SYSTEM.
THEN LET'S GO SEE WHAT WE CAN FIND.

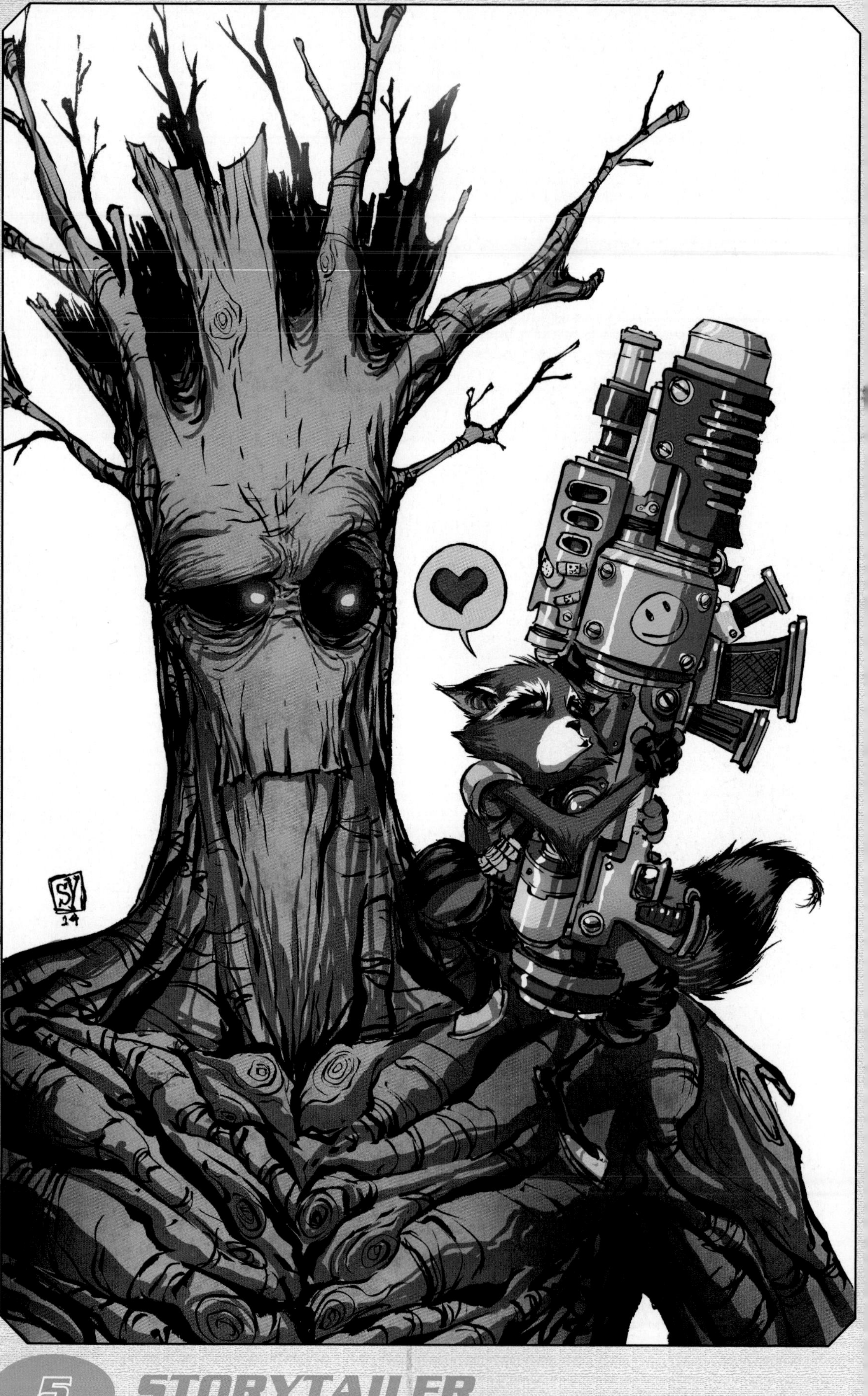

5 STORYTAILER

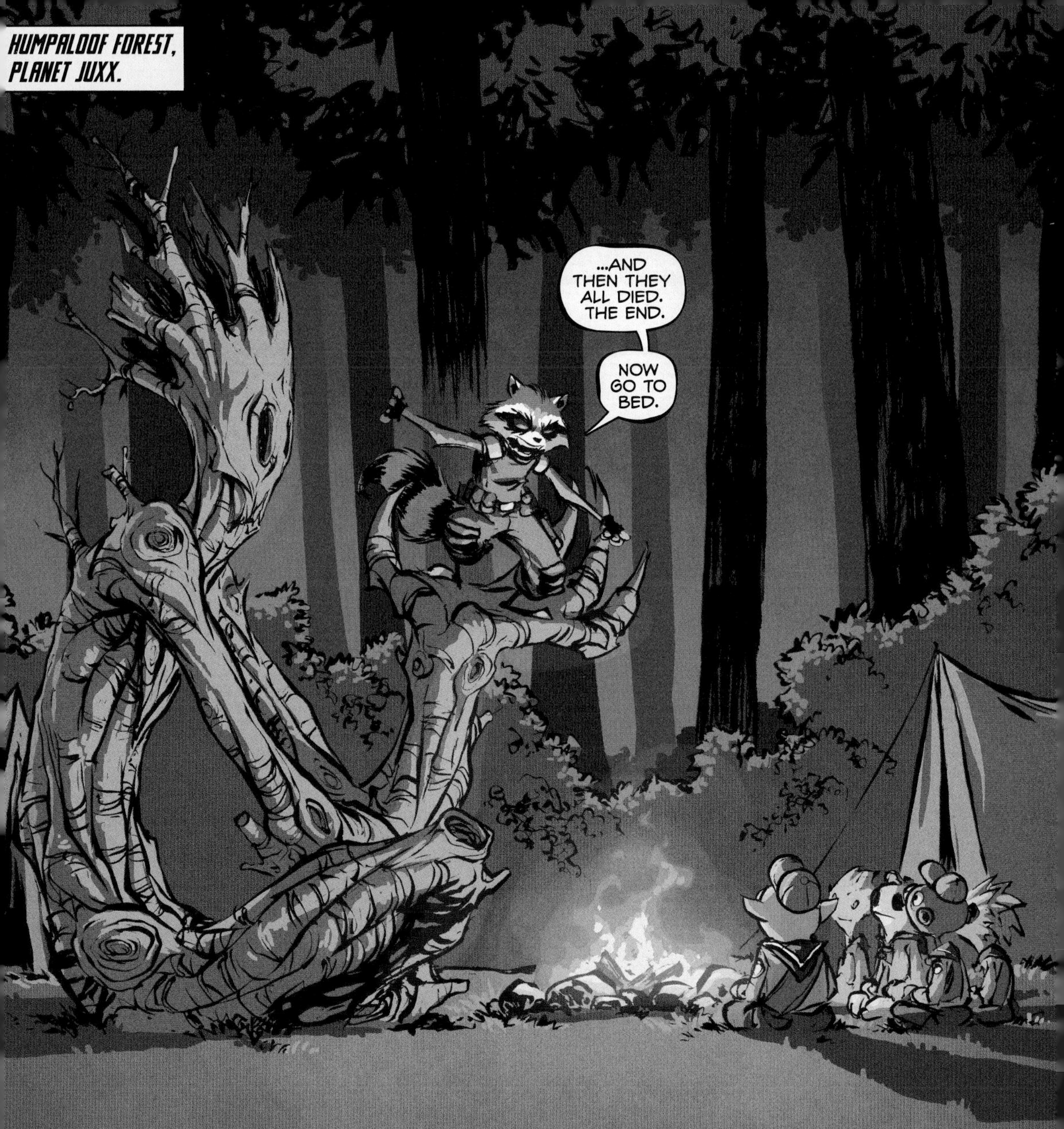
HUMPALOOF FOREST, PLANET JUXX.
...AND THEN THEY ALL DIED. THE END.
NOW GO TO BED.

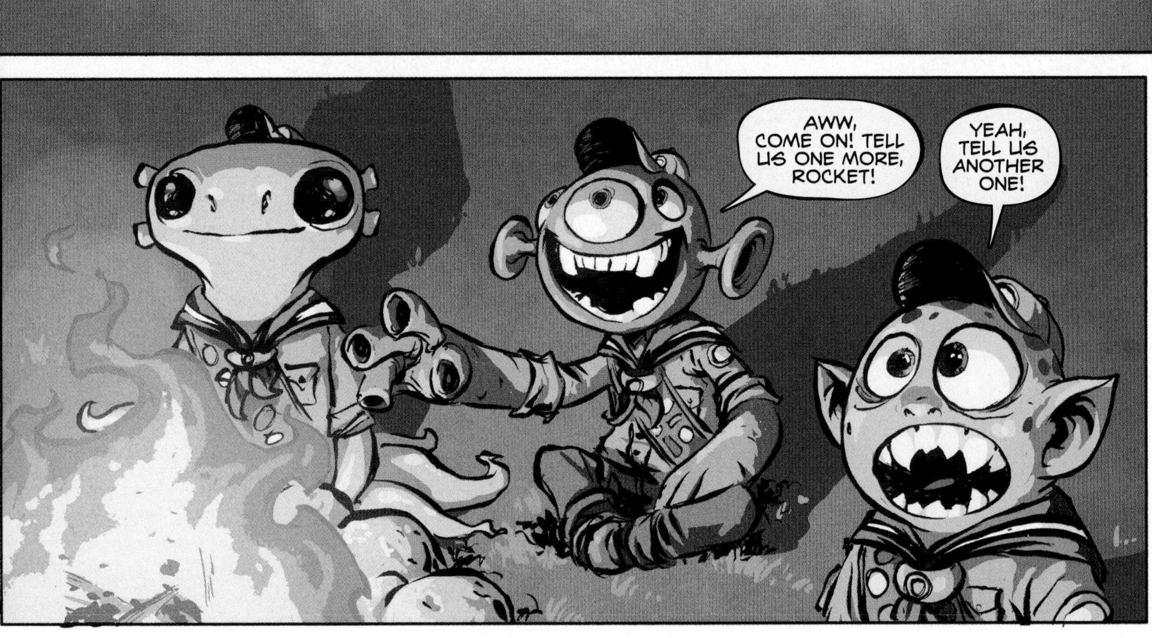
AWW, COME ON! TELL US ONE MORE, ROCKET!
YEAH, TELL US ANOTHER ONE!

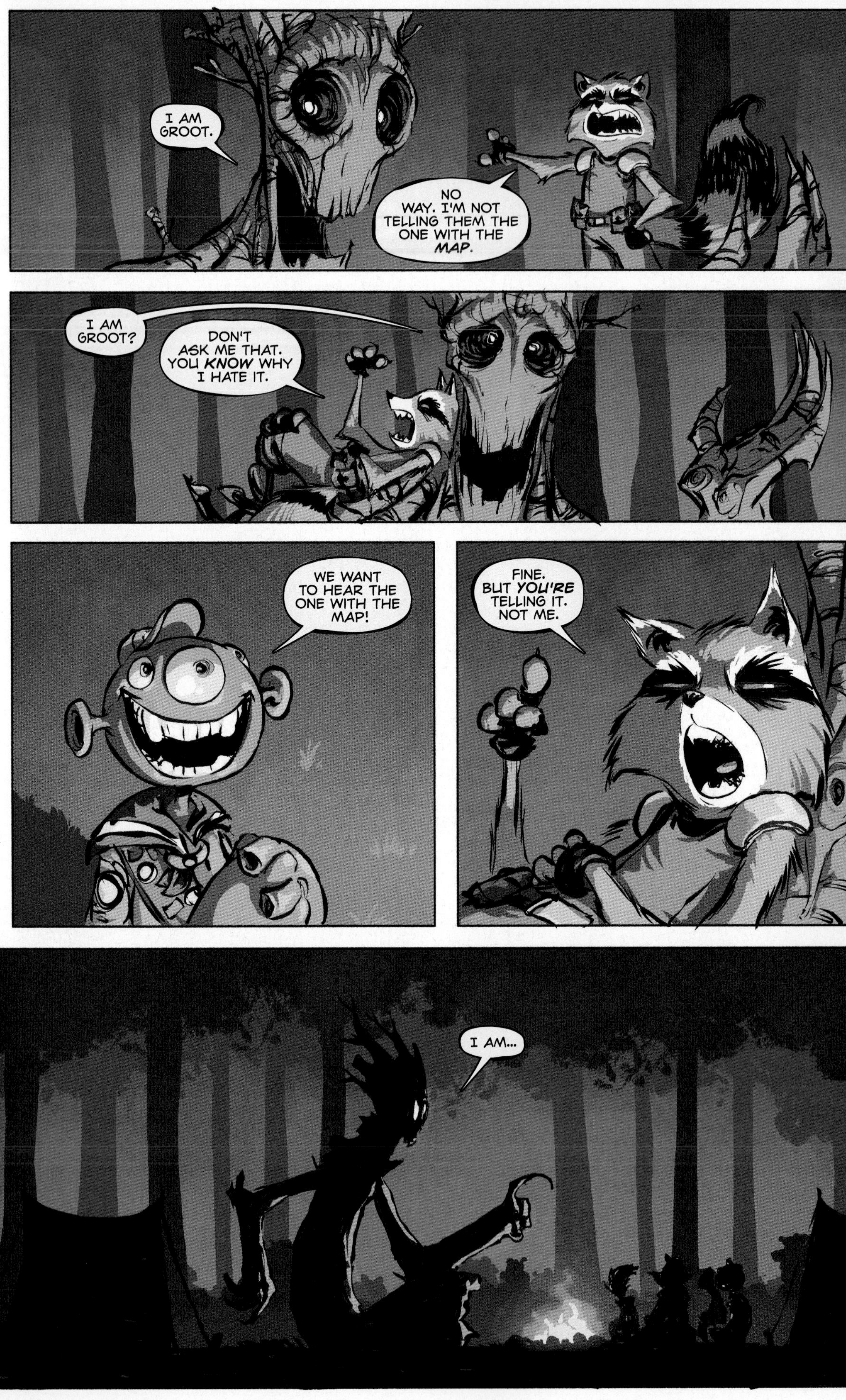
I AM GROOT.
NO WAY. I'M NOT TELLING THEM THE ONE WITH THE *MAP*.
I AM GROOT?
DON'T ASK ME THAT. YOU *KNOW* WHY I HATE IT.
WE WANT TO HEAR THE ONE WITH THE MAP!
FINE. BUT *YOU'RE* TELLING IT. NOT ME.
I AM...

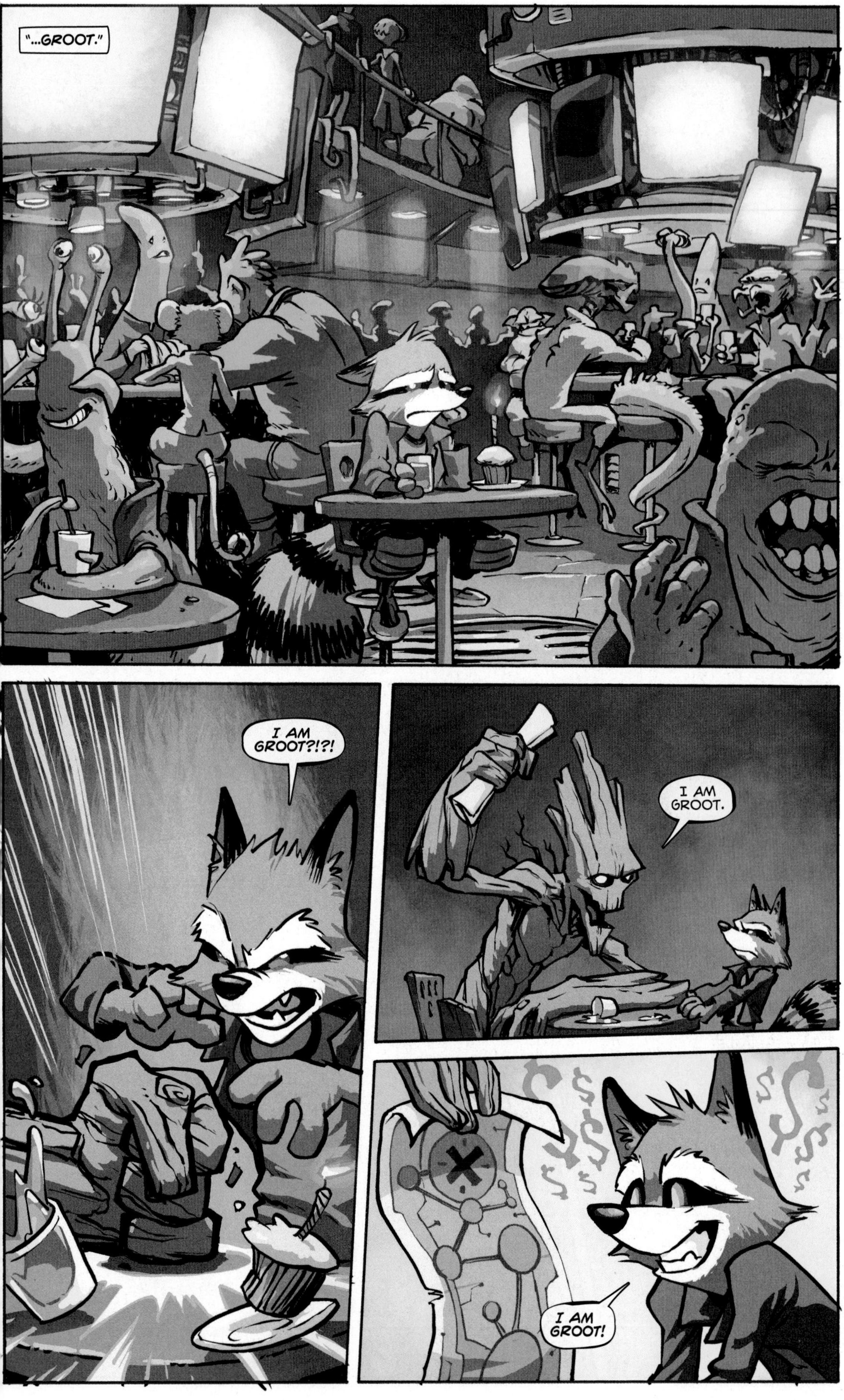
"...GROOT."
I AM GROOT?!?!
I AM GROOT.
I AM GROOT!

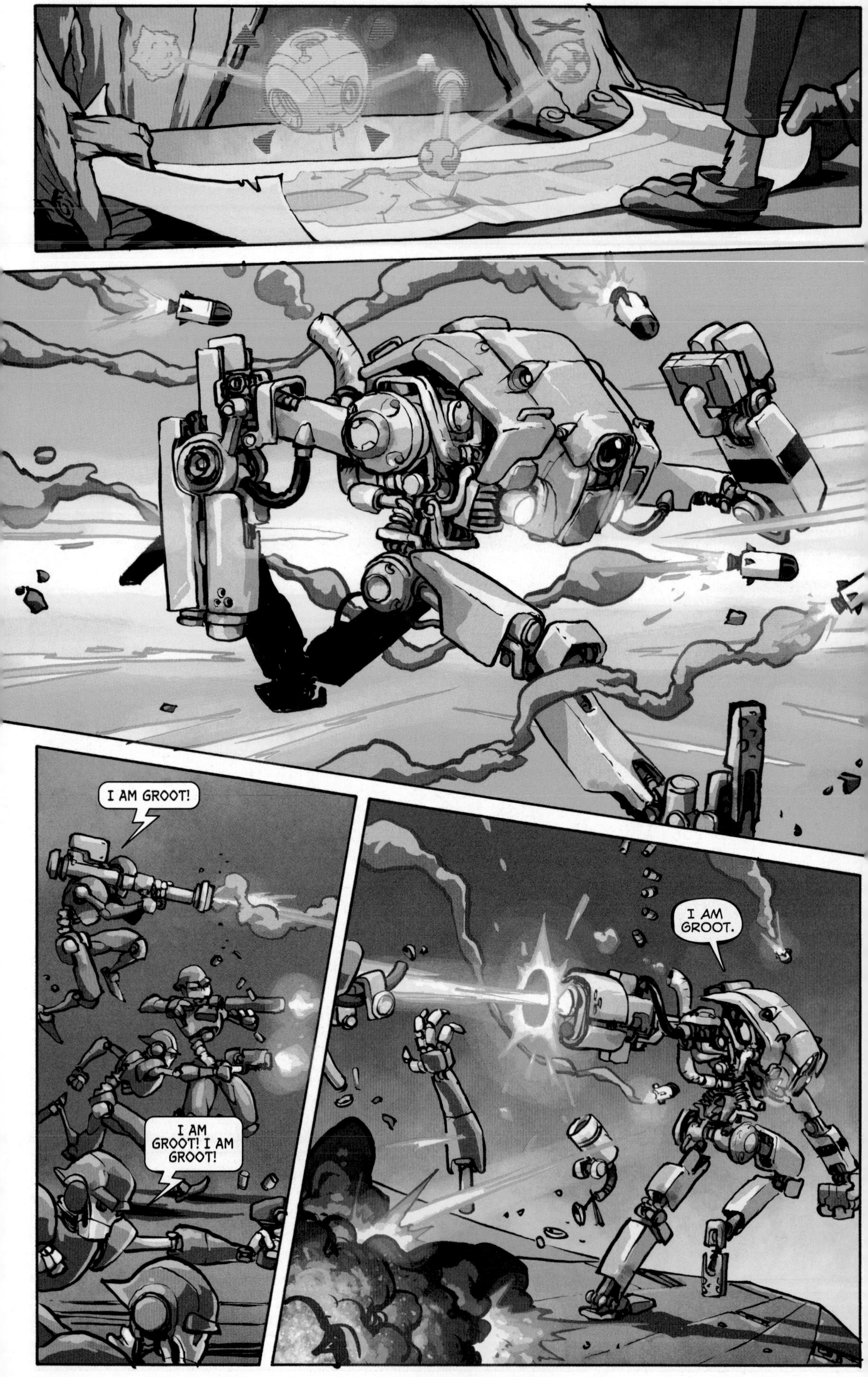
I AM GROOT!
I AM GROOT! I AM GROOT!
I AM GROOT.

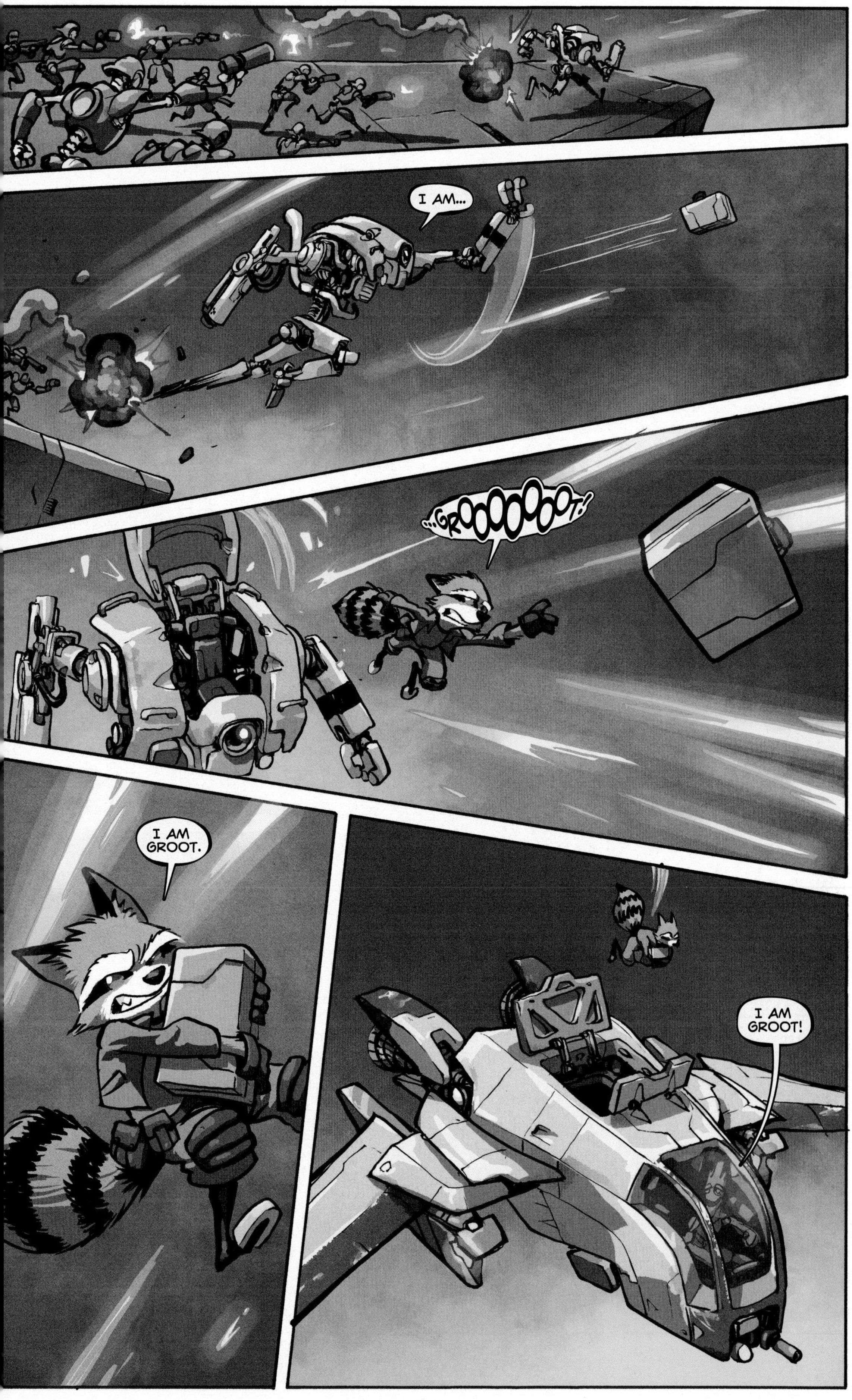
I AM...
...GROOOOOOOOT!
I AM GROOT.
I AM GROOT!

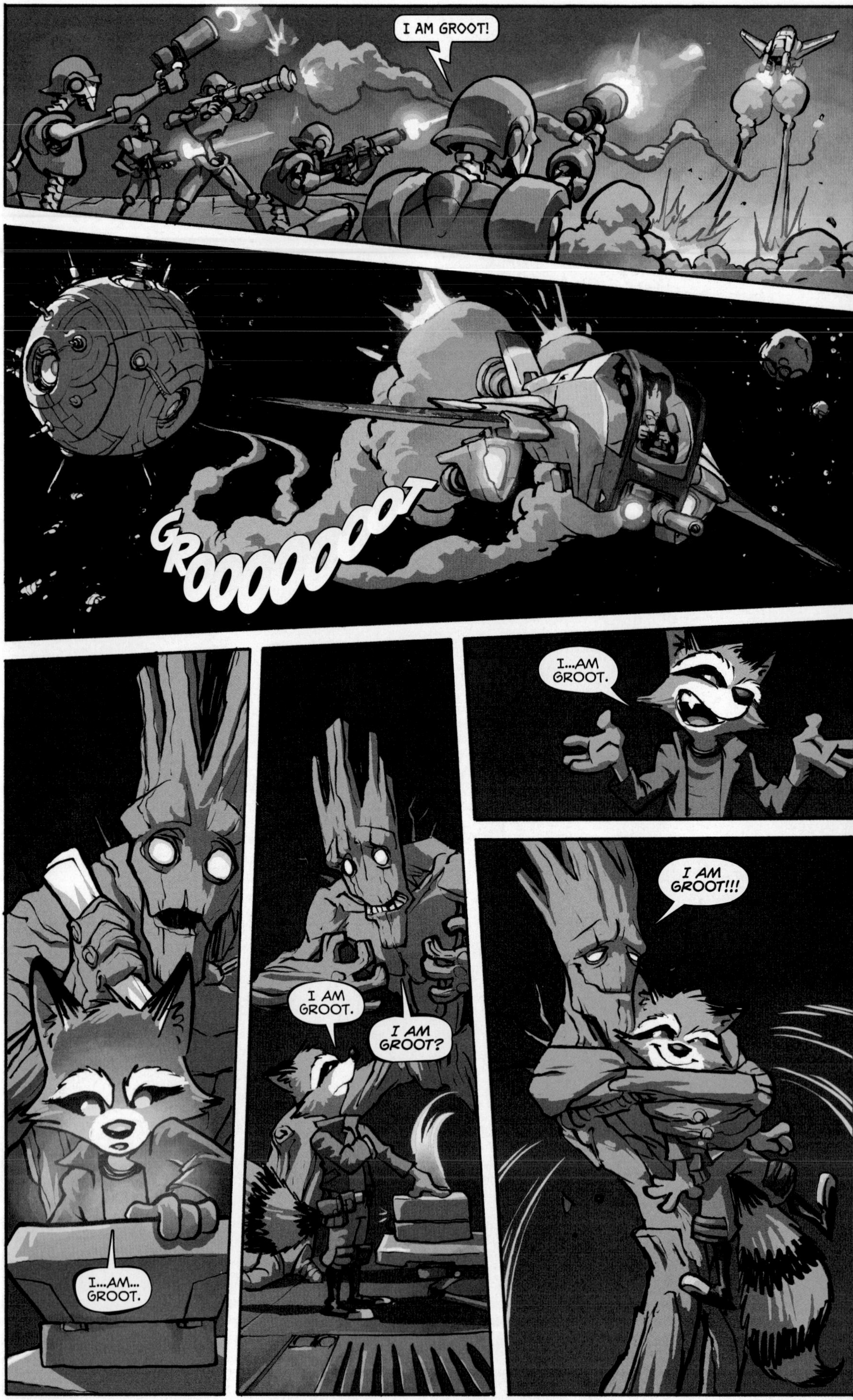
I AM GROOT!
GROOOOOOOOT
I...AM GROOT.
I...AM... GROOT.
I AM GROOT.
I AM GROOT?
I AM GROOT!!!

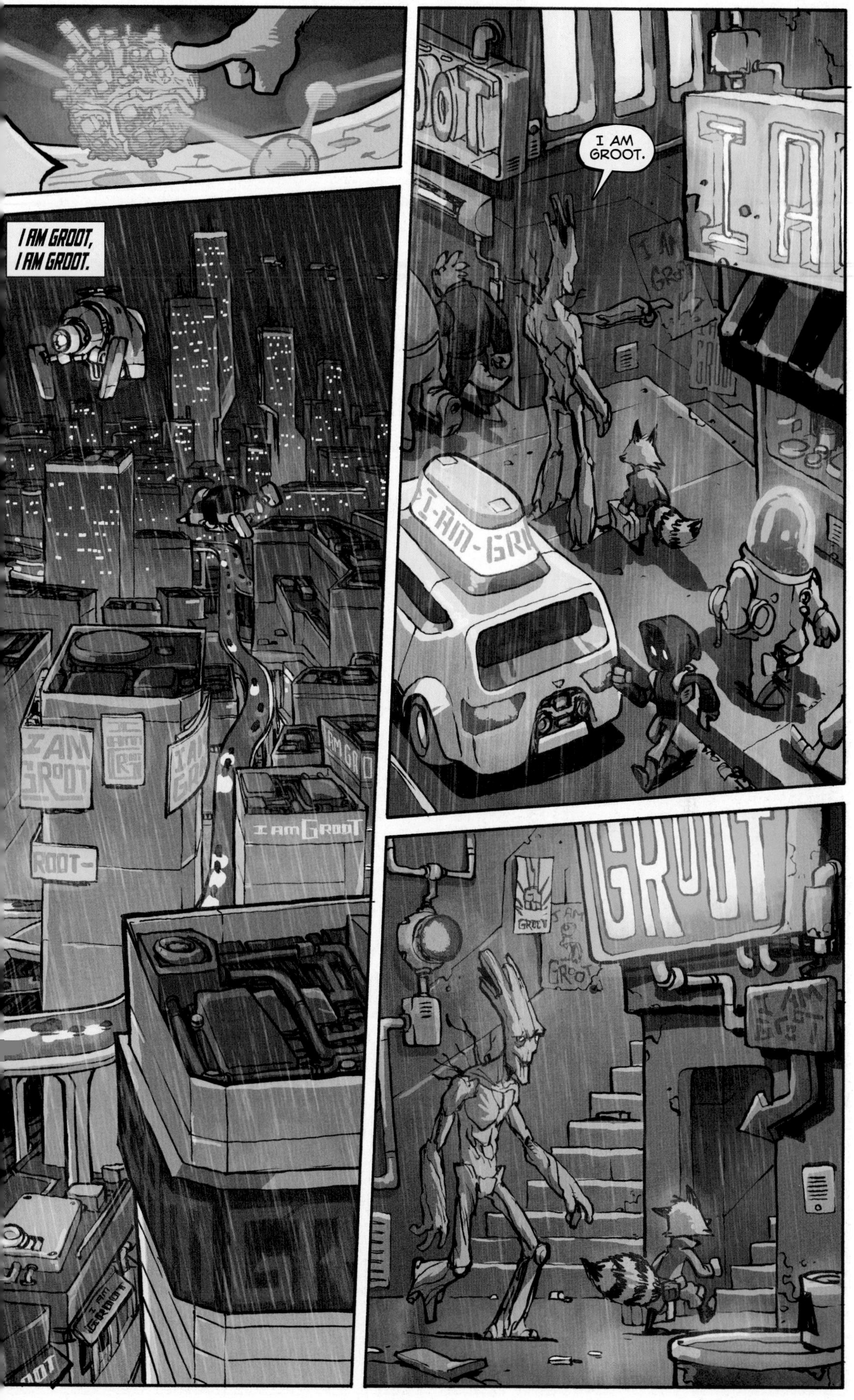
I AM GROOT,
I AM GROOT.
I AM GROOT.
I AM GROOT
I AM GROOT
GROOT-
I AM GROOT
GROOT

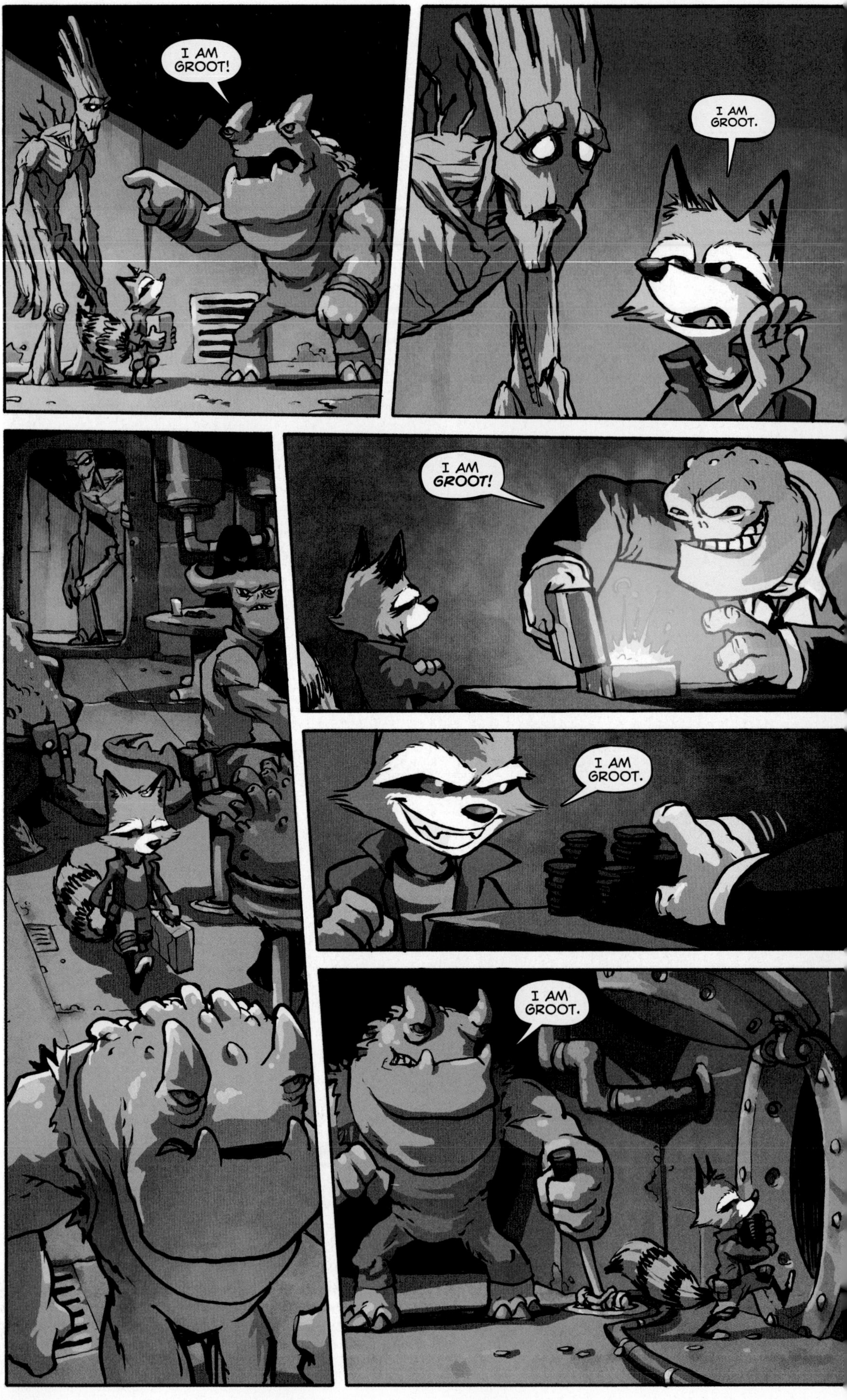
I AM GROOT!
I AM GROOT.
I AM GROOT!
I AM GROOT.
I AM GROOT.

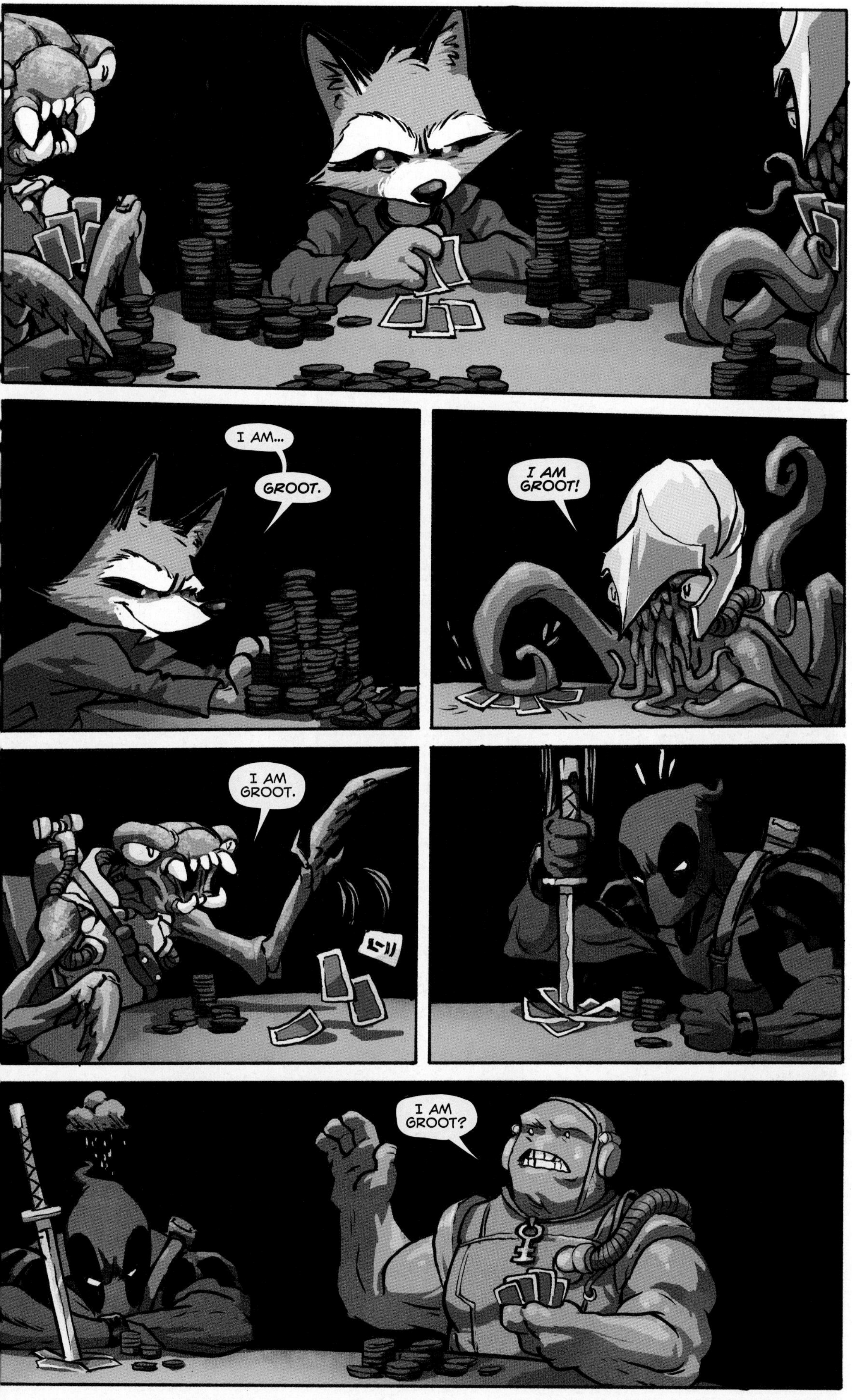
I AM...
GROOT.
I AM GROOT!
I AM GROOT.
I AM GROOT?

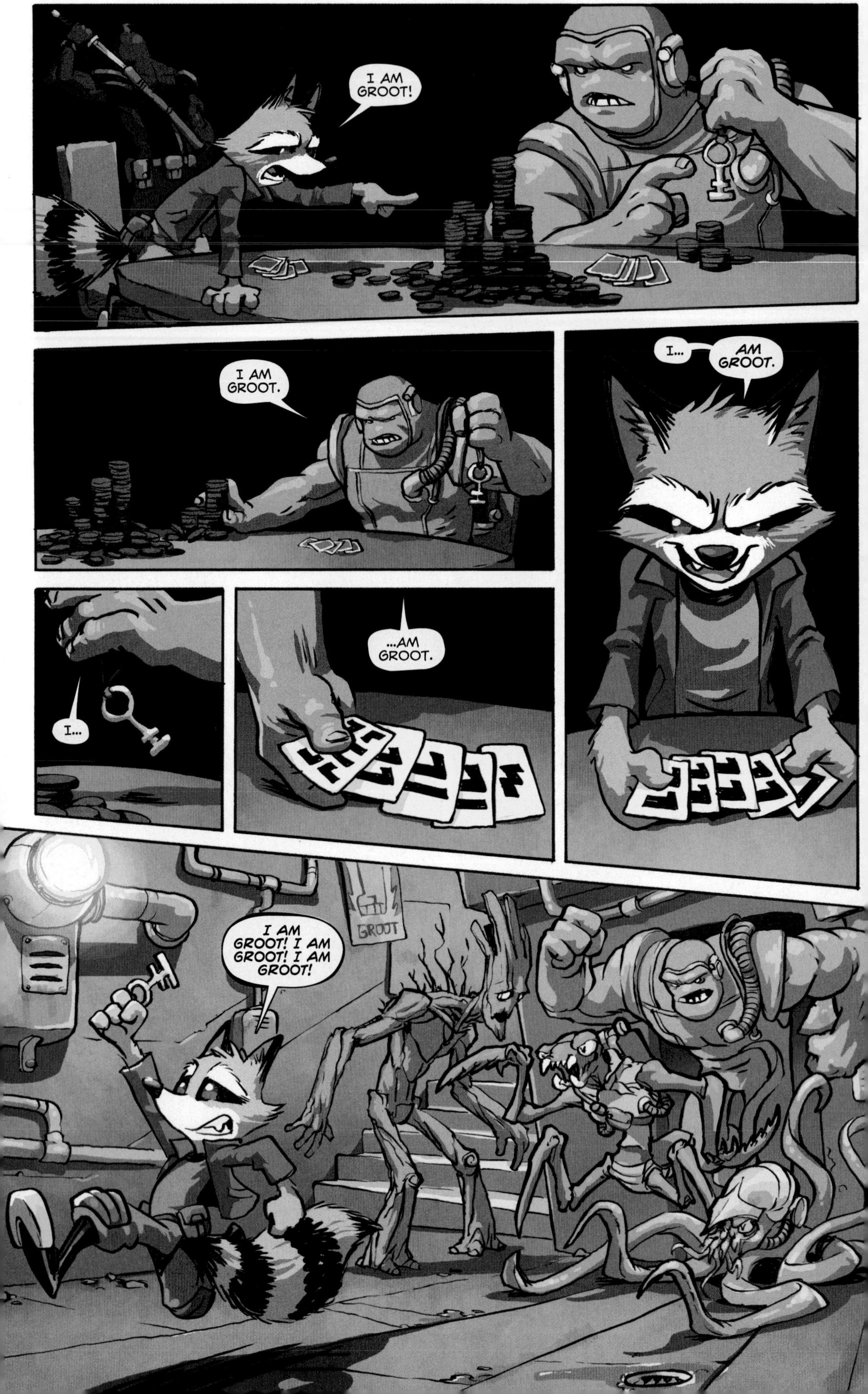
I AM GROOT!
I AM GROOT.
I...
AM GROOT.
I...
...AM GROOT.
GROOT
I AM GROOT! I AM GROOT! I AM GROOT!

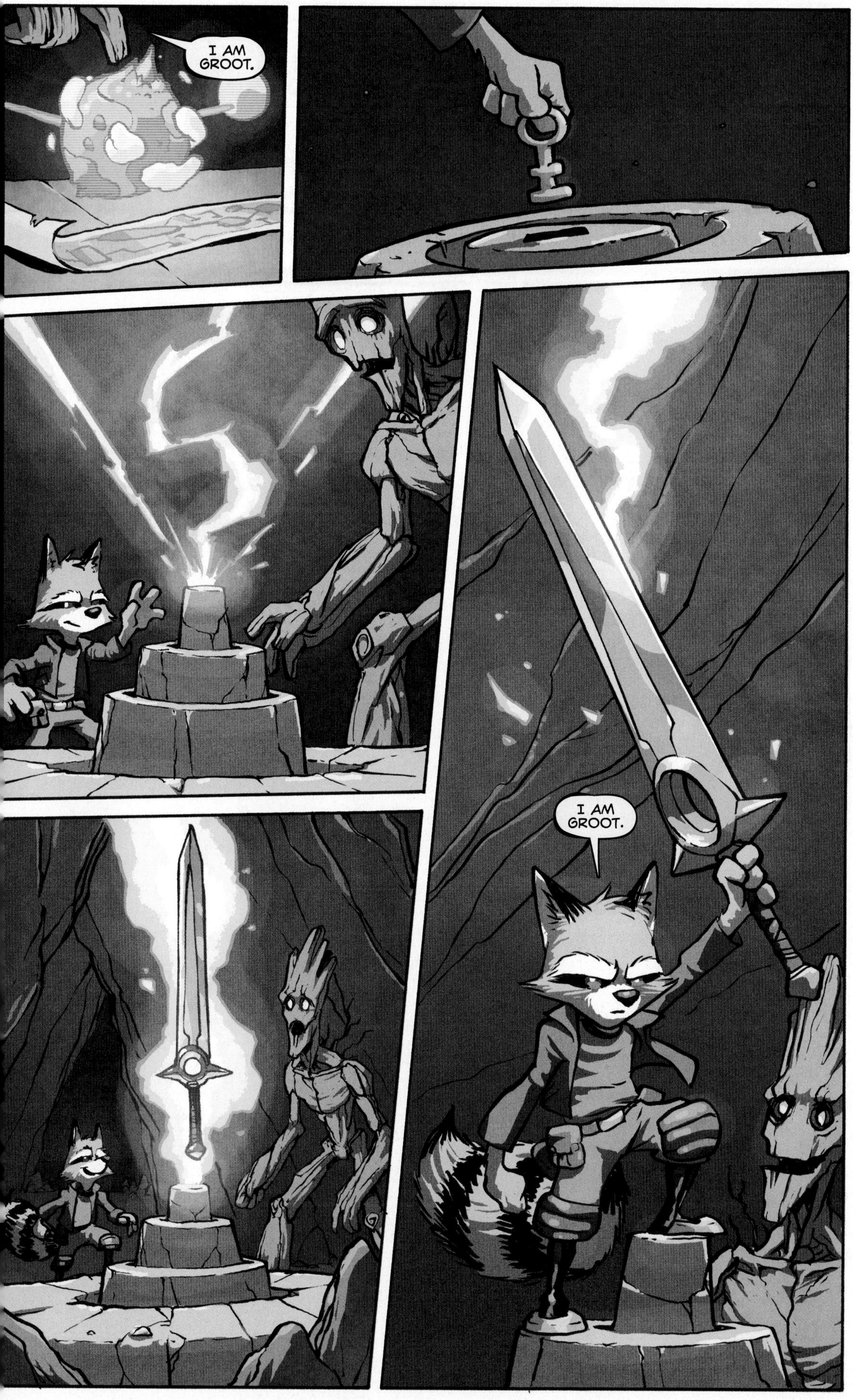
I AM GROOT.
I AM GROOT.

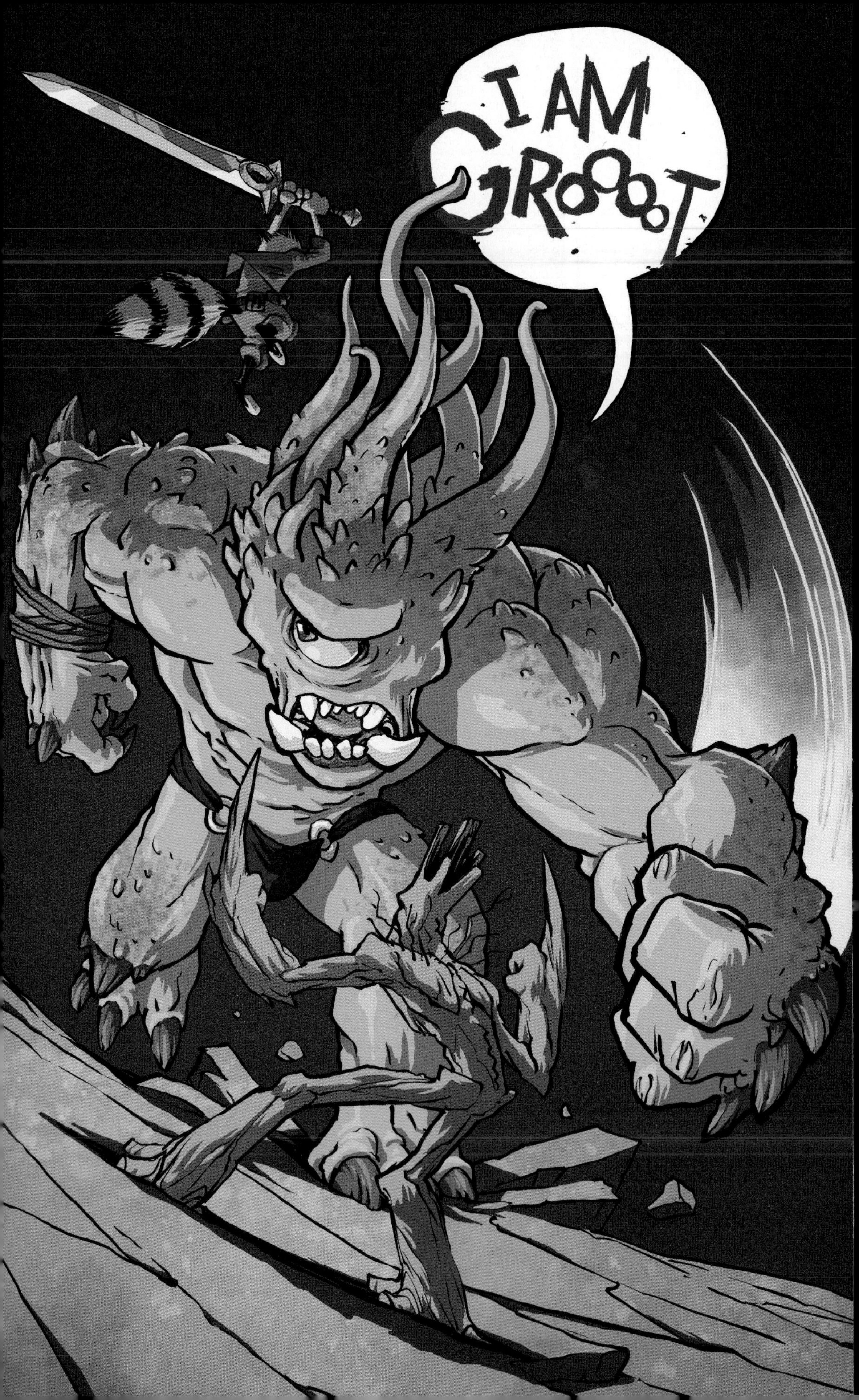
I AM GROOOOT

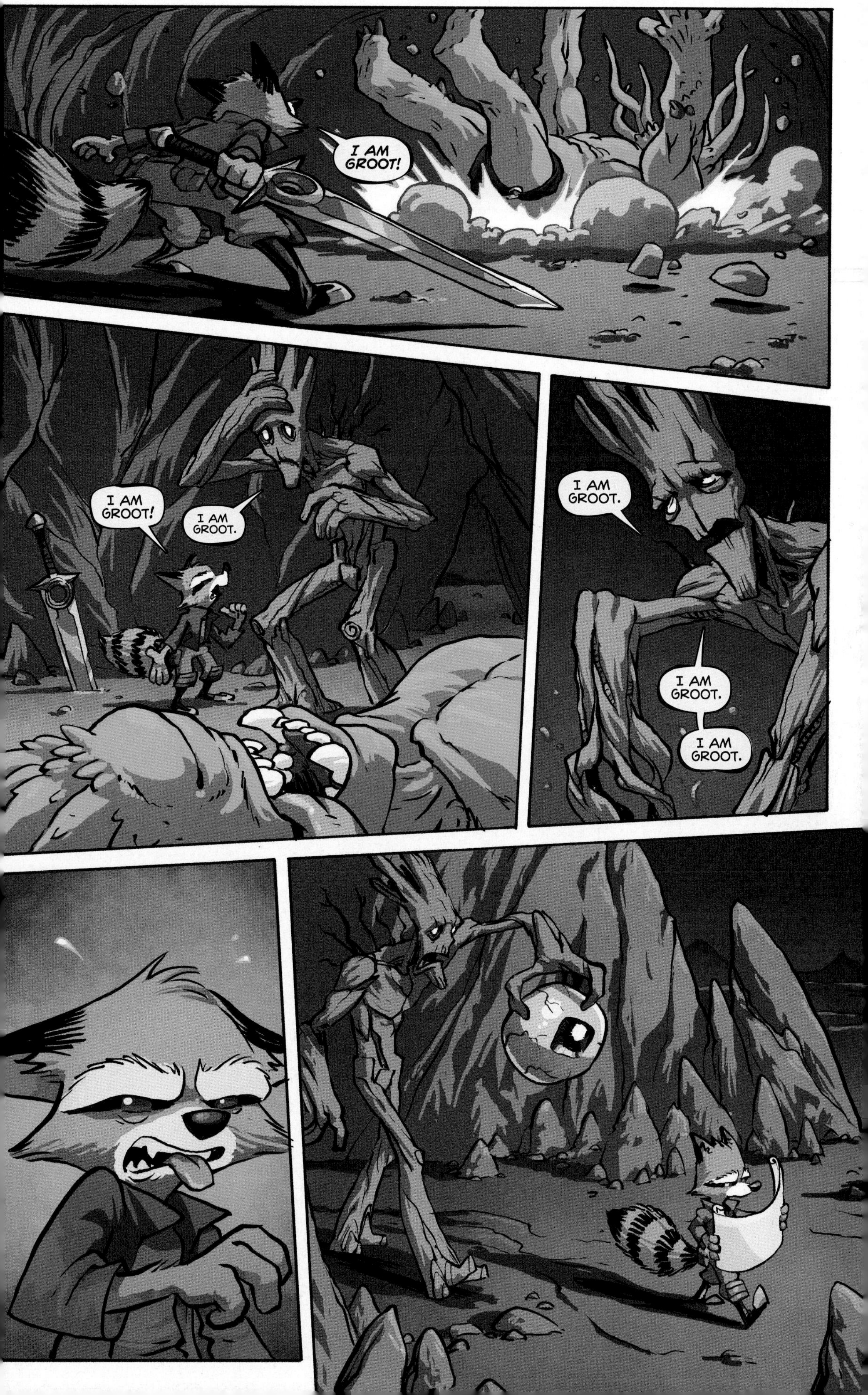
I AM GROOT!
I AM GROOT!
I AM GROOT.
I AM GROOT.
I AM GROOT.
I AM GROOT.

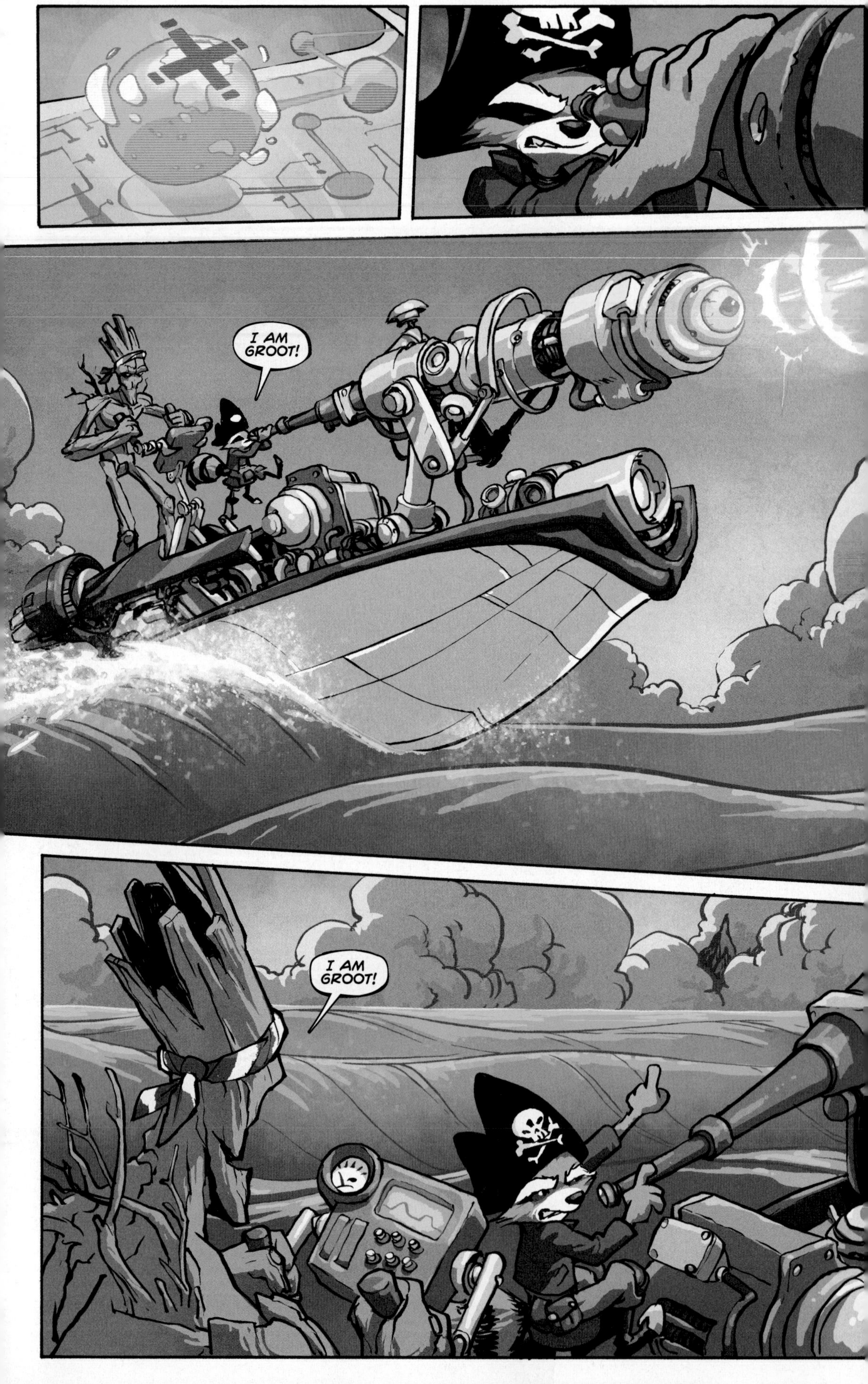

I AM GROOT!
I AM GROOT!

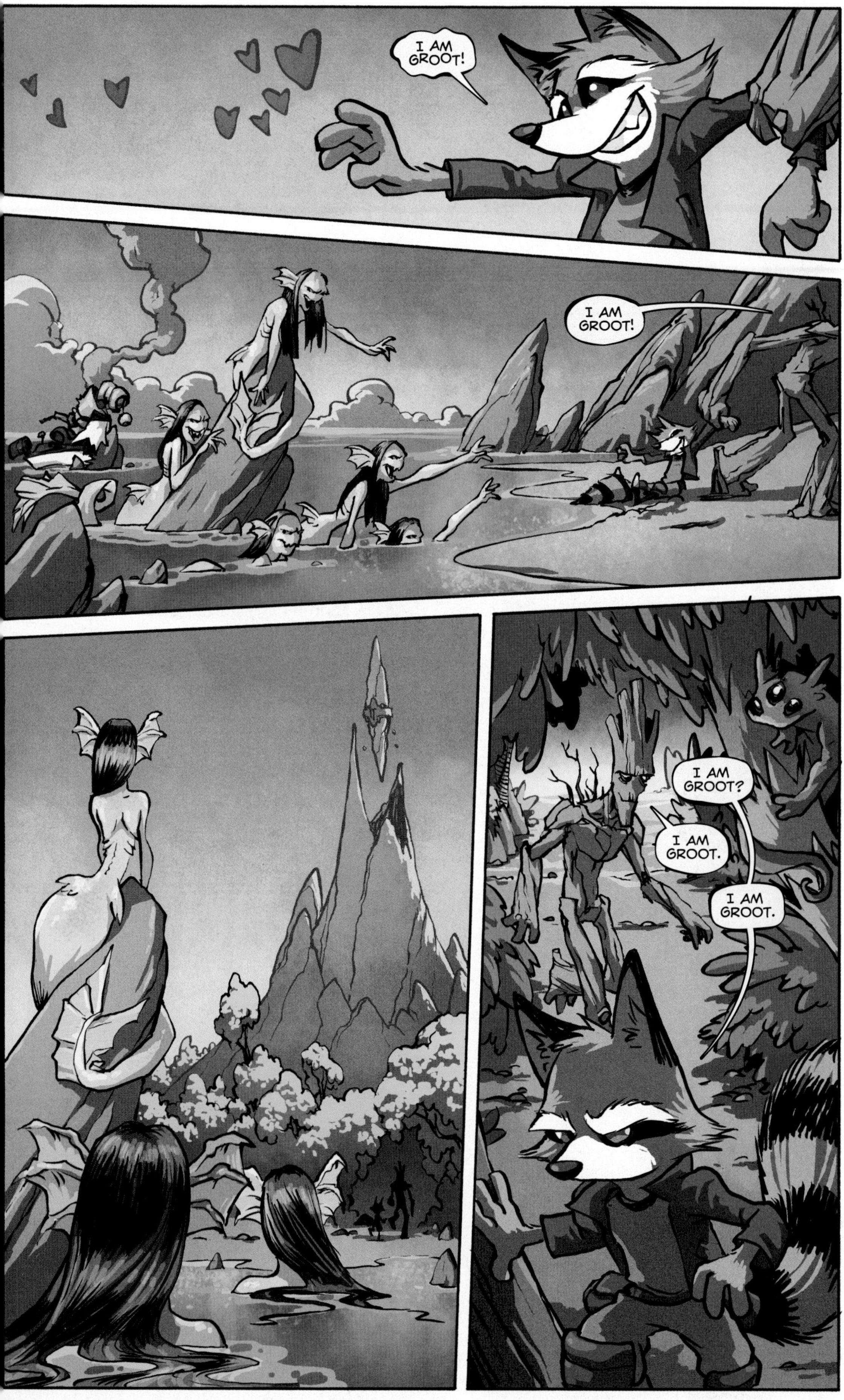
I AM GROOT!
I AM GROOT!
I AM GROOT?
I AM GROOT.
I AM GROOT.

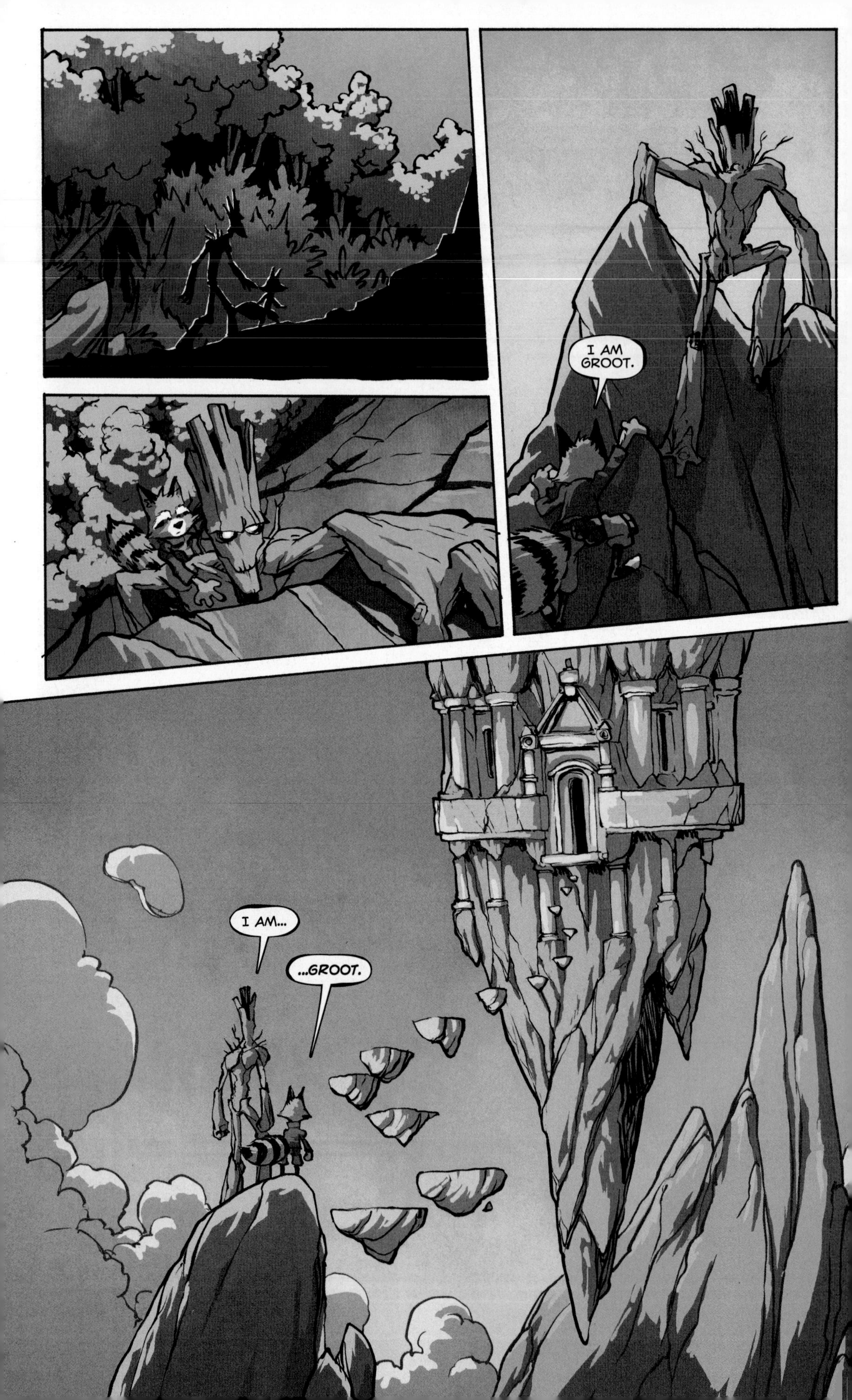
I AM GROOT.
I AM...
...GROOT.

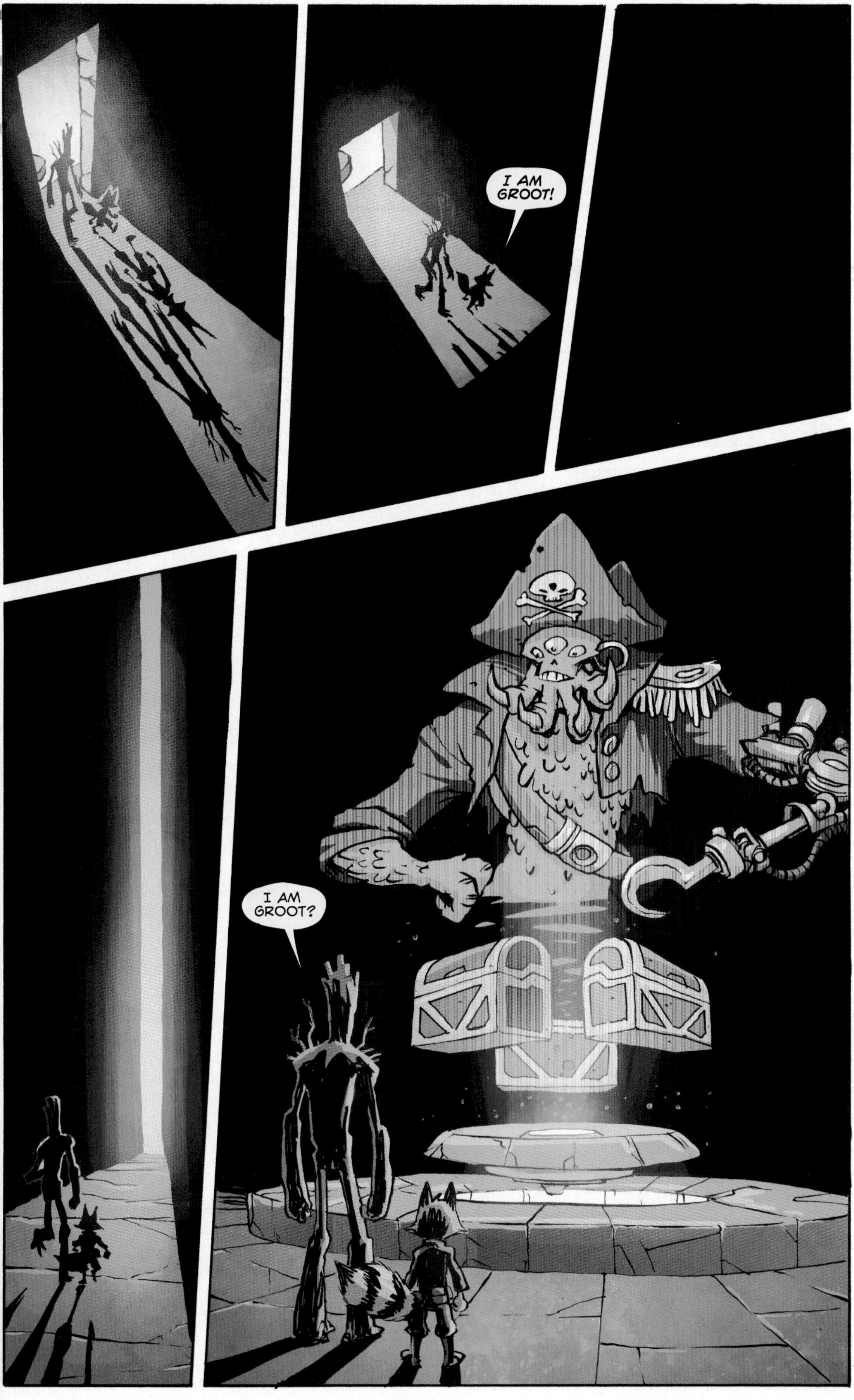
I AM GROOT!
I AM GROOT?

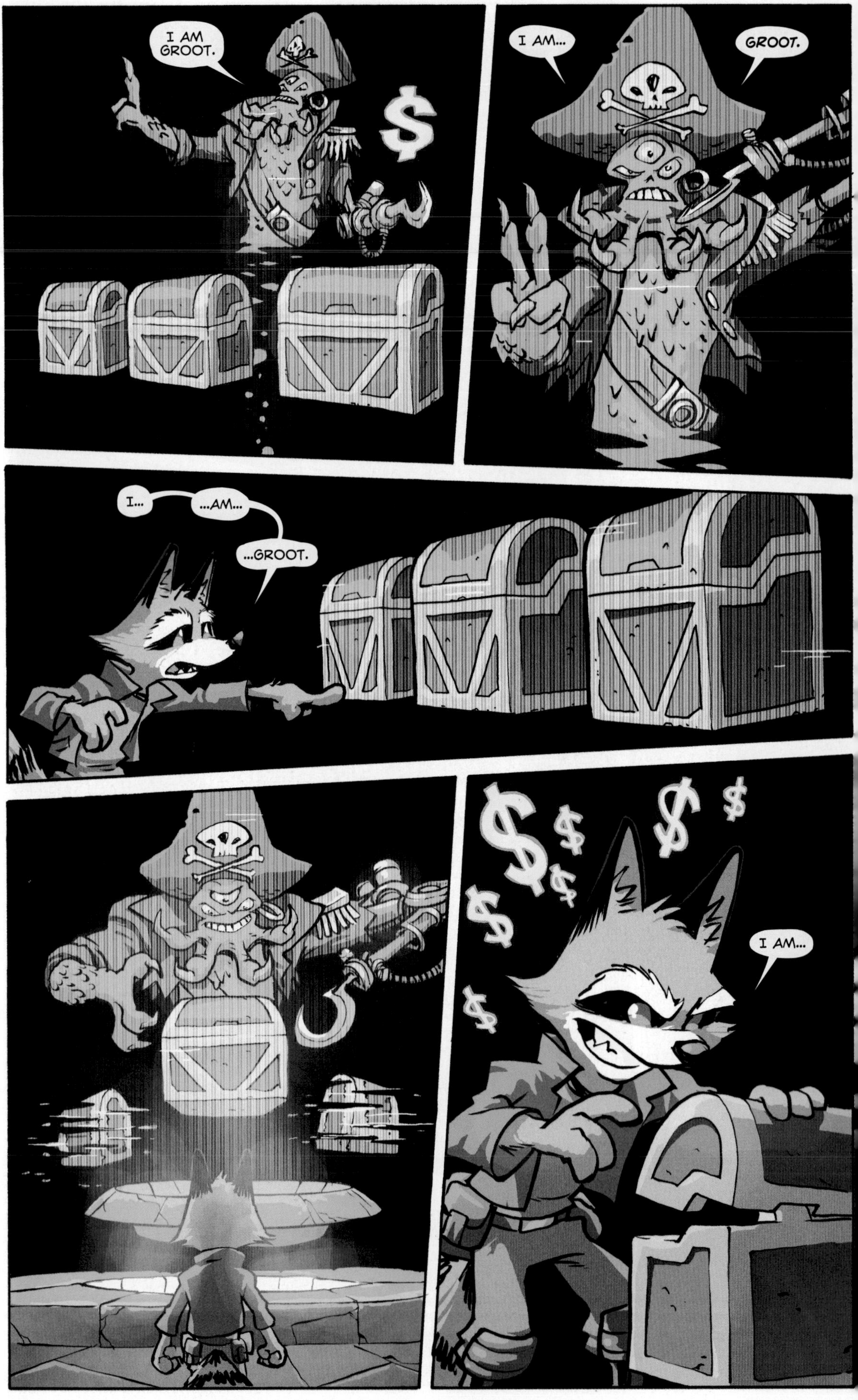
I AM GROOT.
I AM...
GROOT.
I...
...AM...
...GROOT.
I AM...

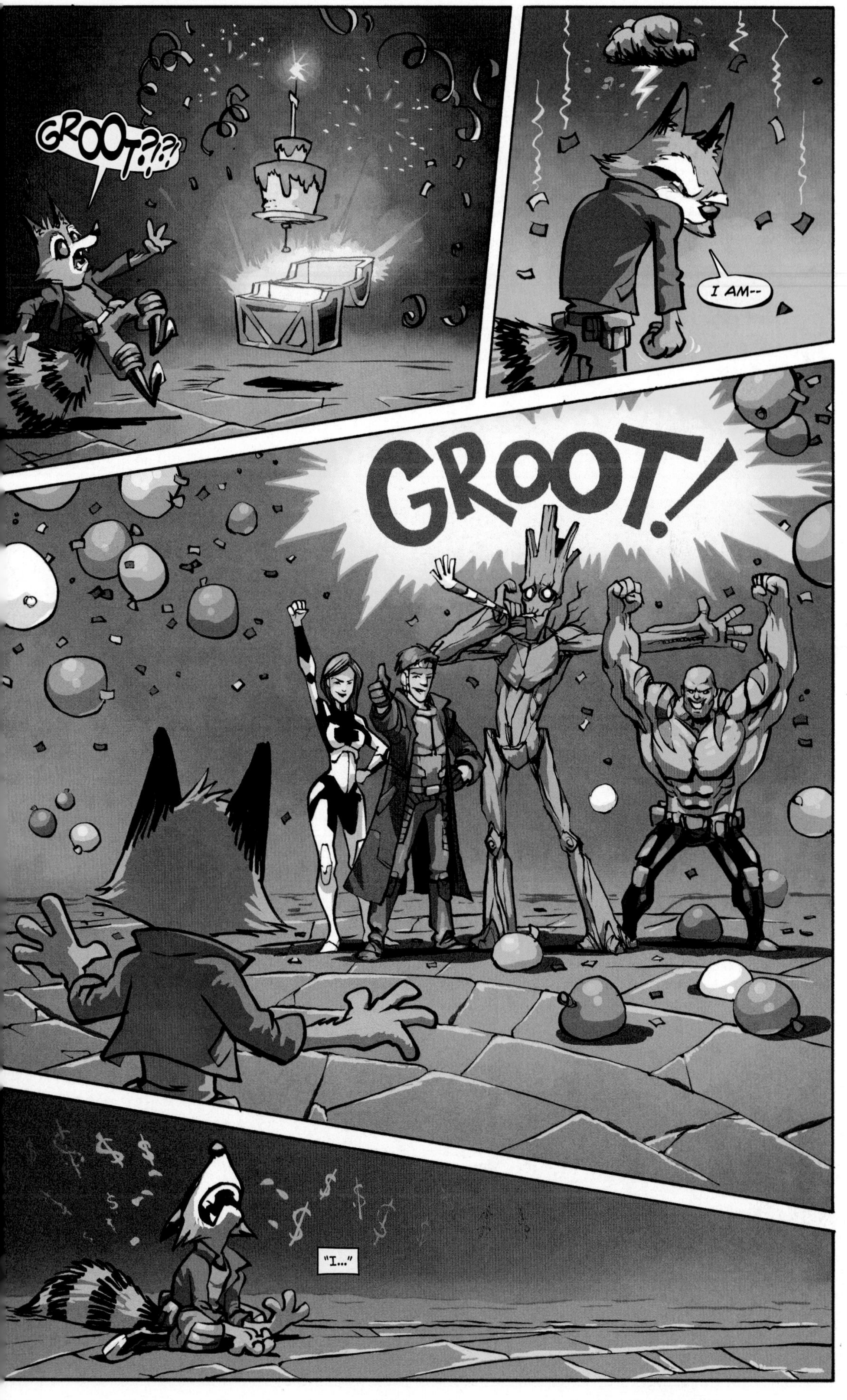
GROOT?!?!
I AM--
GROOT!
"I..."

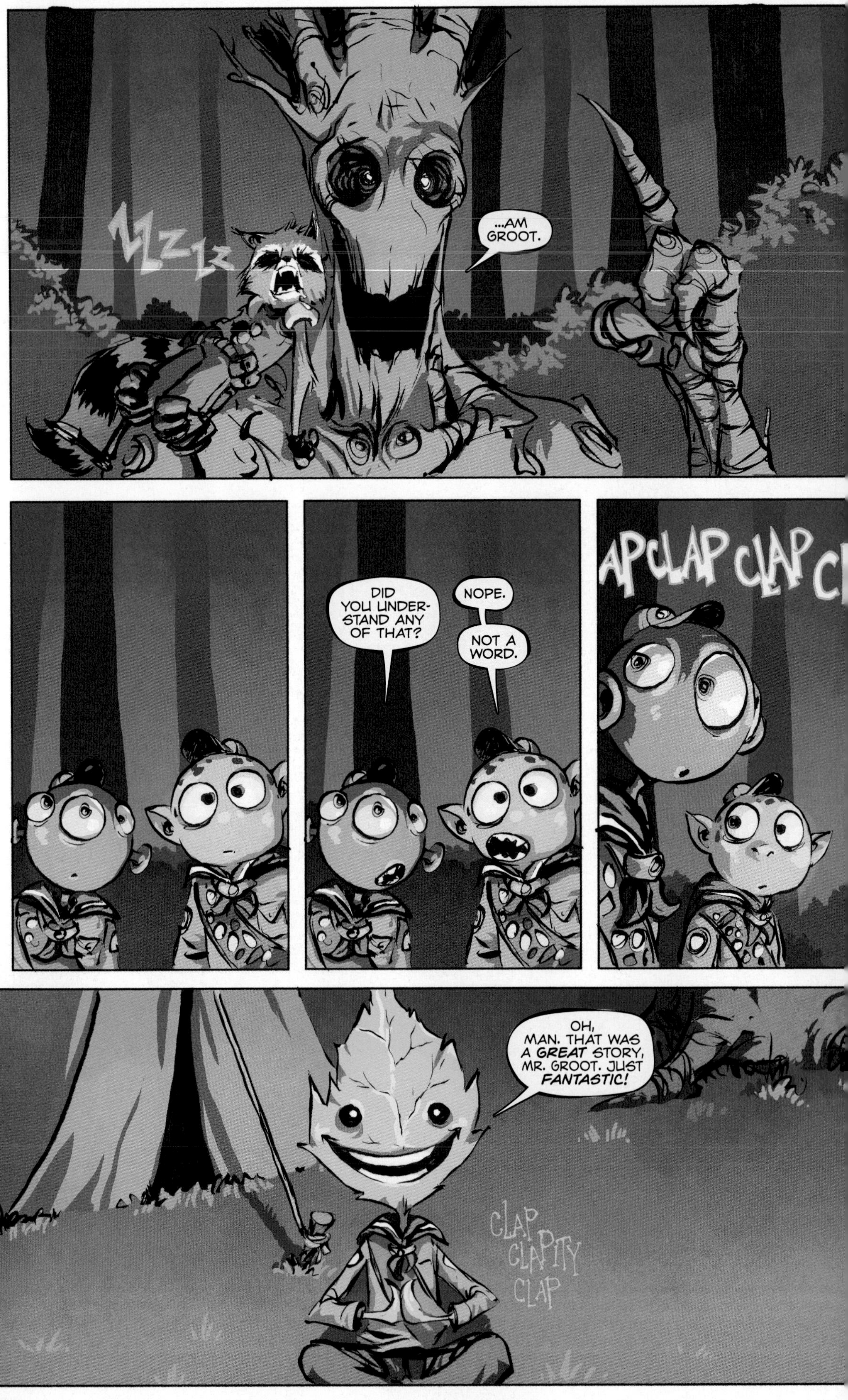
ZZZZZ
...AM GROOT.
DID YOU UNDERSTAND ANY OF THAT?
NOPE.
NOT A WORD.
AP CLAP CLAP CLAP CL
OH, MAN. THAT WAS A **GREAT** STORY, MR. GROOT. JUST ***FANTASTIC!***
CLAP CLAPITY CLAP

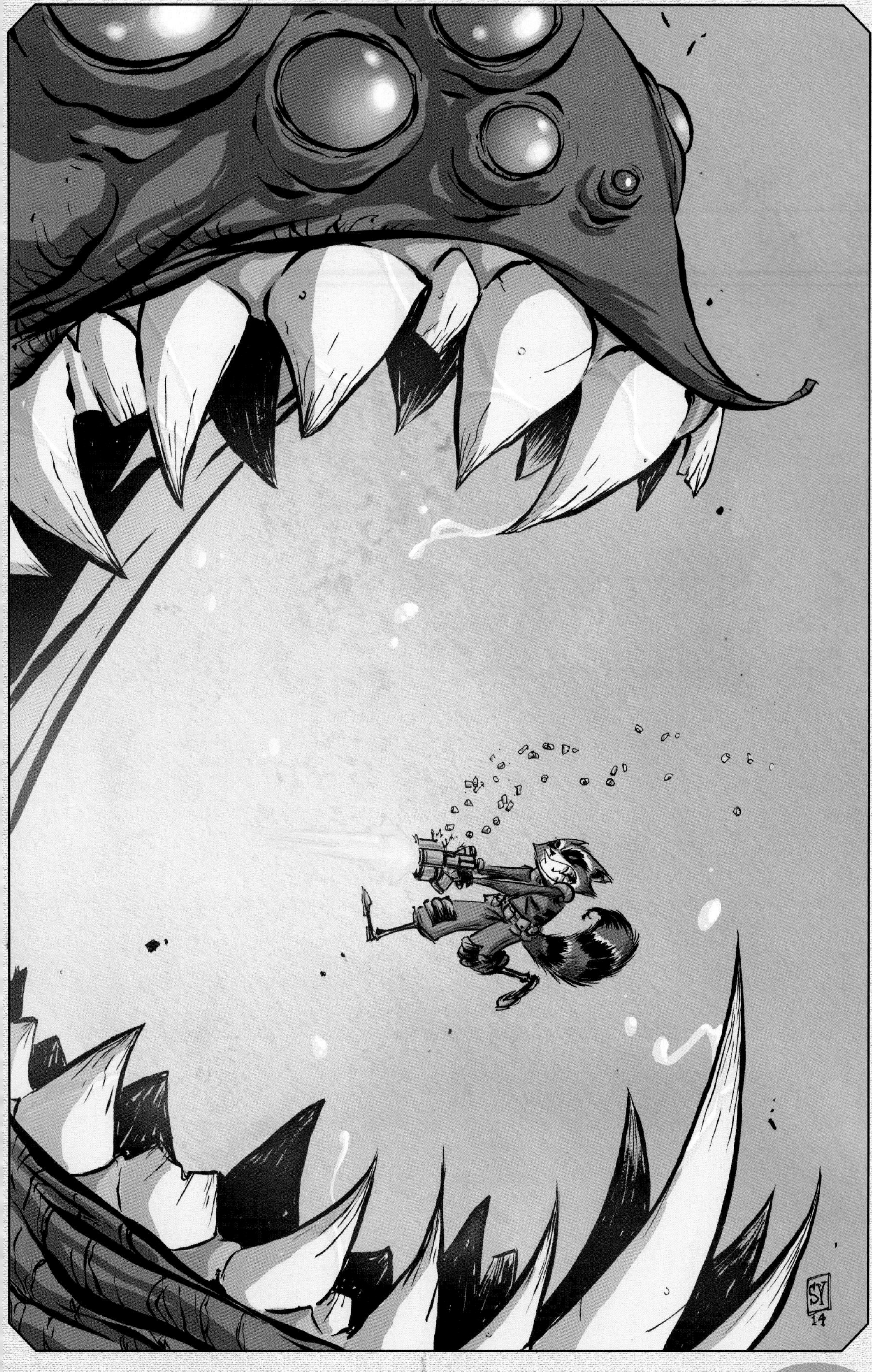

MISFIT MECHS 6

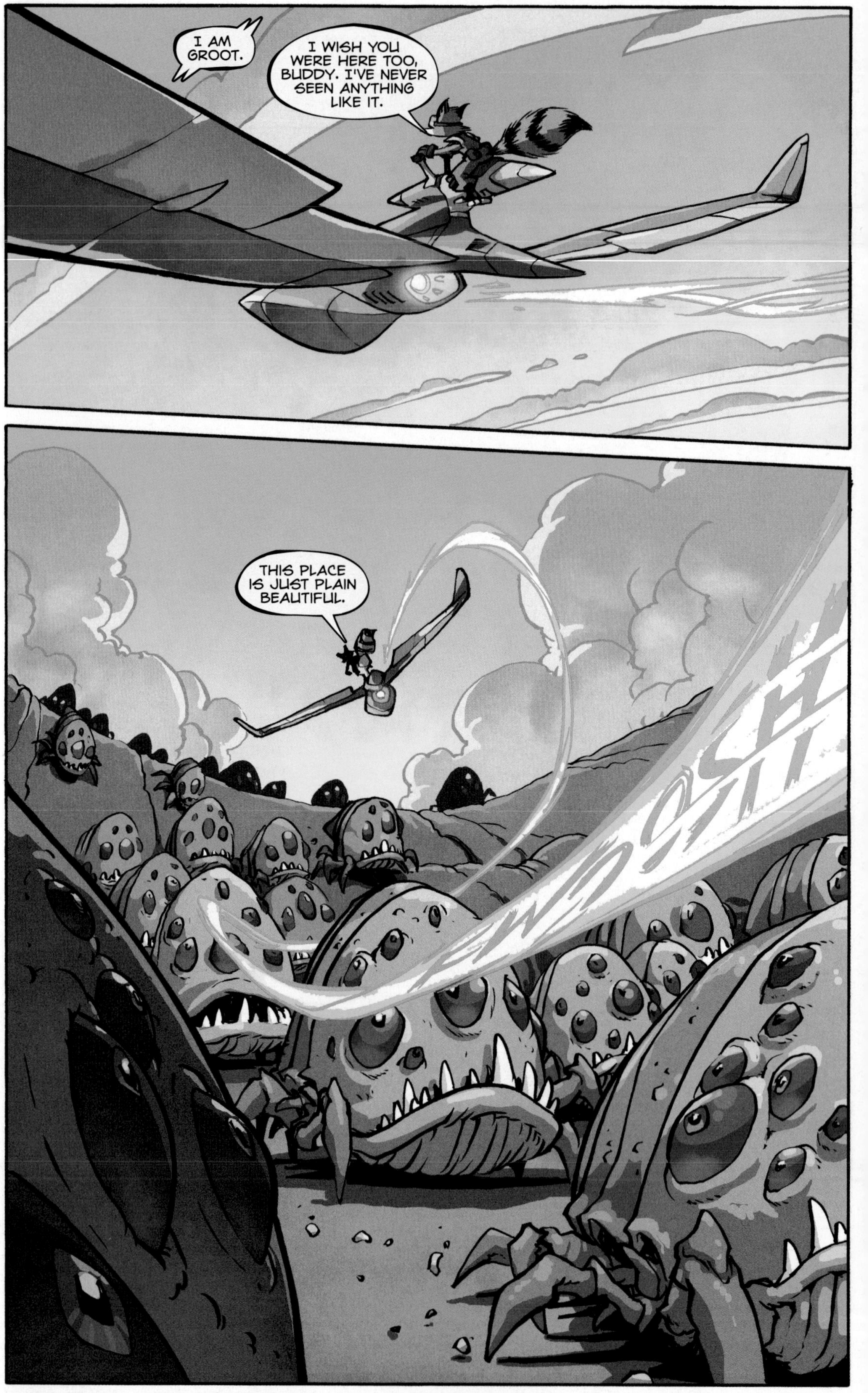
I AM GROOT.
I WISH YOU WERE HERE TOO, BUDDY. I'VE NEVER SEEN ANYTHING LIKE IT.
THIS PLACE IS JUST PLAIN BEAUTIFUL.

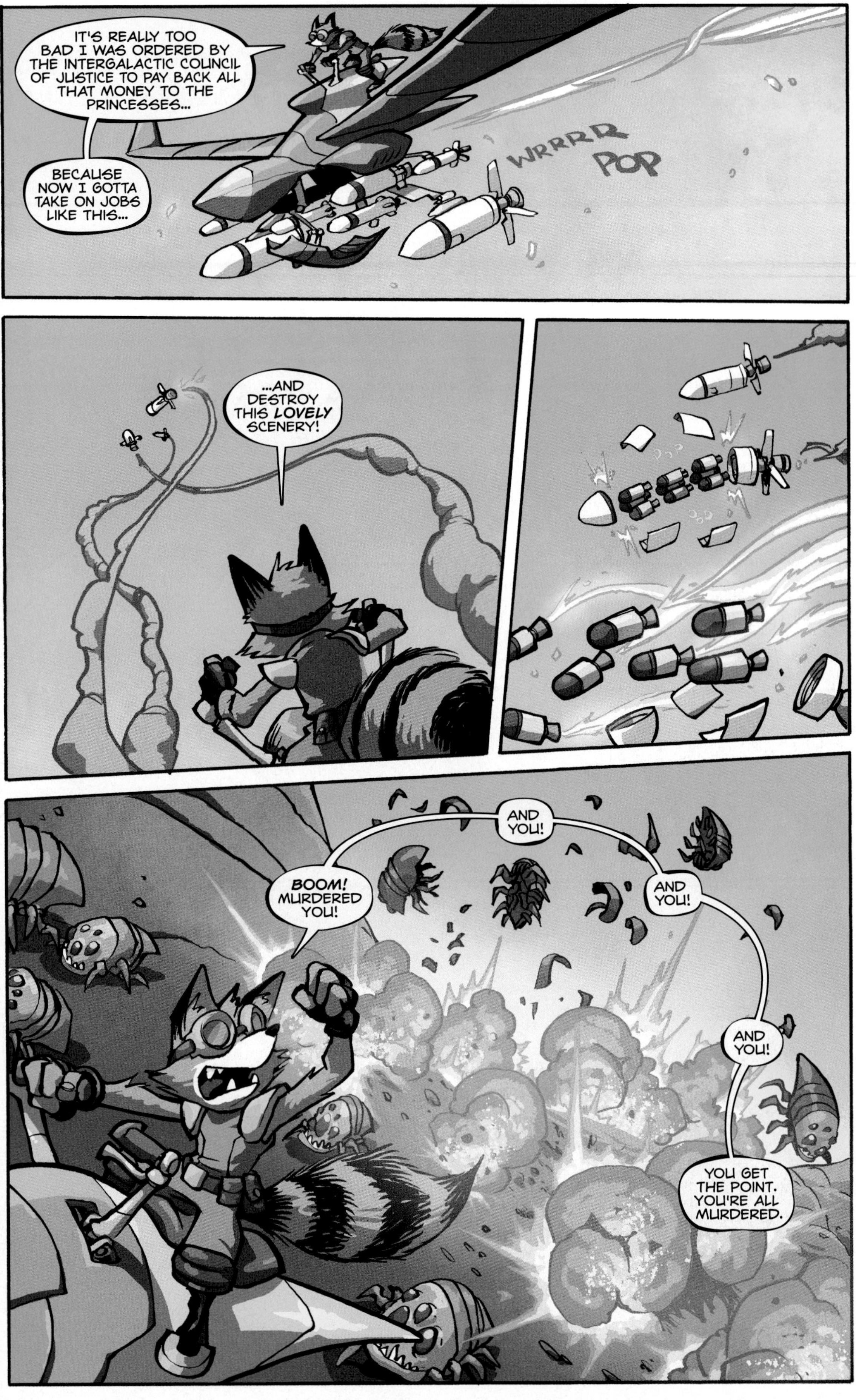
IT'S REALLY TOO BAD I WAS ORDERED BY THE INTERGALACTIC COUNCIL OF JUSTICE TO PAY BACK ALL THAT MONEY TO THE PRINCESSES...
BECAUSE NOW I GOTTA TAKE ON JOBS LIKE THIS...
WRRRR
POP
...AND DESTROY THIS LOVELY SCENERY!
BOOM! MURDERED YOU!
AND YOU!
AND YOU!
AND YOU!
YOU GET THE POINT. YOU'RE ALL MURDERED.

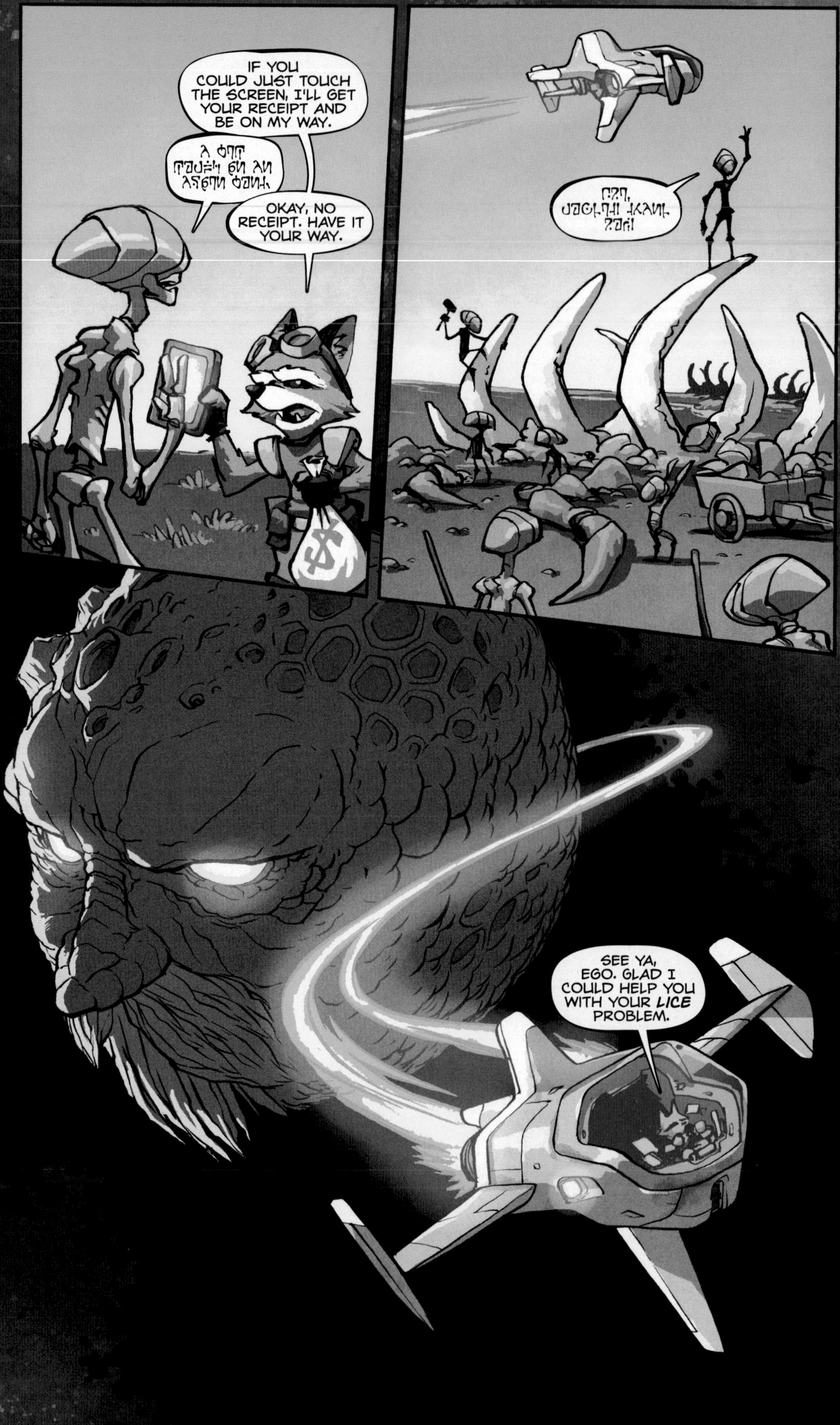
IF YOU COULD JUST TOUCH THE SCREEN, I'LL GET YOUR RECEIPT AND BE ON MY WAY.
OKAY, NO RECEIPT. HAVE IT YOUR WAY.
$
SEE YA, EGO. GLAD I COULD HELP YOU WITH YOUR *LICE* PROBLEM.

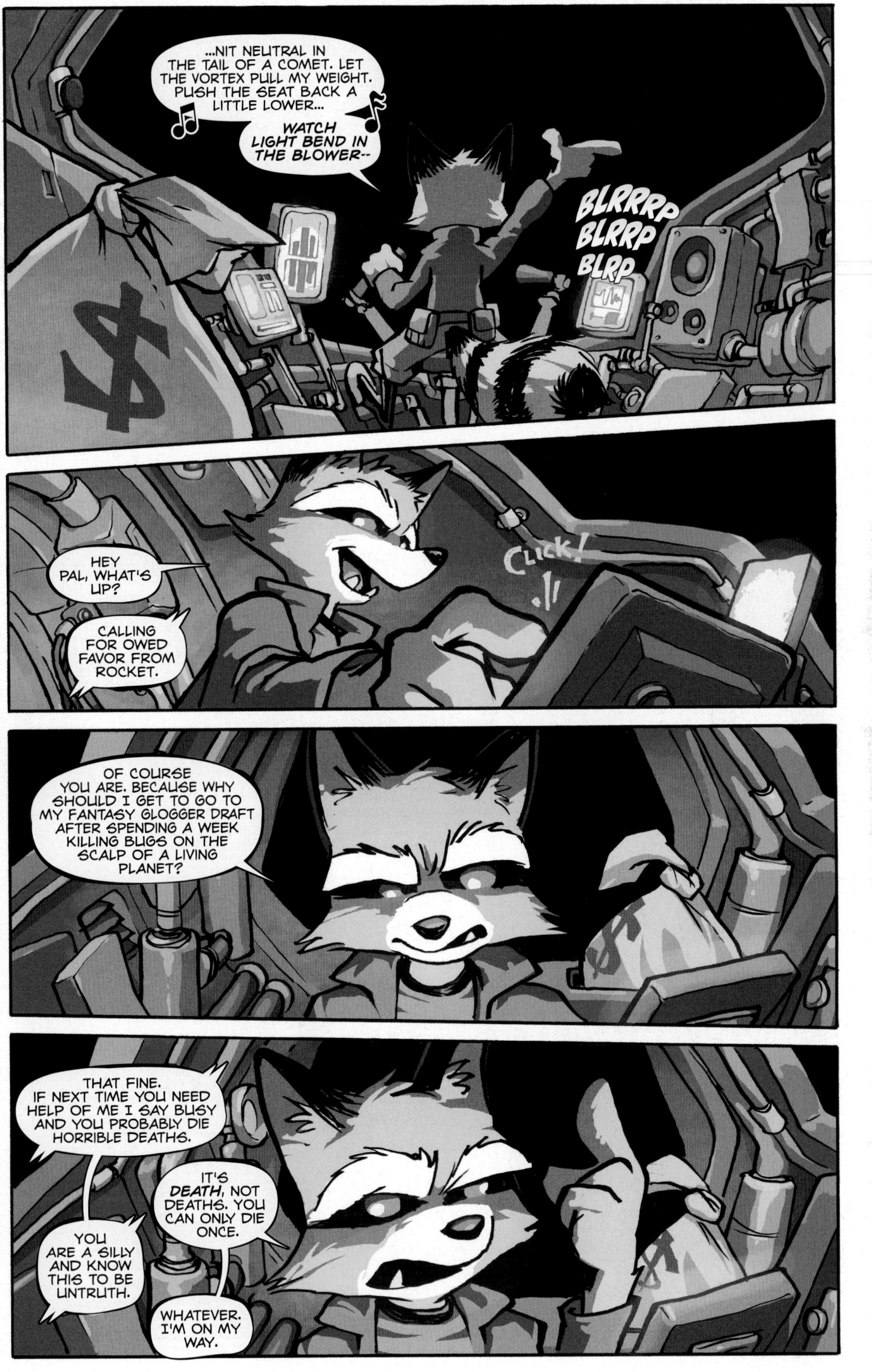

...NIT NEUTRAL IN THE TAIL OF A COMET. LET THE VORTEX PULL MY WEIGHT. PUSH THE SEAT BACK A LITTLE LOWER...
WATCH LIGHT BEND IN THE BLOWER--
BLRRRP BLRRP BLRP
HEY PAL, WHAT'S UP?
CALLING FOR OWED FAVOR FROM ROCKET.
CLICK!
OF COURSE YOU ARE. BECAUSE WHY SHOULD I GET TO GO TO MY FANTASY GLOGGER DRAFT AFTER SPENDING A WEEK KILLING BUGS ON THE SCALP OF A LIVING PLANET?
THAT FINE. IF NEXT TIME YOU NEED HELP OF ME I SAY BUSY AND YOU PROBABLY DIE HORRIBLE DEATHS.
IT'S *DEATH*, NOT DEATHS. YOU CAN ONLY DIE ONCE.
YOU ARE A SILLY AND KNOW THIS TO BE UNTRUTH.
WHATEVER. I'M ON MY WAY.

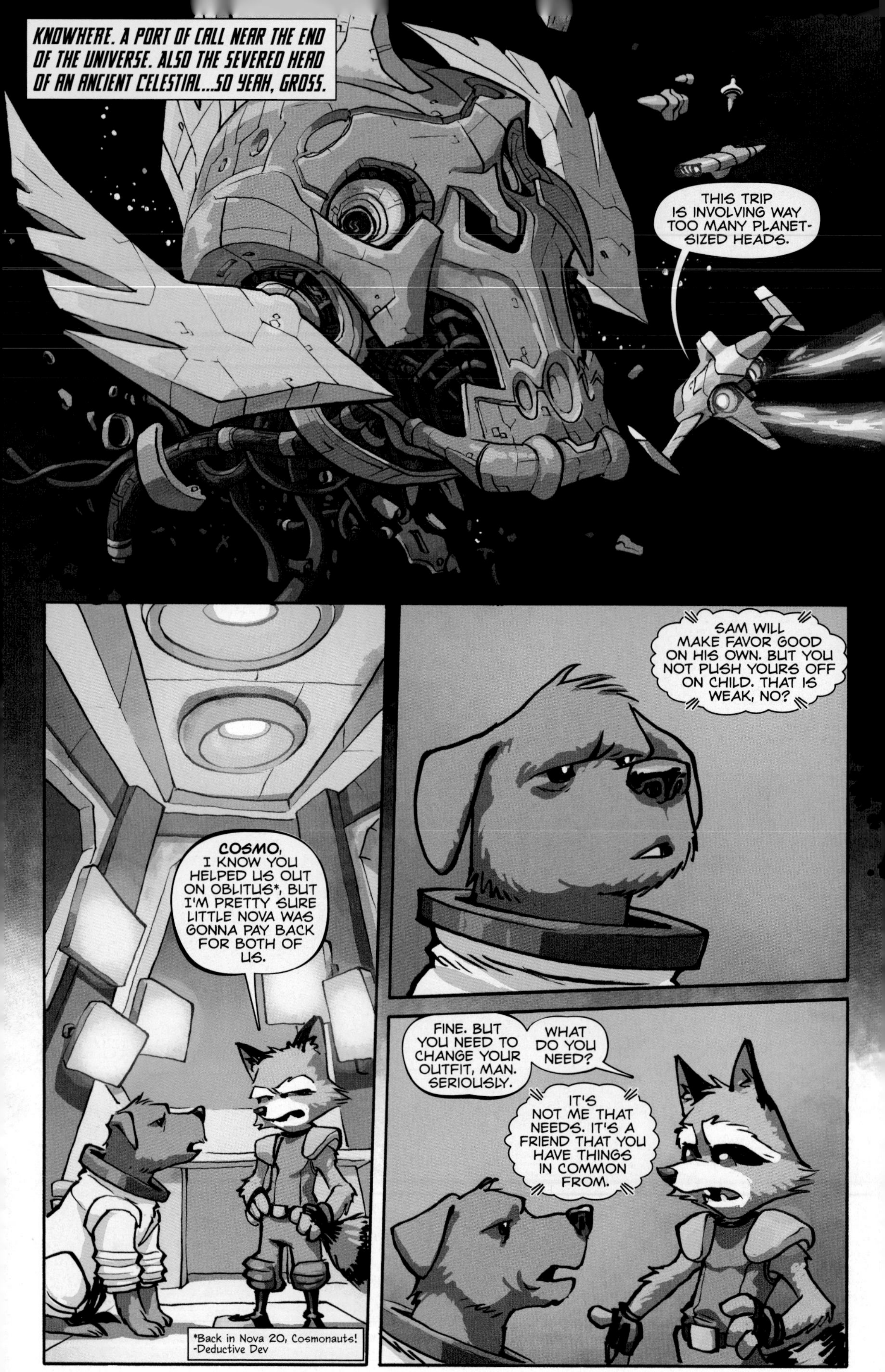
KNOWHERE. A PORT OF CALL NEAR THE END OF THE UNIVERSE. ALSO THE SEVERED HEAD OF AN ANCIENT CELESTIAL...SO YEAH, GROSS.
THIS TRIP IS INVOLVING WAY TOO MANY PLANET-SIZED HEADS.
COSMO, I KNOW YOU HELPED US OUT ON OBLITUS*, BUT I'M PRETTY SURE LITTLE NOVA WAS GONNA PAY BACK FOR BOTH OF US.
*Back in Nova 20, Cosmonauts! -Deductive Dev
SAM WILL MAKE FAVOR GOOD ON HIS OWN. BUT YOU NOT PUSH YOURS OFF ON CHILD. THAT IS WEAK, NO?
FINE. BUT WHAT DO YOU NEED?
YOU NEED TO CHANGE YOUR OUTFIT, MAN. SERIOUSLY.
IT'S NOT ME THAT NEEDS. IT'S A FRIEND THAT YOU HAVE THINGS IN COMMON FROM.

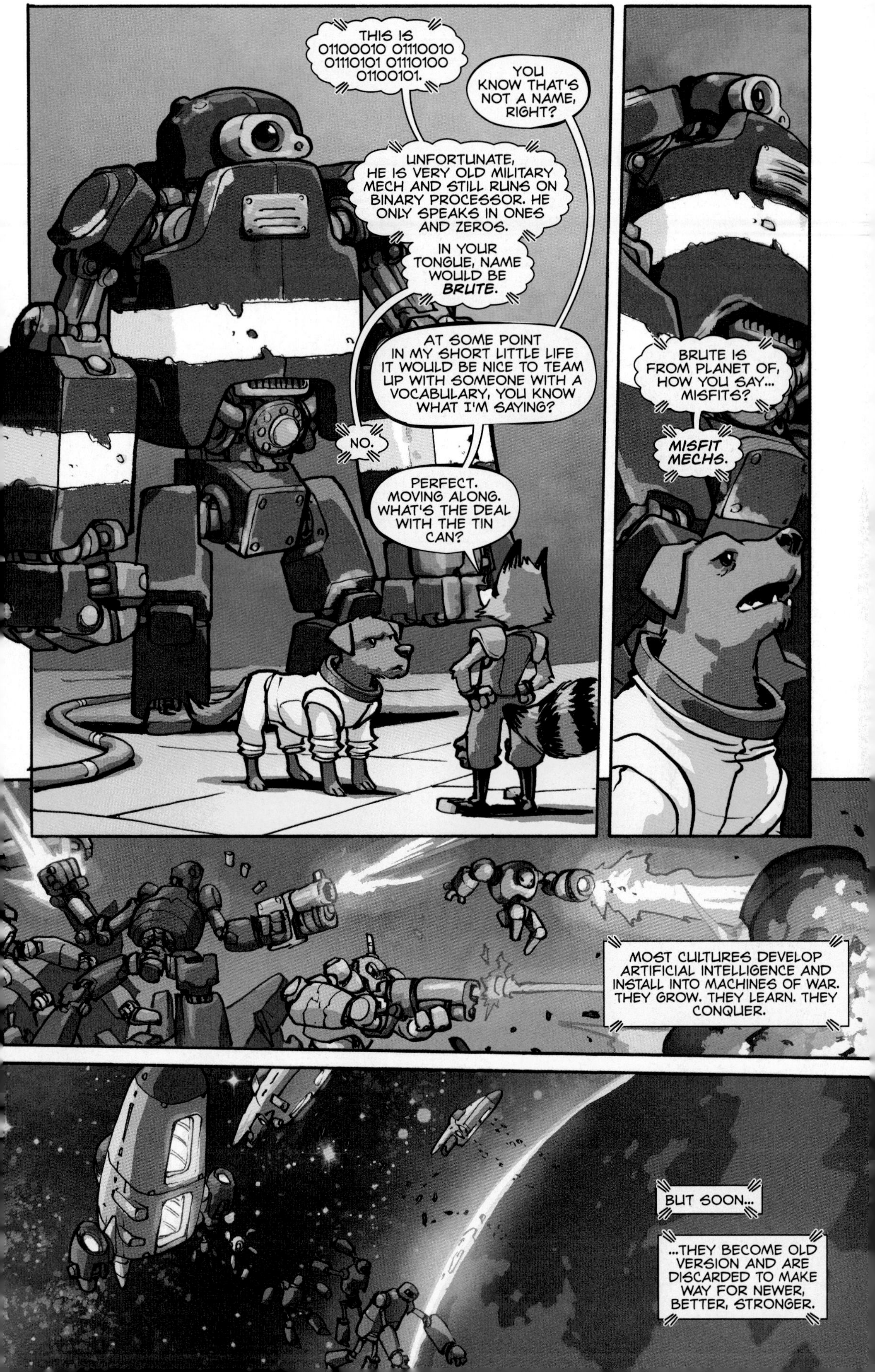

THIS IS 01100010 01110010 01110101 01110100 01100101.
YOU KNOW THAT'S NOT A NAME, RIGHT?
UNFORTUNATE, HE IS VERY OLD MILITARY MECH AND STILL RUNS ON BINARY PROCESSOR. HE ONLY SPEAKS IN ONES AND ZEROS.
IN YOUR TONGUE, NAME WOULD BE *BRUTE*.
AT SOME POINT IN MY SHORT LITTLE LIFE IT WOULD BE NICE TO TEAM UP WITH SOMEONE WITH A VOCABULARY, YOU KNOW WHAT I'M SAYING?
NO.
PERFECT. MOVING ALONG. WHAT'S THE DEAL WITH THE TIN CAN?
BRUTE IS FROM PLANET OF, HOW YOU SAY... MISFITS?
MISFIT MECHS.
MOST CULTURES DEVELOP ARTIFICIAL INTELLIGENCE AND INSTALL INTO MACHINES OF WAR. THEY GROW. THEY LEARN. THEY CONQUER.
BUT SOON...
...THEY BECOME OLD VERSION AND ARE DISCARDED TO MAKE WAY FOR NEWER, BETTER, STRONGER.

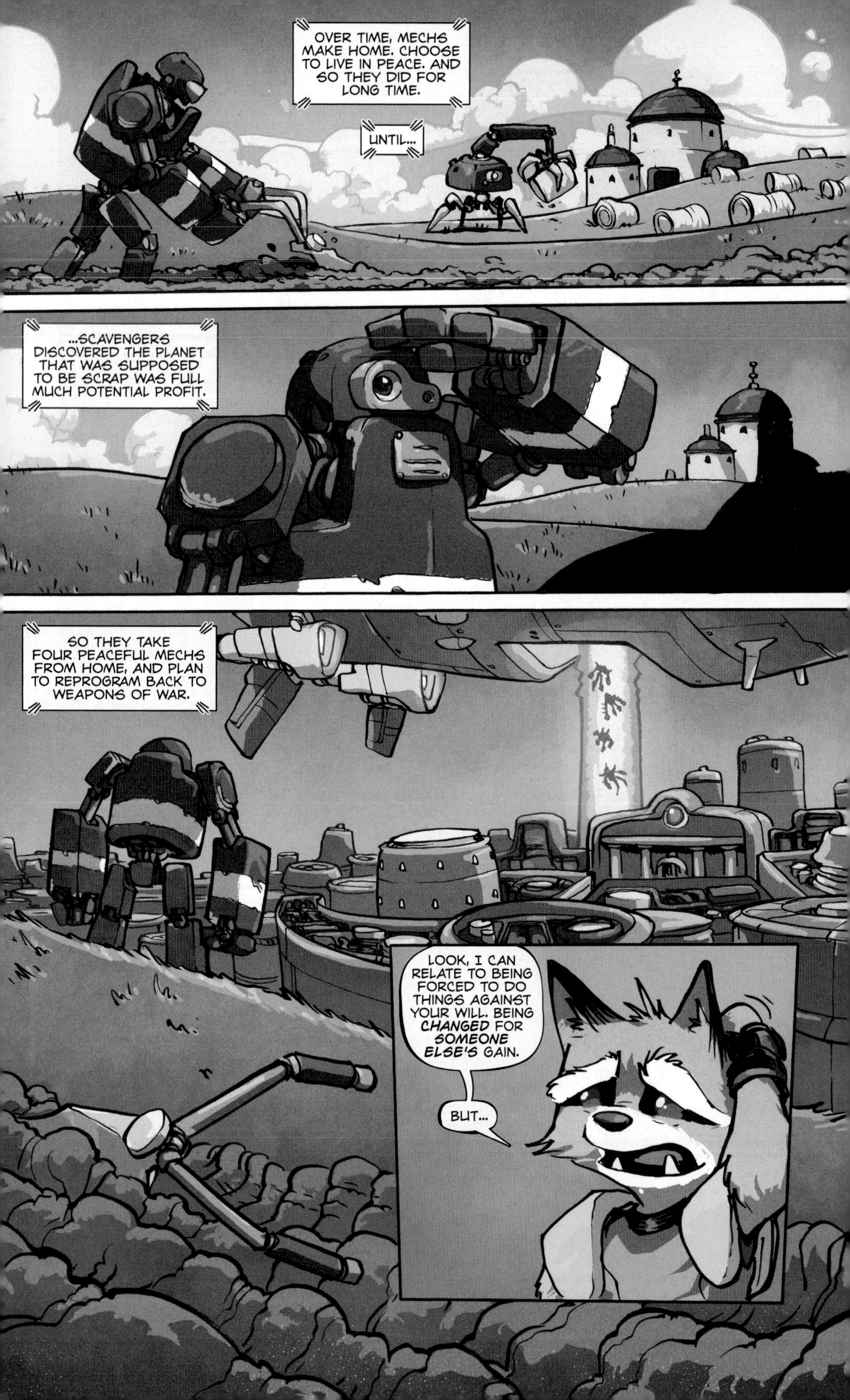
OVER TIME, MECHS MAKE HOME. CHOOSE TO LIVE IN PEACE. AND SO THEY DID FOR LONG TIME.
UNTIL...
...SCAVENGERS DISCOVERED THE PLANET THAT WAS SUPPOSED TO BE SCRAP WAS FULL MUCH POTENTIAL PROFIT.
SO THEY TAKE FOUR PEACEFUL MECHS FROM HOME, AND PLAN TO REPROGRAM BACK TO WEAPONS OF WAR.
LOOK, I CAN RELATE TO BEING FORCED TO DO THINGS AGAINST YOUR WILL. BEING CHANGED FOR SOMEONE ELSE'S GAIN.
BUT...

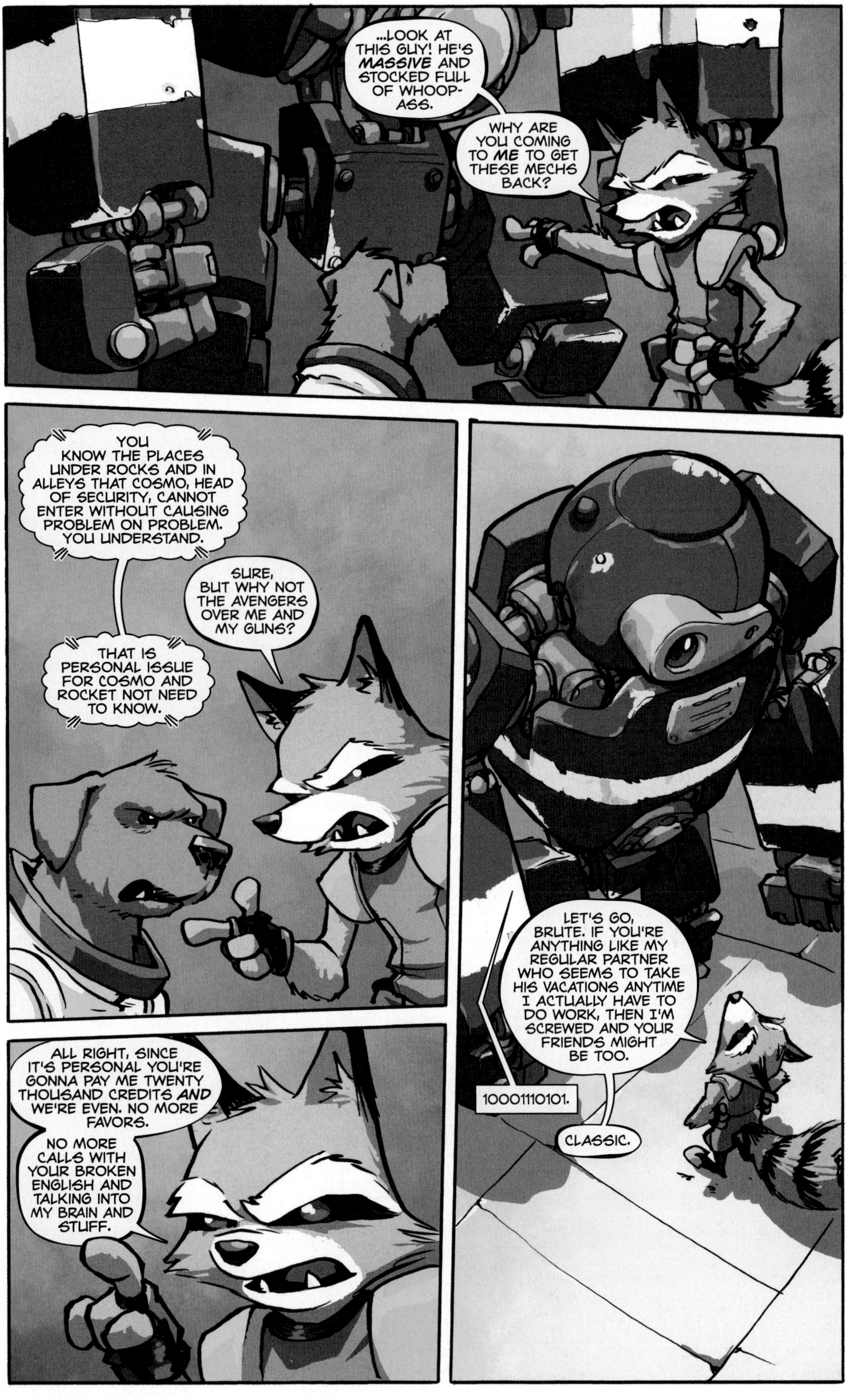
...LOOK AT THIS GUY! HE'S *MASSIVE* AND STOCKED FULL OF WHOOP-ASS.
WHY ARE YOU COMING TO *ME* TO GET THESE MECHS BACK?
YOU KNOW THE PLACES UNDER ROCKS AND IN ALLEYS THAT COSMO, HEAD OF SECURITY, CANNOT ENTER WITHOUT CAUSING PROBLEM ON PROBLEM. YOU UNDERSTAND.
SURE, BUT WHY NOT THE AVENGERS OVER ME AND MY GUNS?
THAT IS PERSONAL ISSUE FOR COSMO AND ROCKET NOT NEED TO KNOW.
ALL RIGHT, SINCE IT'S PERSONAL YOU'RE GONNA PAY ME TWENTY THOUSAND CREDITS *AND* WE'RE EVEN. NO MORE FAVORS.
NO MORE CALLS WITH YOUR BROKEN ENGLISH AND TALKING INTO MY BRAIN AND STUFF.
LET'S GO, BRUTE. IF YOU'RE ANYTHING LIKE MY REGULAR PARTNER WHO SEEMS TO TAKE HIS VACATIONS ANYTIME I ACTUALLY HAVE TO DO WORK, THEN I'M SCREWED AND YOUR FRIENDS MIGHT BE TOO.
10001110101.
CLASSIC.

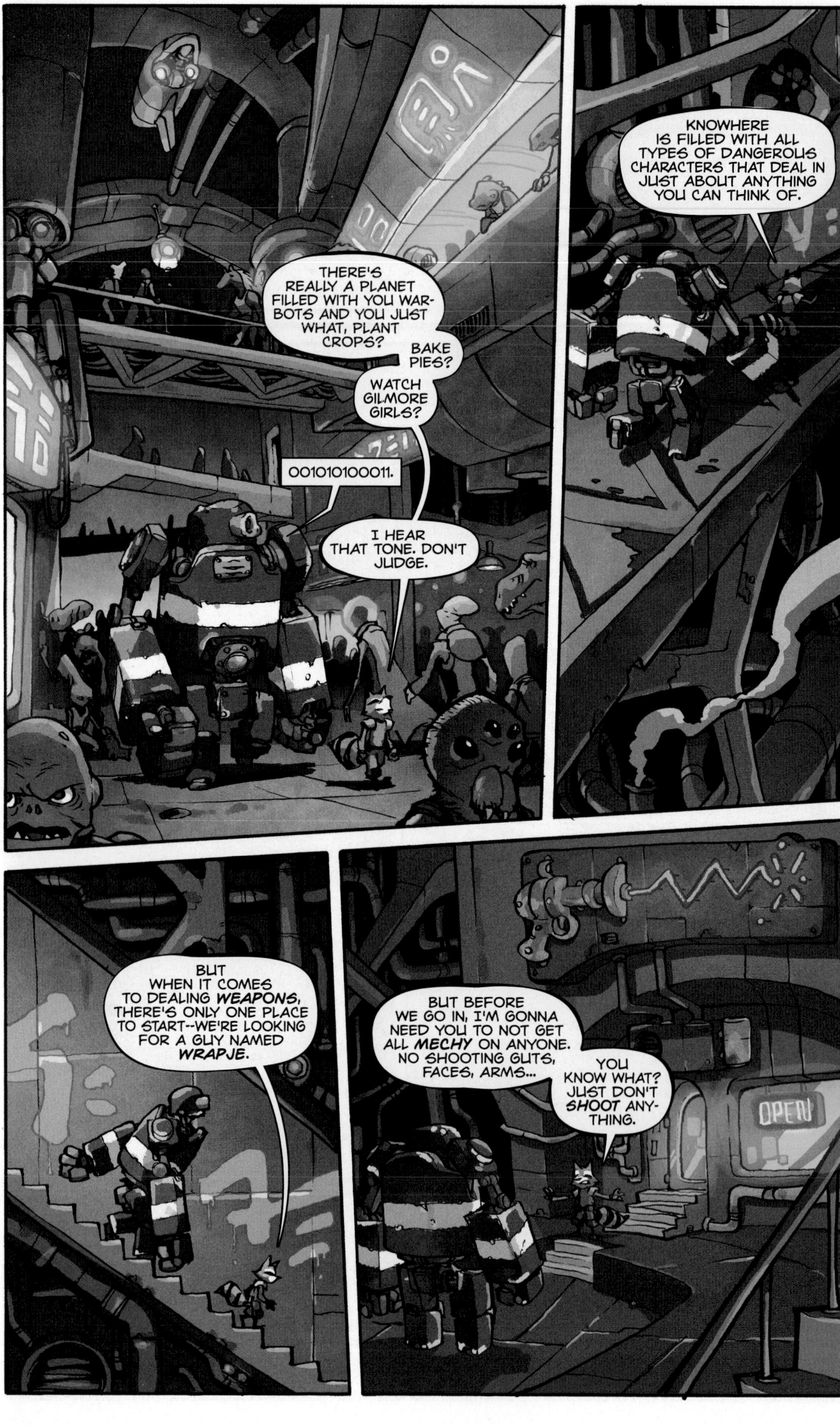
THERE'S REALLY A PLANET FILLED WITH YOU WAR-BOTS AND YOU JUST WHAT, PLANT CROPS?
BAKE PIES?
WATCH GILMORE GIRLS?
001010100011.
I HEAR THAT TONE. DON'T JUDGE.
KNOWHERE IS FILLED WITH ALL TYPES OF DANGEROUS CHARACTERS THAT DEAL IN JUST ABOUT ANYTHING YOU CAN THINK OF.
BUT WHEN IT COMES TO DEALING *WEAPONS*, THERE'S ONLY ONE PLACE TO START--WE'RE LOOKING FOR A GUY NAMED *WRAPJE*.
BUT BEFORE WE GO IN, I'M GONNA NEED YOU TO NOT GET ALL *MECHY* ON ANYONE. NO SHOOTING GUTS, FACES, ARMS...
YOU KNOW WHAT? JUST DON'T *SHOOT* ANY-THING.
OPEN

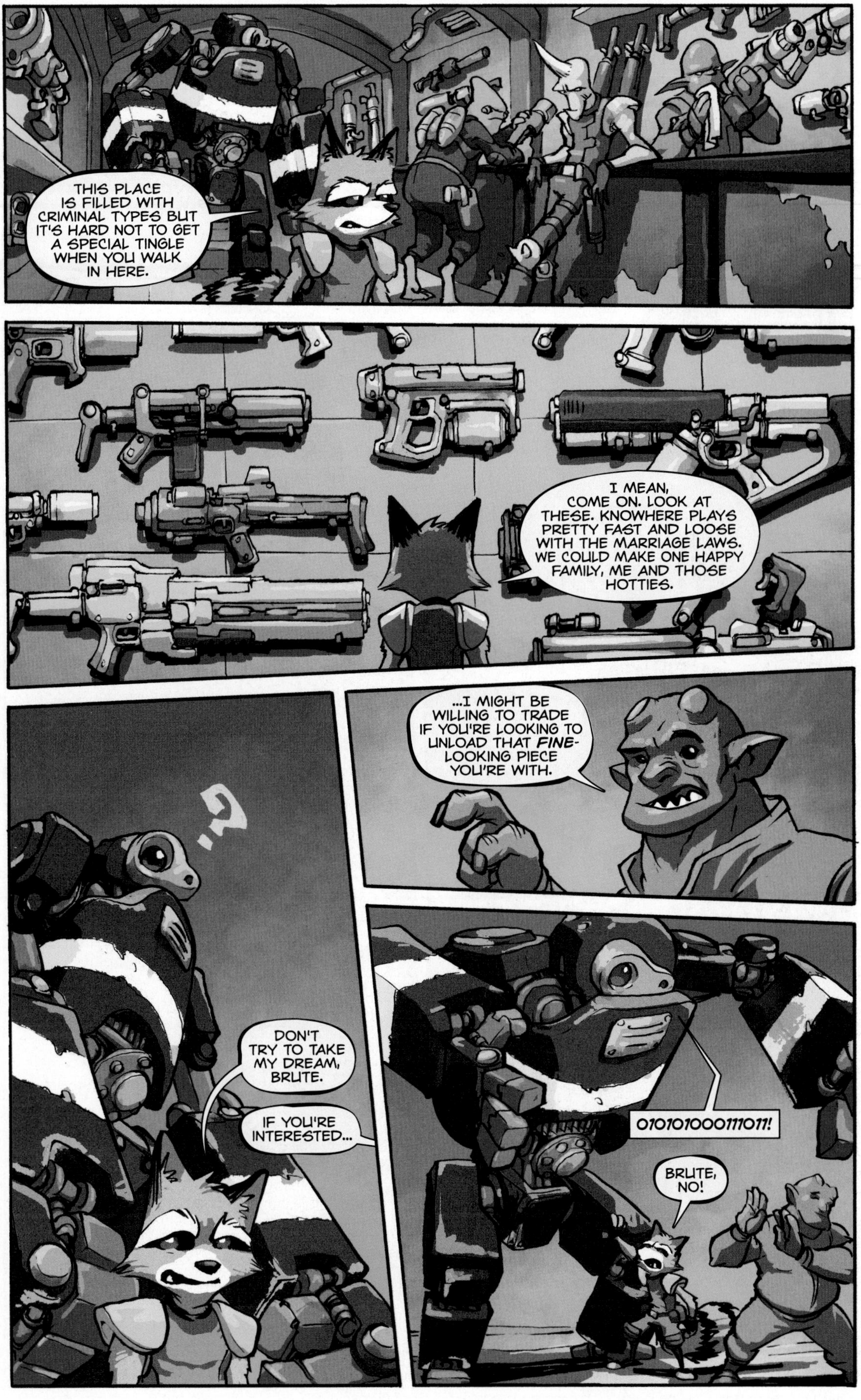
THIS PLACE IS FILLED WITH CRIMINAL TYPES BUT IT'S HARD NOT TO GET A SPECIAL TINGLE WHEN YOU WALK IN HERE.
I MEAN, COME ON. LOOK AT THESE. KNOWHERE PLAYS PRETTY FAST AND LOOSE WITH THE MARRIAGE LAWS. WE COULD MAKE ONE HAPPY FAMILY, ME AND THOSE HOTTIES.
...I MIGHT BE WILLING TO TRADE IF YOU'RE LOOKING TO UNLOAD THAT *FINE*-LOOKING PIECE YOU'RE WITH.
?
DON'T TRY TO TAKE MY DREAM, BRUTE.
IF YOU'RE INTERESTED...
0101010001110 11!
BRUTE, NO!

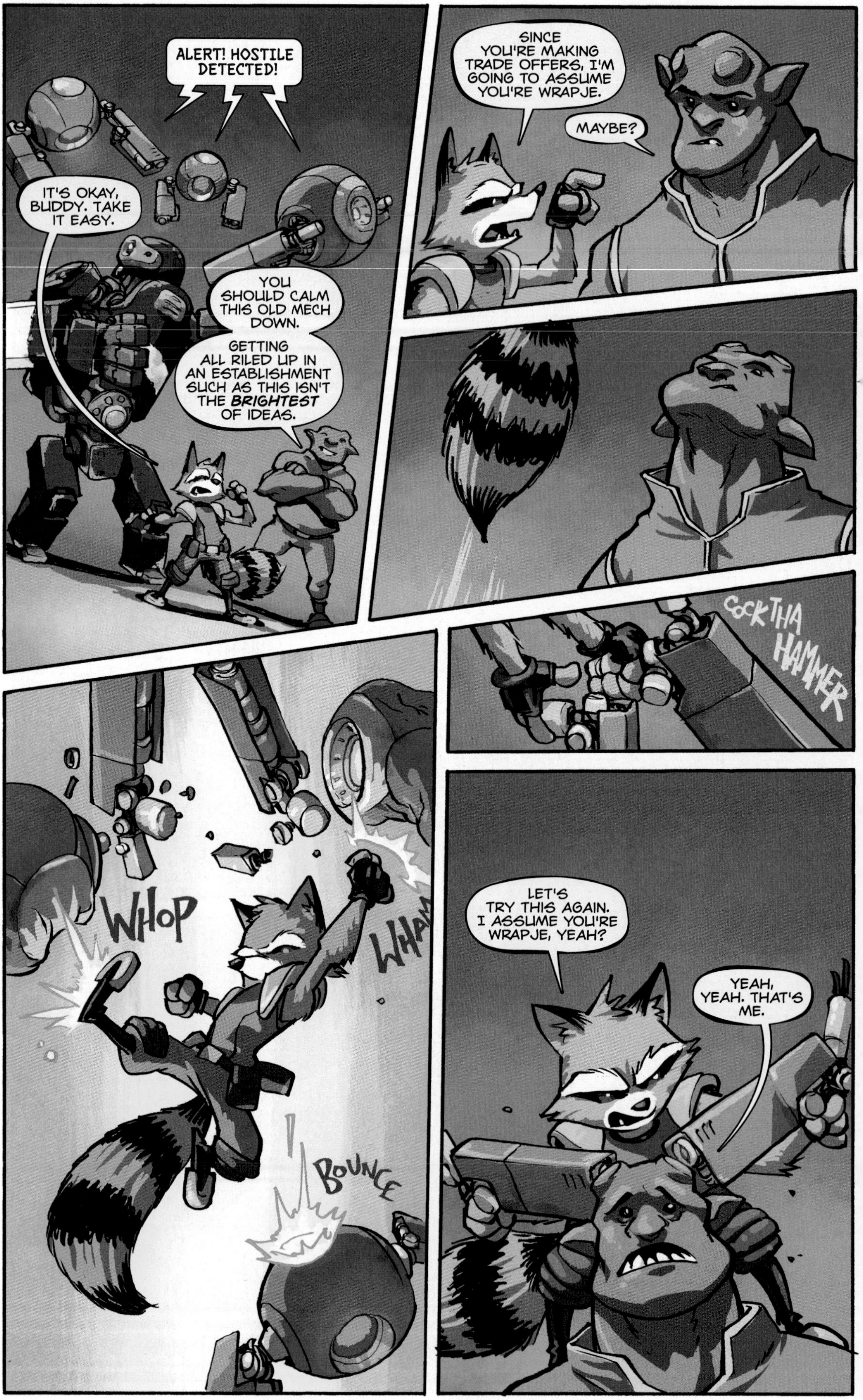
ALERT! HOSTILE DETECTED!
IT'S OKAY, BUDDY. TAKE IT EASY.
YOU SHOULD CALM THIS OLD MECH DOWN.
GETTING ALL RILED UP IN AN ESTABLISHMENT SUCH AS THIS ISN'T THE **BRIGHTEST** OF IDEAS.
SINCE YOU'RE MAKING TRADE OFFERS, I'M GOING TO ASSUME YOU'RE WRAPJE.
MAYBE?
COCK THA HAMMER
WHOP
WHAM
BOUNCE
LET'S TRY THIS AGAIN. I ASSUME YOU'RE WRAPJE, YEAH?
YEAH, YEAH. THAT'S ME.

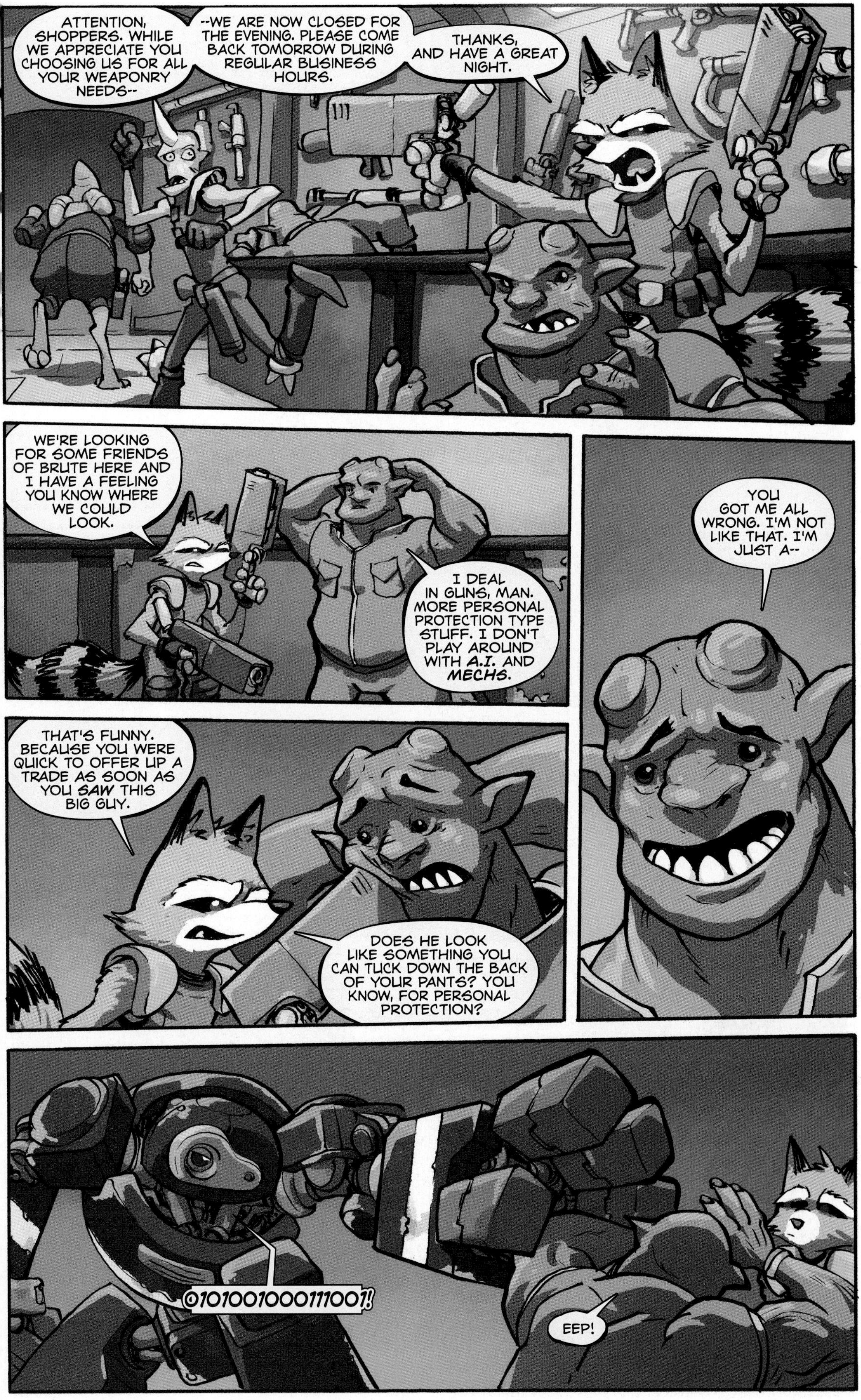
ATTENTION, SHOPPERS. WHILE WE APPRECIATE YOU CHOOSING US FOR ALL YOUR WEAPONRY NEEDS--
--WE ARE NOW CLOSED FOR THE EVENING. PLEASE COME BACK TOMORROW DURING REGULAR BUSINESS HOURS.
THANKS, AND HAVE A GREAT NIGHT.
WE'RE LOOKING FOR SOME FRIENDS OF BRUTE HERE AND I HAVE A FEELING YOU KNOW WHERE WE COULD LOOK.
I DEAL IN GUNS, MAN. MORE PERSONAL PROTECTION TYPE STUFF. I DON'T PLAY AROUND WITH A.I. AND MECHS.
YOU GOT ME ALL WRONG. I'M NOT LIKE THAT. I'M JUST A--
THAT'S FUNNY. BECAUSE YOU WERE QUICK TO OFFER UP A TRADE AS SOON AS YOU SAW THIS BIG GUY.
DOES HE LOOK LIKE SOMETHING YOU CAN TUCK DOWN THE BACK OF YOUR PANTS? YOU KNOW, FOR PERSONAL PROTECTION?
©101001000111001!
EEP!

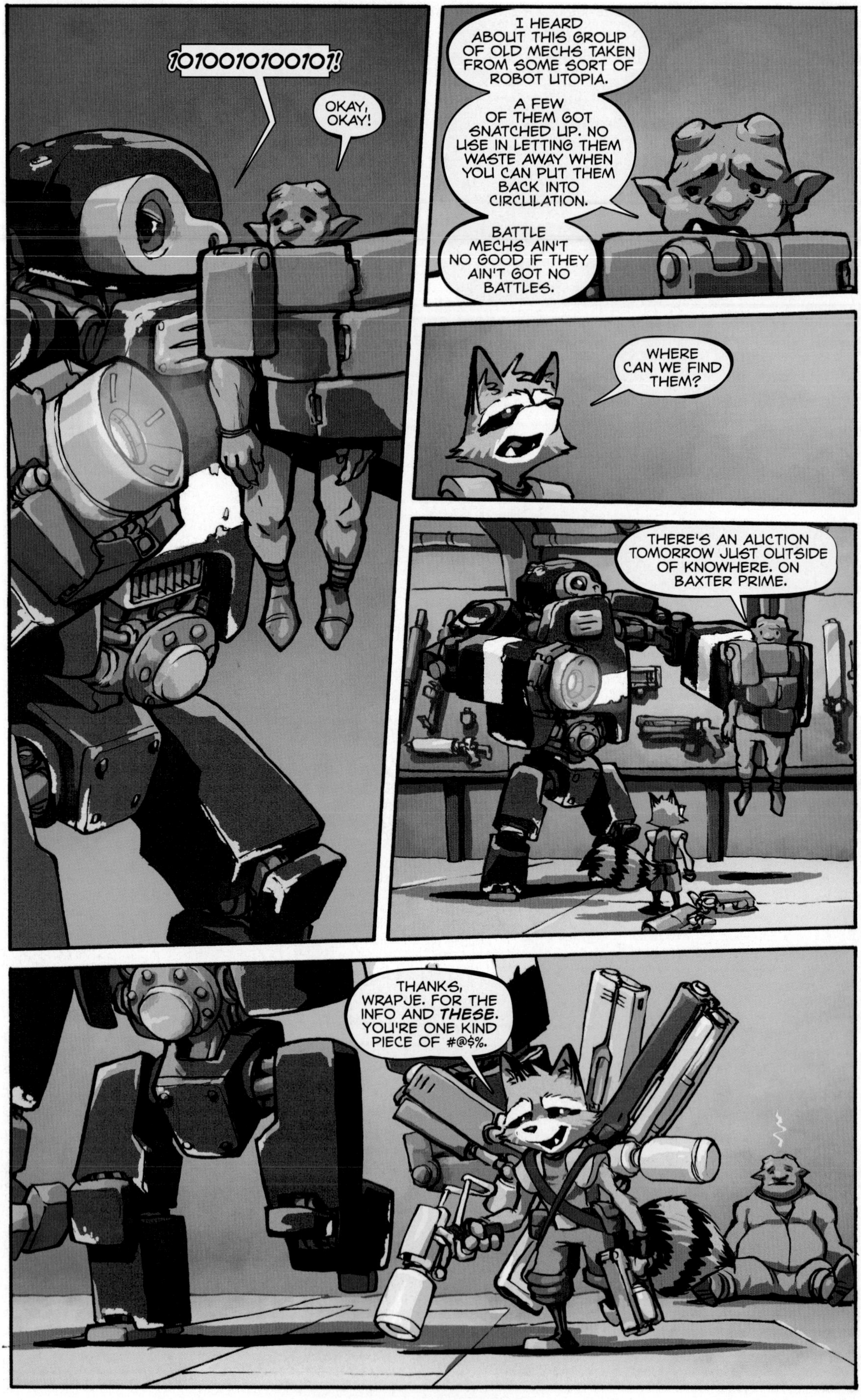
1010010100101!
OKAY, OKAY!
I HEARD ABOUT THIS GROUP OF OLD MECHS TAKEN FROM SOME SORT OF ROBOT UTOPIA.
A FEW OF THEM GOT SNATCHED UP. NO USE IN LETTING THEM WASTE AWAY WHEN YOU CAN PUT THEM BACK INTO CIRCULATION.
BATTLE MECHS AIN'T NO GOOD IF THEY AIN'T GOT NO BATTLES.
WHERE CAN WE FIND THEM?
THERE'S AN AUCTION TOMORROW JUST OUTSIDE OF KNOWHERE. ON BAXTER PRIME.
THANKS, WRAPJE. FOR THE INFO AND *THESE*. YOU'RE ONE KIND PIECE OF #@$%.

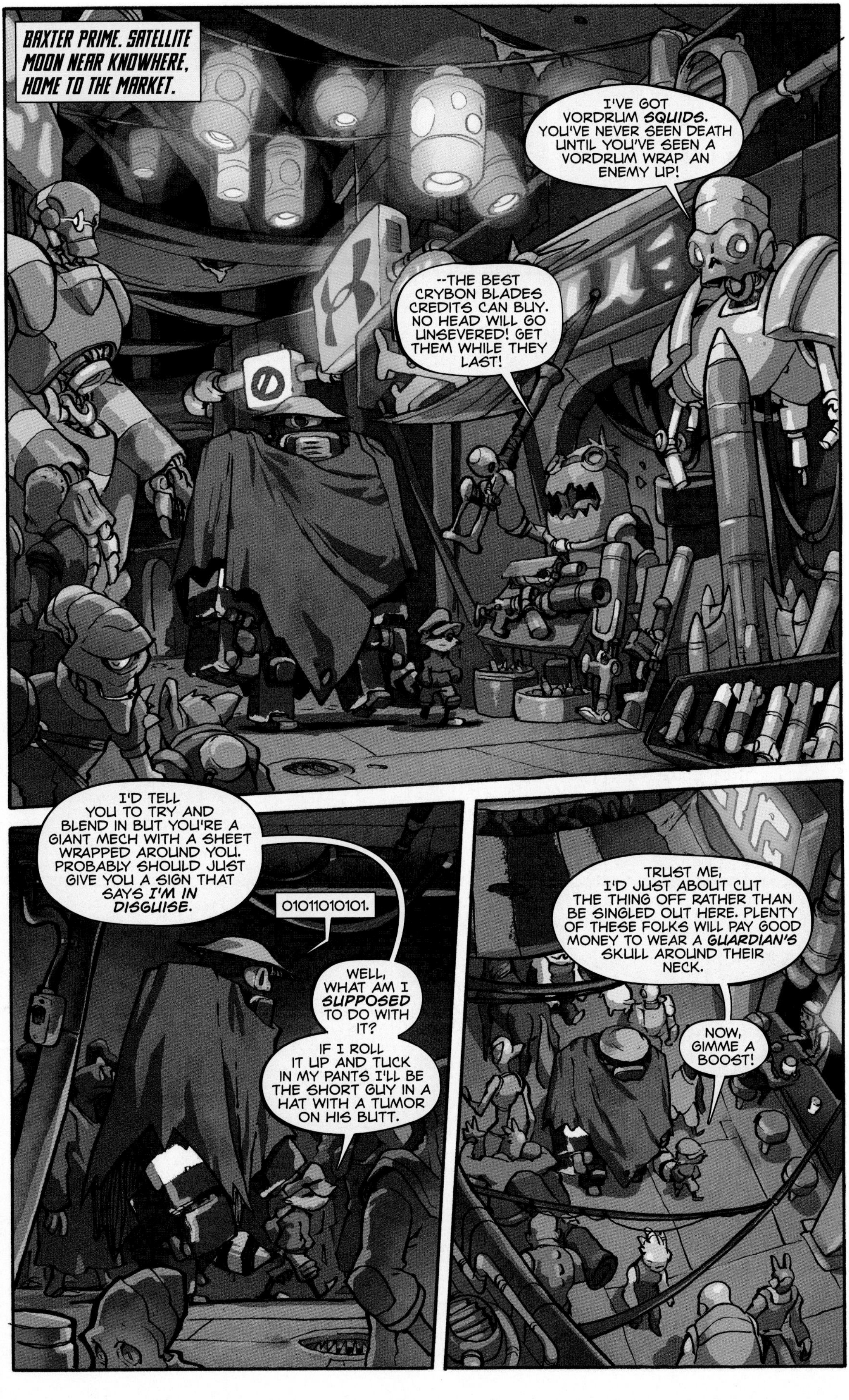
BAXTER PRIME. SATELLITE MOON NEAR KNOWHERE, HOME TO THE MARKET.
I'VE GOT VORDRUM SQUIDS. YOU'VE NEVER SEEN DEATH UNTIL YOU'VE SEEN A VORDRUM WRAP AN ENEMY UP!
--THE BEST CRYBON BLADES CREDITS CAN BUY. NO HEAD WILL GO UNSEVERED! GET THEM WHILE THEY LAST!
I'D TELL YOU TO TRY AND BLEND IN BUT YOU'RE A GIANT MECH WITH A SHEET WRAPPED AROUND YOU. PROBABLY SHOULD JUST GIVE YOU A SIGN THAT SAYS I'M IN DISGUISE.
01011010101.
WELL, WHAT AM I SUPPOSED TO DO WITH IT?
IF I ROLL IT UP AND TUCK IN MY PANTS I'LL BE THE SHORT GUY IN A HAT WITH A TUMOR ON HIS BUTT.
TRUST ME, I'D JUST ABOUT CUT THE THING OFF RATHER THAN BE SINGLED OUT HERE. PLENTY OF THESE FOLKS WILL PAY GOOD MONEY TO WEAR A GUARDIAN'S SKULL AROUND THEIR NECK.
NOW, GIMME A BOOST!

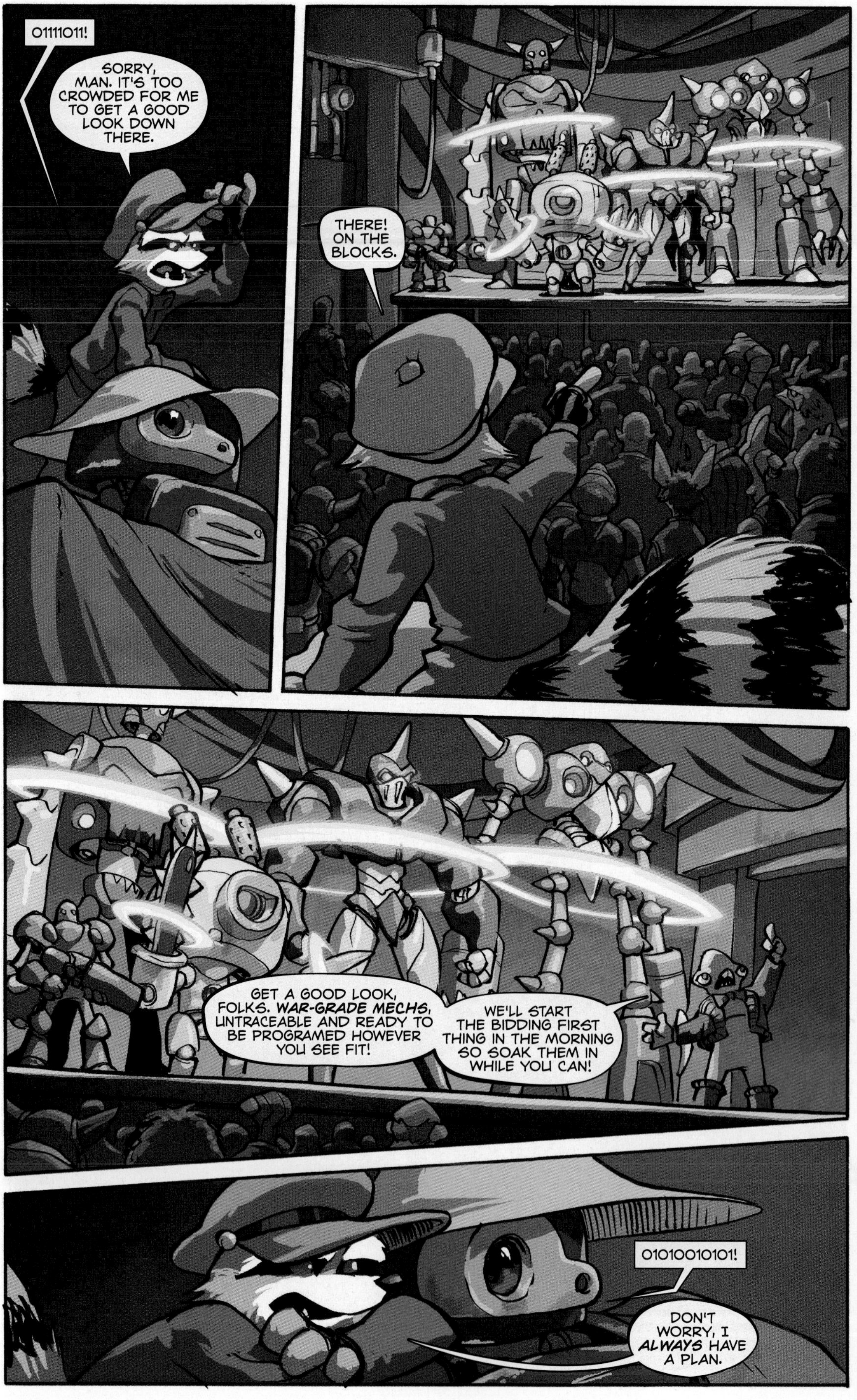
01111011!
SORRY, MAN. IT'S TOO CROWDED FOR ME TO GET A GOOD LOOK DOWN THERE.
THERE! ON THE BLOCKS.
GET A GOOD LOOK, FOLKS. WAR-GRADE MECHS, UNTRACEABLE AND READY TO BE PROGRAMED HOWEVER YOU SEE FIT!
WE'LL START THE BIDDING FIRST THING IN THE MORNING SO SOAK THEM IN WHILE YOU CAN!
01010010101!
DON'T WORRY, I ALWAYS HAVE A PLAN.

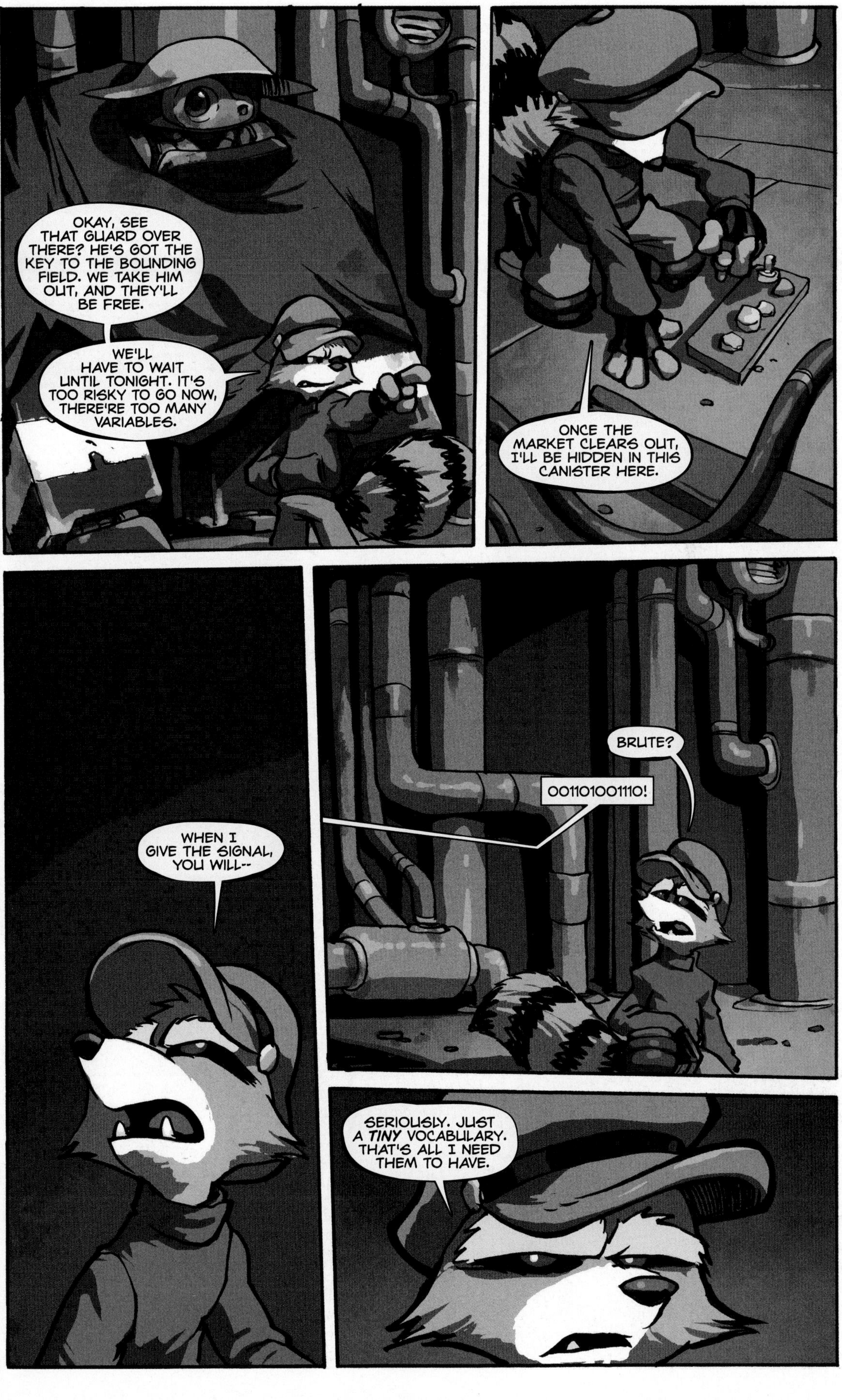
OKAY, SEE THAT GUARD OVER THERE? HE'S GOT THE KEY TO THE BOUNDING FIELD. WE TAKE HIM OUT, AND THEY'LL BE FREE.
WE'LL HAVE TO WAIT UNTIL TONIGHT. IT'S TOO RISKY TO GO NOW, THERE'RE TOO MANY VARIABLES.
ONCE THE MARKET CLEARS OUT, I'LL BE HIDDEN IN THIS CANISTER HERE.
WHEN I GIVE THE SIGNAL, YOU WILL--
BRUTE?
001101001110!
SERIOUSLY. JUST A *TINY* VOCABULARY. THAT'S ALL I NEED THEM TO HAVE.

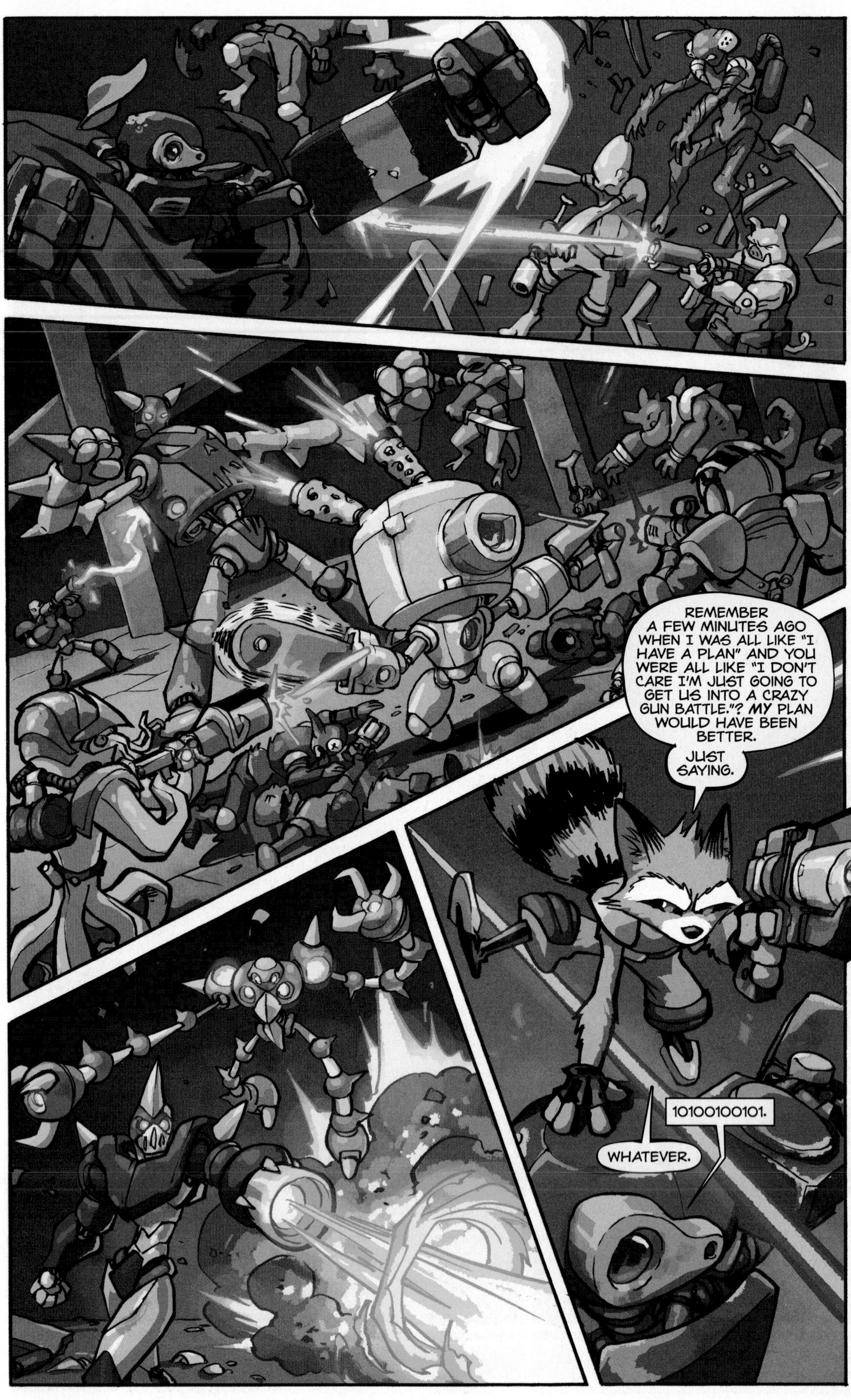
REMEMBER A FEW MINUTES AGO WHEN I WAS ALL LIKE "I HAVE A PLAN" AND YOU WERE ALL LIKE "I DON'T CARE I'M JUST GOING TO GET US INTO A CRAZY GUN BATTLE."? MY PLAN WOULD HAVE BEEN BETTER.
JUST SAYING.
10100100101.
WHATEVER.

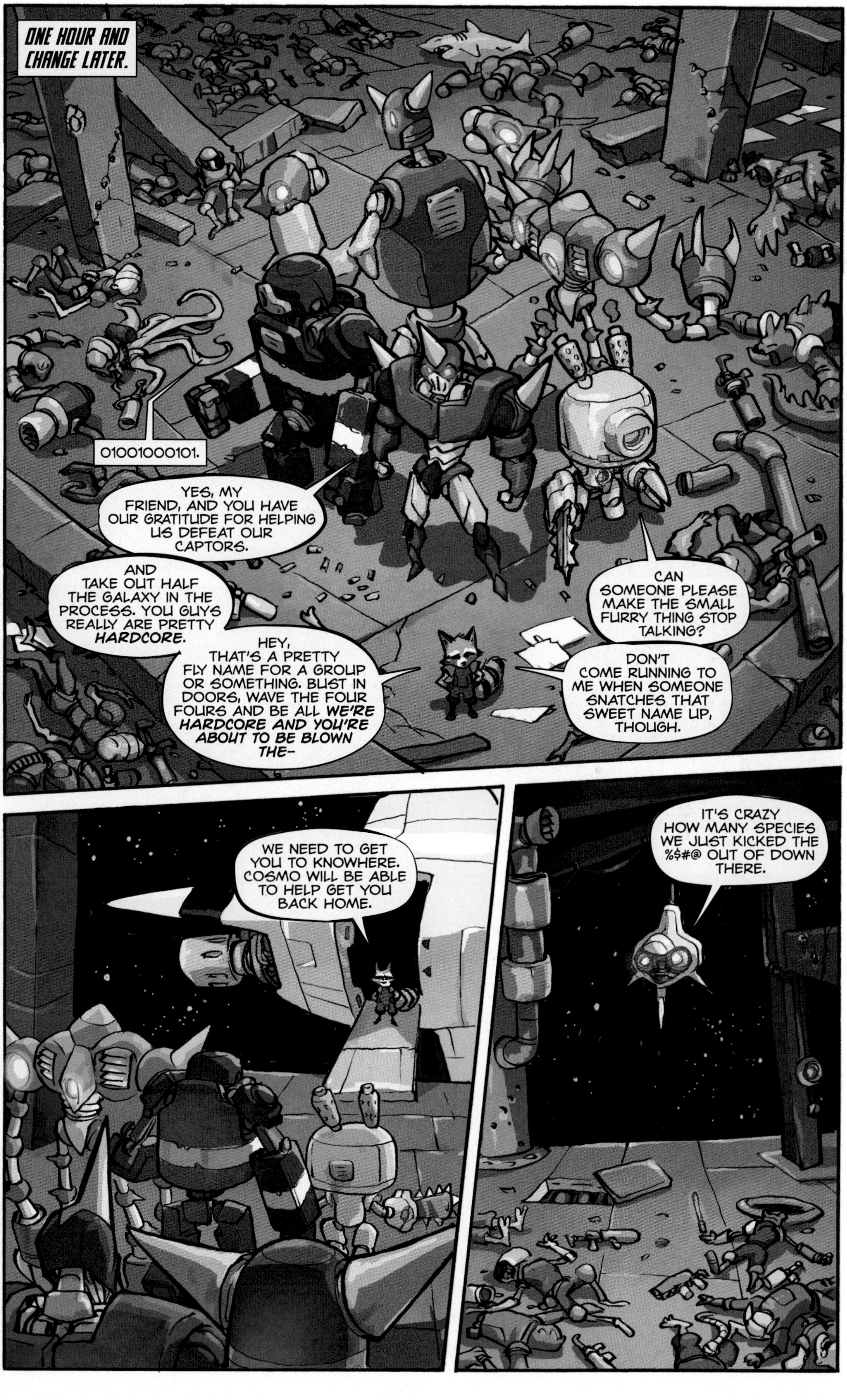
ONE HOUR AND CHANGE LATER.
01001000101.
YES, MY FRIEND, AND YOU HAVE OUR GRATITUDE FOR HELPING US DEFEAT OUR CAPTORS.
AND TAKE OUT HALF THE GALAXY IN THE PROCESS. YOU GUYS REALLY ARE PRETTY *HARDCORE*.
CAN SOMEONE PLEASE MAKE THE SMALL FURRY THING STOP TALKING?
HEY, THAT'S A PRETTY FLY NAME FOR A GROUP OR SOMETHING. BUST IN DOORS, WAVE THE FOUR FOURS AND BE ALL *WE'RE HARDCORE AND YOU'RE ABOUT TO BE BLOWN THE-*
DON'T COME RUNNING TO ME WHEN SOMEONE SNATCHES THAT SWEET NAME UP, THOUGH.
WE NEED TO GET YOU TO KNOWHERE. COSMO WILL BE ABLE TO HELP GET YOU BACK HOME.
IT'S CRAZY HOW MANY SPECIES WE JUST KICKED THE %$#@ OUT OF DOWN THERE.

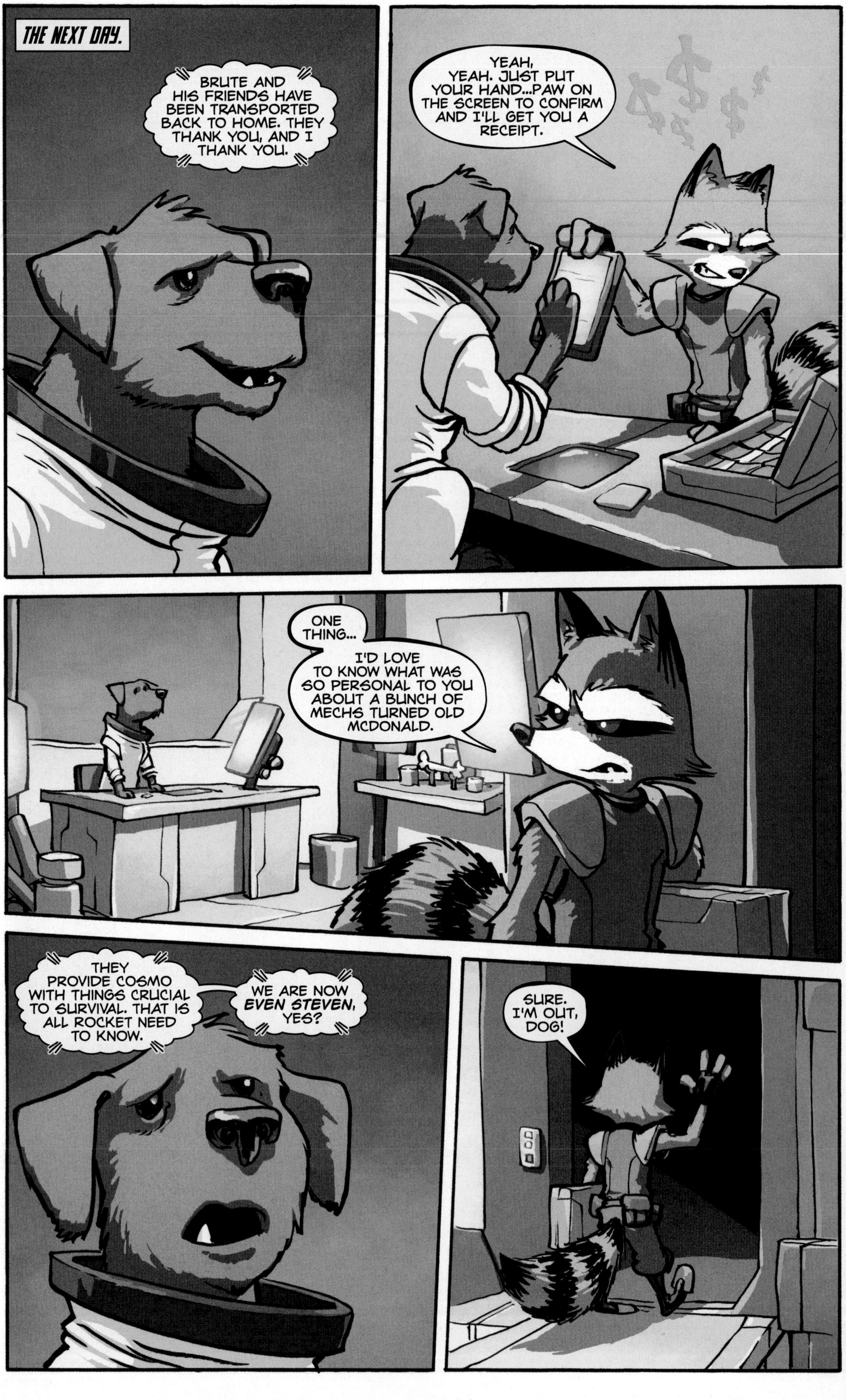
THE NEXT DAY.
BRUTE AND HIS FRIENDS HAVE BEEN TRANSPORTED BACK TO HOME. THEY THANK YOU, AND I THANK YOU.
YEAH, YEAH. JUST PUT YOUR HAND...PAW ON THE SCREEN TO CONFIRM AND I'LL GET YOU A RECEIPT.
ONE THING...
I'D LOVE TO KNOW WHAT WAS SO PERSONAL TO YOU ABOUT A BUNCH OF MECHS TURNED OLD MCDONALD.
THEY PROVIDE COSMO WITH THINGS CRUCIAL TO SURVIVAL. THAT IS ALL ROCKET NEED TO KNOW.
WE ARE NOW *EVEN STEVEN*, YES?
SURE. I'M OUT, DOG!

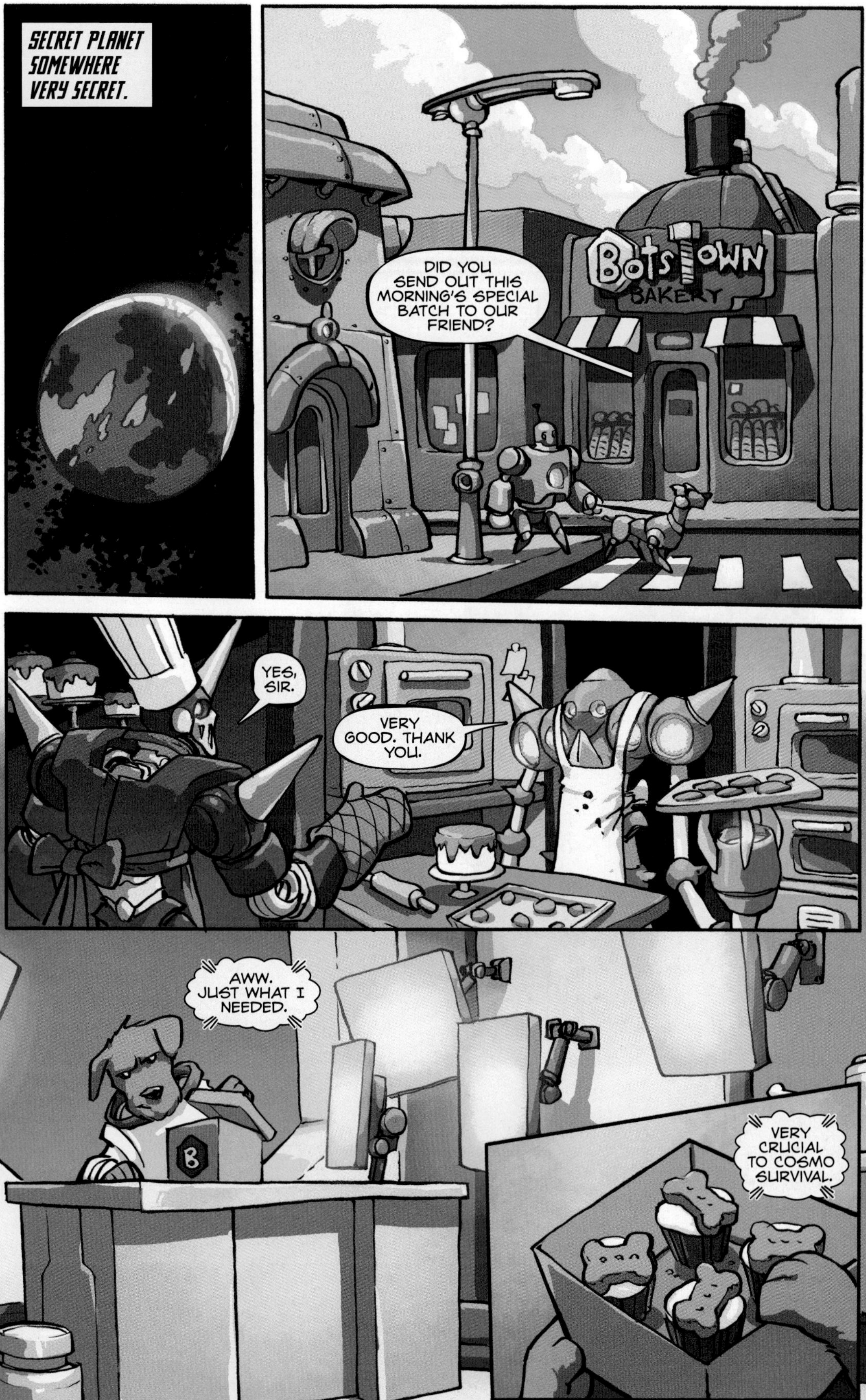

SECRET PLANET SOMEWHERE VERY SECRET.
BOTS TOWN BAKERY
DID YOU SEND OUT THIS MORNING'S SPECIAL BATCH TO OUR FRIEND?
YES, SIR.
VERY GOOD. THANK YOU.
AWW. JUST WHAT I NEEDED.
VERY CRUCIAL TO COSMO SURVIVAL.
THE END.

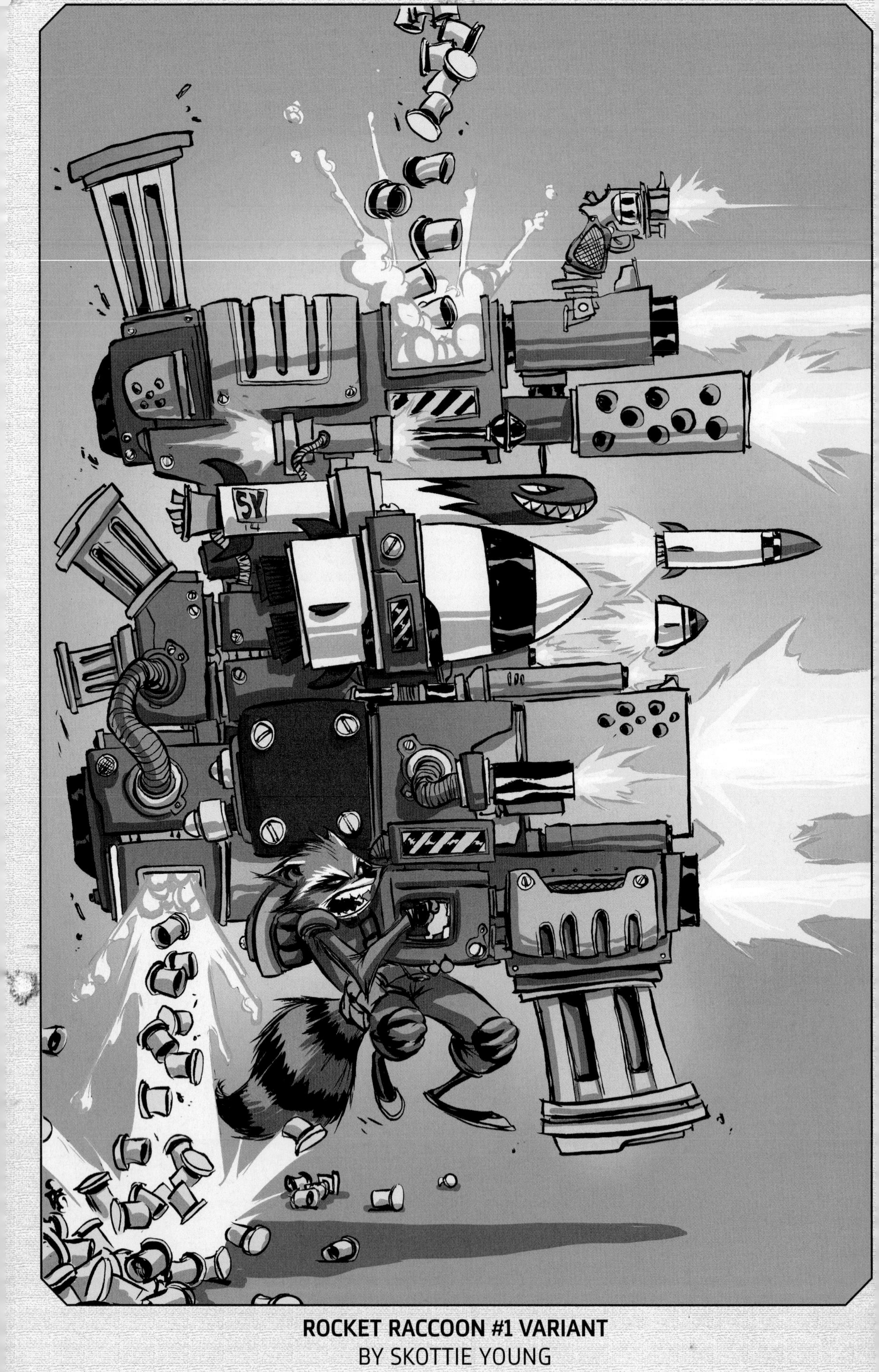
SY

ROCKET RACCOON #1 VARIANT
BY SKOTTIE YOUNG

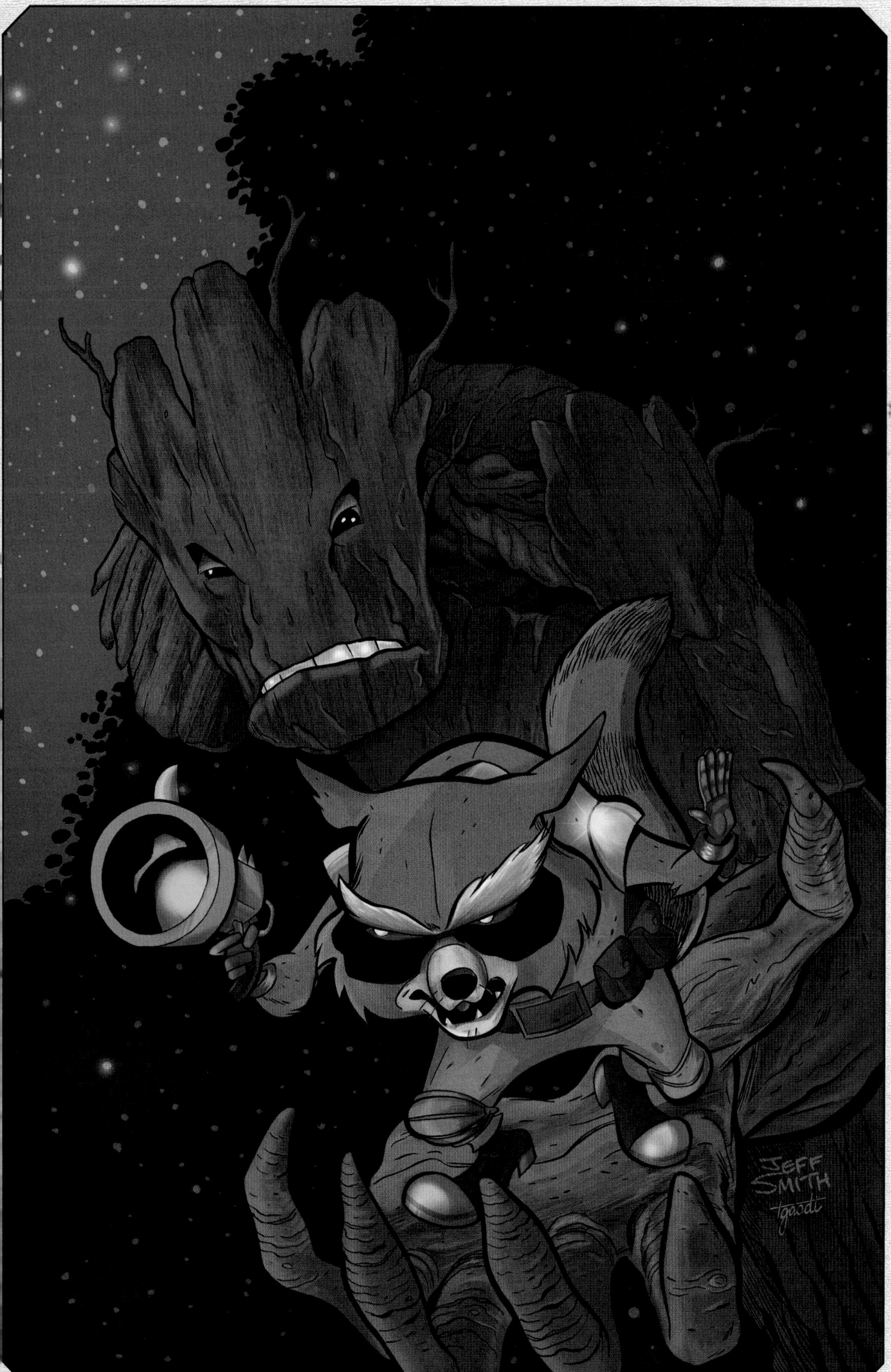
JEFF SMITH
tgaadt

ROCKET RACCOON #1 SDCC VARIANT
BY JEFF SMITH & TOM GAADT

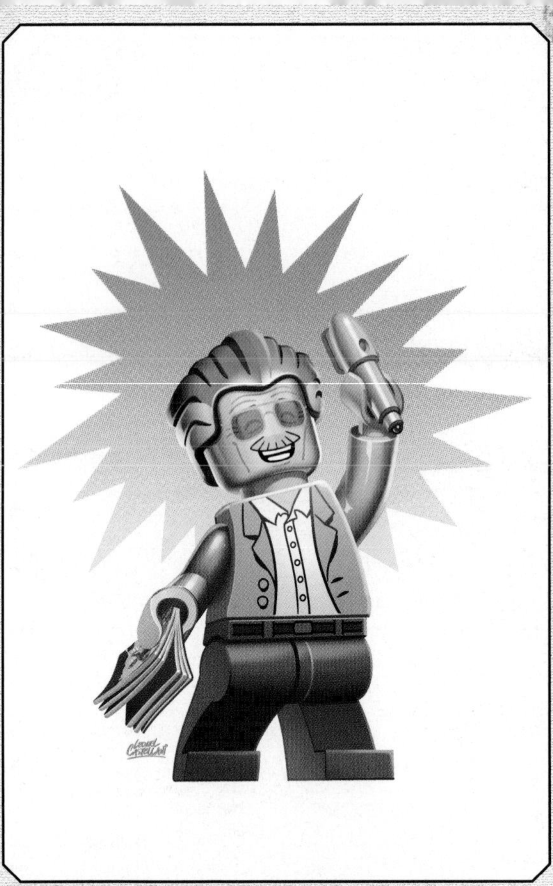

ROCKET RACCOON #1 STAN LEE LEGO VARIANT
BY LEONEL CASTELLANI

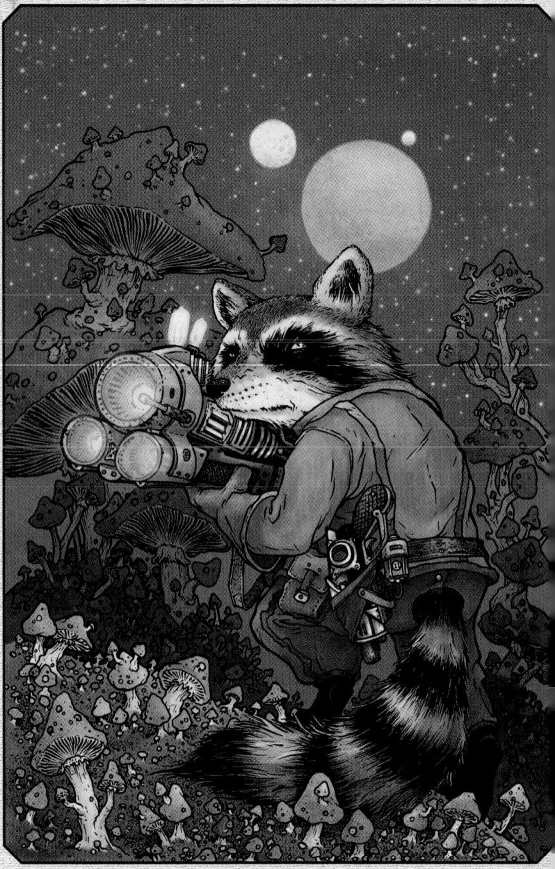

ROCKET RACCOON #1 VARIANT
BY DAVID PETERSON

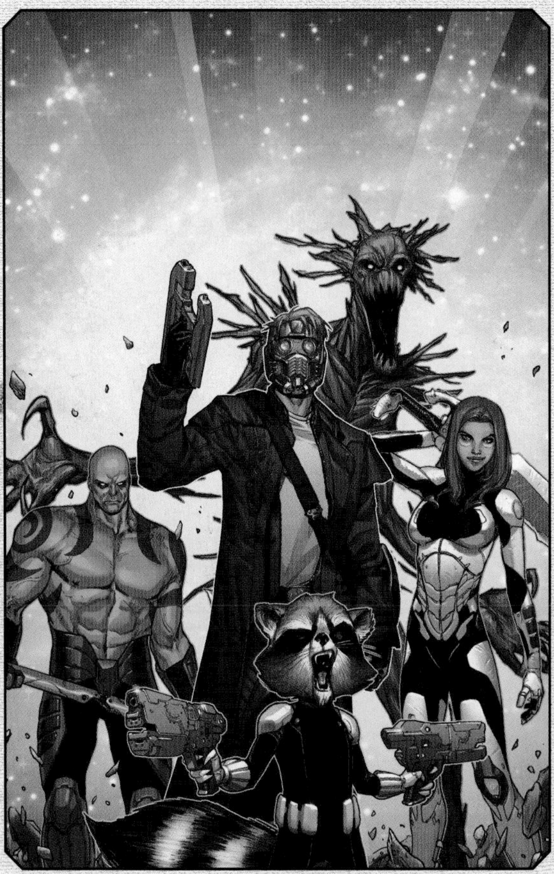

ROCKET RACCOON #1 MU PLUS VARIANT
BY SARAH PICHELLI & JUSTIN PONSOR

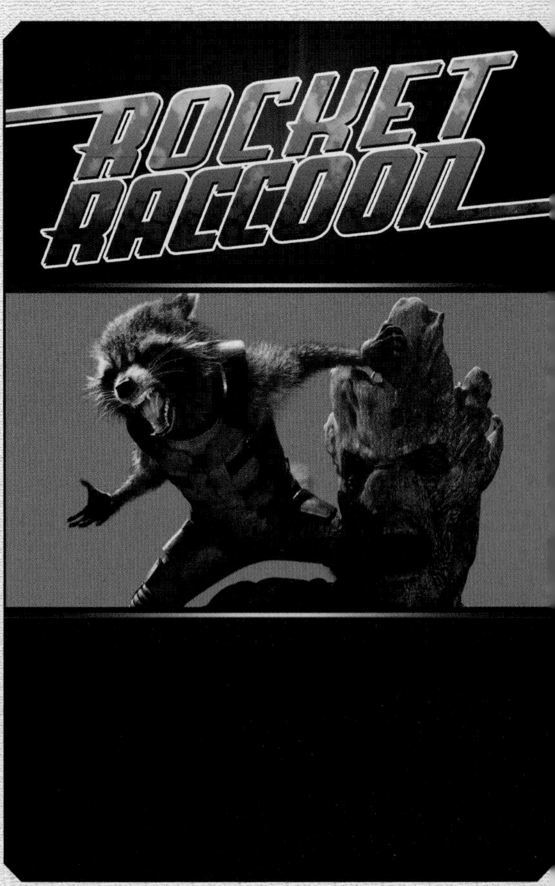
ROCKET RACCOON

ROCKET RACCOON #1 MOVIE VARIANT

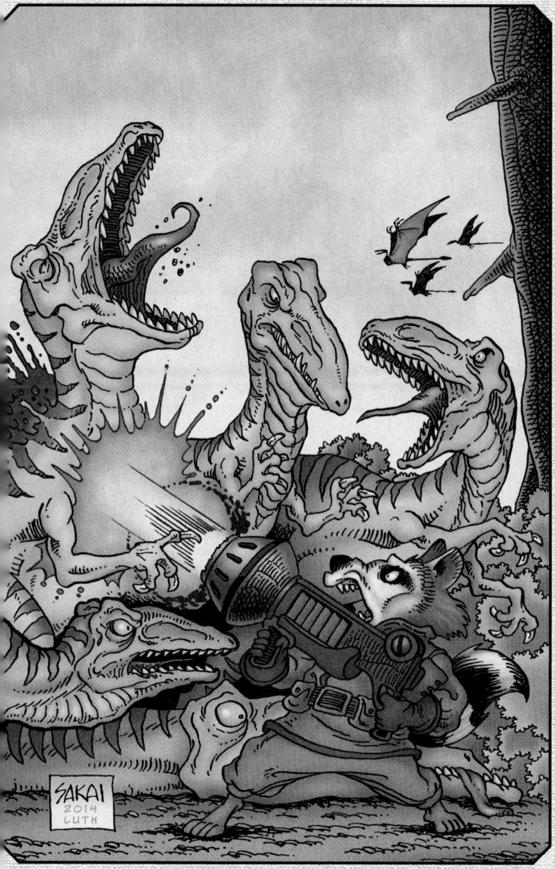
SAKAI
2014
LUTH

ROCKET RACCOON #2 VARIANT
BY STAN SAKAI & TOM LUTH

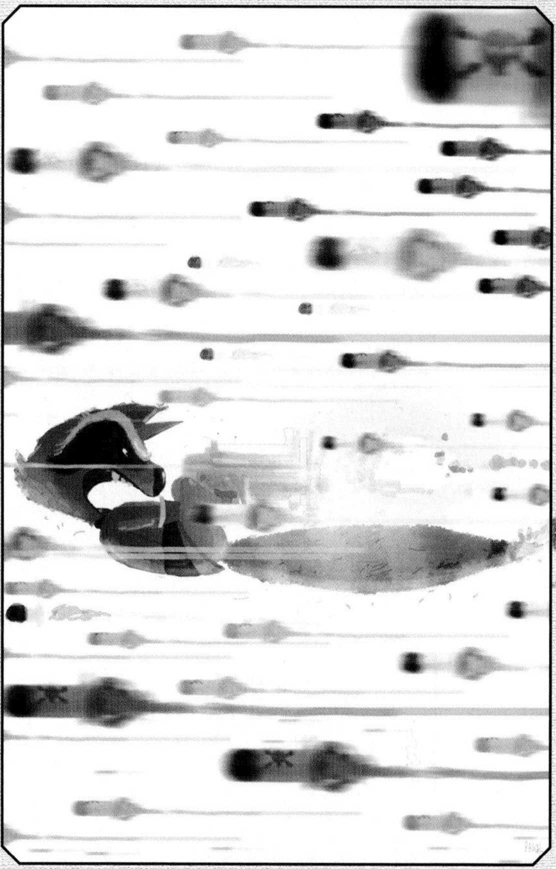

ROCKET RACCOON #3 VARIANT
BY PASCAL CAMPION

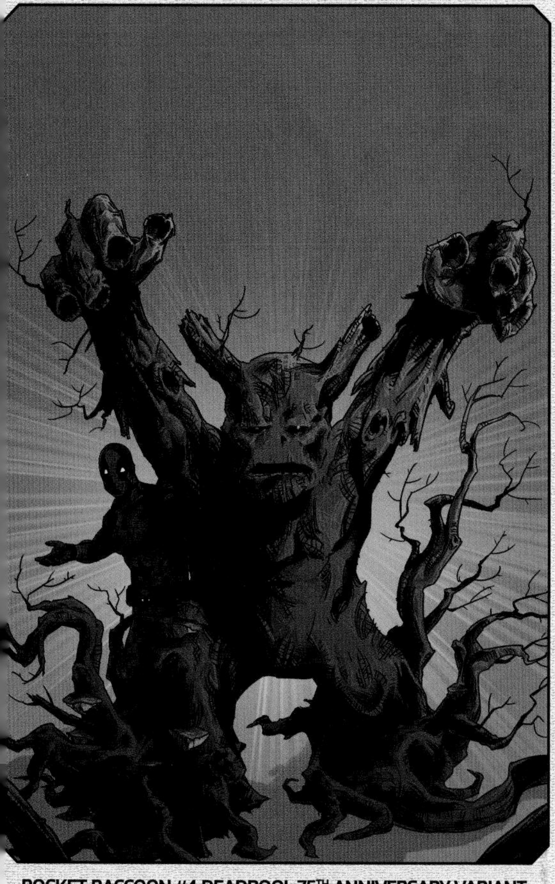

ROCKET RACCOON #4 DEADPOOL 75TH ANNIVERSARY VARIANT
BY KALMAN ANDRASOFSZKY

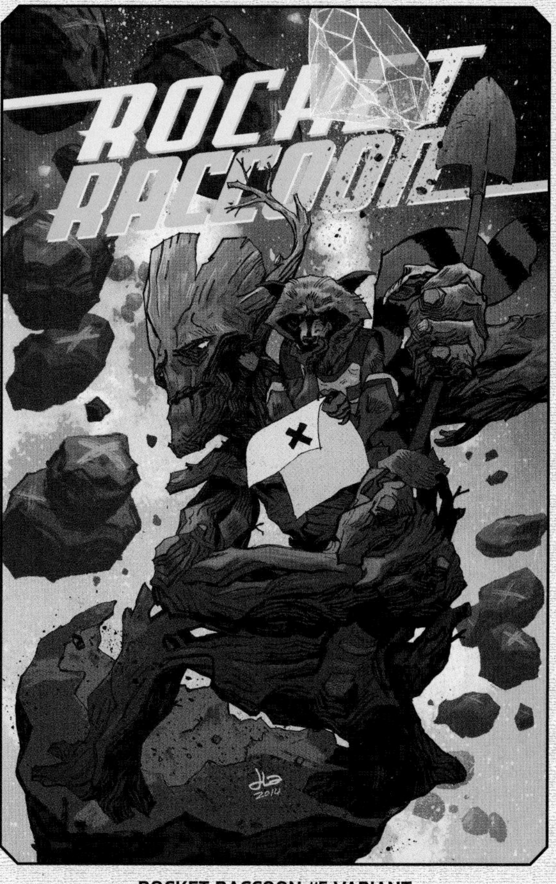

ROCKET RACCOON #5 VARIANT
BY JASON LATOUR

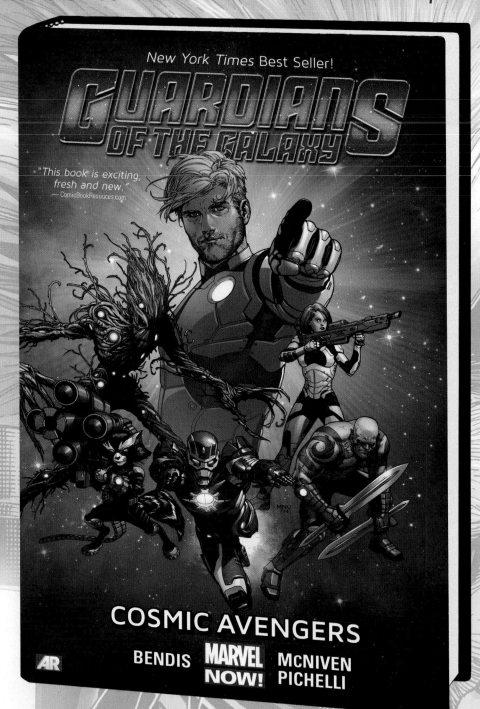